A

POPULAR MUSIC IN ADVERTISING

As Heard on TV:
Popular Music in Advertising

BETHANY KLEIN
University of Leeds, UK

ASHGATE

First published in paperback 2010

Published by
Ashgate Publishing Limited
Wey Court East
Union Road
Farnham
Surrey, GU9 7PT
England

Ashgate Publishing Company
Suite 420
101 Cherry Street
Burlington
VT 05401-4405
USA

www.ashgate.com

British Library Cataloguing in Publication Data
Klein, Bethany
  As heard on TV: popular music in advertising. – (Ashgate popular and folk music series)
    1. Music in advertising 2. Popular music – History and criticism 3. Television advertising
  I. Title
  306.4'8424

Library of Congress Cataloging-in-Publication Data
Klein, Bethany
  As heard on TV: popular music in advertising / Bethany Klein.
    p. cm. – (Ashgate popular and folk music series)
  Includes bibliographical references and index.
  ISBN 978-0-7546-6665-3 (hardcover : alk. paper) 1. Music in advertising. 2. Popular music–History and criticism. 3. Television advertising. I. Title.
  ML3790.K467 2009
  781.5'4–dc22

2008037174

ISBN 9780754666653 (hbk)
ISBN 9781409407645 (pbk)
ISBN 9780754693345 (ebk)

Contents

General Editor's Preface

The upheaval that occurred in musicology during the last two decades of the twentieth century has created a new urgency for the study of popular music alongside the development of new critical and theoretical models. A relativistic outlook has replaced the universal perspective of modernism (the international ambitions of the 12-note style); the grand narrative of the evolution and dissolution of tonality has been challenged, and emphasis has shifted to cultural context, reception and subject position. Together, these have conspired to eat away at the status of canonical composers and categories of high and low in music. A need has arisen, also, to recognize and address the emergence of crossovers, mixed and new genres, to engage in debates concerning the vexed problem of what constitutes authenticity in music and to offer a critique of musical practice as the product of free, individual expression.

Popular musicology is now a vital and exciting area of scholarship, and the *Ashgate Popular and Folk Music Series* presents some of the best research in the field. Authors are concerned with locating musical practices, values and meanings in cultural context, and draw upon methodologies and theories developed in cultural studies, semiotics, poststructuralism, psychology and sociology. The series focuses on popular musics of the twentieth and twenty-first centuries. It is designed to embrace the world's popular musics from Acid Jazz to Zydeco, whether high tech or low tech, commercial or non-commercial, contemporary or traditional.

Professor Derek B. Scott
Professor of Critical Musicology
University of Leeds

Acknowledgements

This book and the PhD dissertation from which it originates have benefited from the involvement of a variety of people on two continents. At the University of Pennsylvania, I thank Klaus Krippendorff, Katherine Sender, and David Grazian for their interest in and counsel on this project, as committee members and mentors, and especially my advisor Barbie Zelizer, for her unwavering support and invaluable advice. In the UK, I am grateful to Dave Hesmondhalgh for his encouragement of my research and transatlantic move, and Simon Frith for his early suggestions regarding scope and organization. Thanks to series editor Derek Scott and Ashgate senior commissioning editor Heidi May for their enthusiasm and guidance during the publishing process. Portions of Chapter 4 appeared in *Media, Culture & Society* and an earlier version of Chapter 5 appeared in *Popular Music and Society*; I thank the publishers for allowing me to include the revised versions here.

I am indebted to my informants, for sharing their time and their thoughtful perspectives with me. Each interview allowed me to sharpen the details of the cultural practice I have attempted to map, and I owe the richness of these descriptions entirely to them. I hope that my portrayals come close to representing their intelligence, passion, and humor.

A number of friends have kindly combed sections for typos and unclear logic, and provided a trusty sounding board for my ideas. I thank my current collaborator Claire Wardle, and former Annenberg peers Nicole Maurantonio, Matt Carlson, and the Culture Club for their helpful comments. I am especially grateful to Adela Smith, full-time best friend and part-time copyeditor, for keeping my prose clean and my mind sane. Thanks to my family for being proud of me, whether or not they understand what I do, and to the many friends who supported me in more subtle ways, by reminding me to attend music events, enjoy restaurants, and share pub quiz duties, when I could have been reading and writing; Nicole Mercurio, Reyna Howkins, and Jeff Perkins were particularly proficient and entertaining distractions during the research process. Finally, I thank Morrissey, who taught me to take popular music seriously: I will never forget the songs that saved my life.

Introduction

In recent years it has become increasingly common to hear popular music outside of the expected and traditional vehicles of radio and personal stereos. In marketing, and particularly in television commercials, popular music has become ubiquitous. The presumed significance and power of popular music are revealed both by its persistent use in advertising, as well as by the sometimes disapproving responses of fans, critics, and musicians concerned with the problems raised by such usage.

Deregulation, digitization, and an overall increase in media commercialism in the past decade have resulted in a radio industry that displays an ever-narrowing range of music and a music industry that, confronted with potential threats to record sales, is seeking out alternative options to ensure financial viability. The industrial processes involved in the production of popular music and the creative processes of music culture are linked: as the supporting structures—organizational, legal, technological—transform, so too will the creation of music culture undergo change. The growing attraction to advertising is partly a reaction to changes within and dilemmas currently being confronted by the radio and music industries, yet the advertising industry presents its own set of problems for recording artists. As music culture nurtures a relationship with advertising, traditional ideological stances of popular music are challenged. Although popular music has always had commercial objectives, many musicians have nonetheless vowed to commit to an anti-commercial ideology. Moreover, as record companies and musicians become gradually more reliant on advertising as a means of revenue and exposure, the concern is that certain types of music will be favored in production, distribution, and consumption channels, endangering, or at any rate further marginalizing, less commercially feasible forms. The continuing debate about the use of popular music in advertising is evidence that the commercialization of the popular arts comes inbuilt not only with advantages but also with strain.

Through a close investigation of emblematic case studies, this book traces the continuities and unpacks the complexities of the increasingly common marketing practice of licensing music to advertising. I consider the discourse surrounding the adoption of popular music for television commercials through analysis of popular and trade press coverage and through interviews with involved parties, in order to explore the various arguments and issues activated by the changing relationship between popular music and advertising. The use of popular music in advertising is one example of a larger debate about the seemingly appropriate role of commercial objectives in the dissemination of culture and, as such, provides a lens through which a wide range of practices that have flourished as a result of hypercommercialism can be understood. From the renaming of sports and entertainment venues for corporate backers to product placement in film and on television, advertisers are insinuated in nearly all aspects of leisure and entertainment today. This book addresses what the role of advertising means for popular music culture, weighing the celebrated benefits of corporate support against the negative implications of growing advertiser control.

The use of popular music in advertising revisits some issues that popular music has confronted in the past and generates some new issues as well. Among the issues relevant to song licensing for commercials are the relationship between authorship and ownership in popular music, the artistic legitimization of advertising, transformations in the radio and music industries, the role of music in branding, and the restructuring of texts that results from commercial placements of popular music. This book is structured around these topics by focusing on six relatively high-profile cases or collections of cases of popular music in television commercials, each of which underscores one of the aforementioned subjects. I have chosen cases that I believe "will help generate, to the fullest extent, as many properties of the categories as possible, and that will help relate categories to each other and to their properties" (Glaser and Strauss 1999/1967: 49). The cases were selected for study both because they are emblematic of one or more of the aforementioned issues and because all received a great deal of attention from fans and critics at the time of the ad campaigns and, in some instances, for years after. These cases can thus be understood as critical incidents in the use of music in advertising, and a close analysis of the cases allows for the identification of underlying values and patterns.

Chapter 1 provides a contextualization of the use of popular music in advertising by considering the historic predecessors to this modern practice, and popular music's unsettled relationship to notions of both art and commerce. Subsequent chapters explore the tensions inherent to the practice, the reasons for its increasing presence, and the wider cultural debates invoked by the appearance of popular music in television commercials.

Chapter 2 examines the role of authorship in music licensing through an analysis of the 1987 watershed event that saw the Beatles' "Revolution" licensed to Nike by Michael Jackson, who purchased the publishing rights to much of the group's song catalog. Legal permission to grant the use of a song in a commercial, gained by Jackson through his purchase, is a regular element of the debate over music in advertising. While authorship is commonly associated with copyright and ownership in Western culture (Jaszi 1994: 31), in the music industry, the copyright system muddles the connection between authorship and ownership. That a band featured in a commercial is famous and successful does not necessarily mean the artists agreed to license the song. Though the three living Beatles protested the commercial usage of "Revolution," even filing a lawsuit against Nike, its ad agency, and Capitol-EMI Records, they were legally helpless. Beatles fans witnessed the song being used to sell athletic footwear and, not for the last time, the use of popular music in advertising became a focus of debate. The extent of press coverage had much to do with the lawsuit, and, for this reason, it is a case that speaks to issues of authorship and ownership in mergers between popular music and advertising.

The high-profile case of Nike licensing "Revolution" had the incidental result of informing the public about copyright law; it became clear that among fans and music experts, the response to art being licensed against the artist's wishes is a disapproving one. I suggest in Chapter 2 that the system of copyright favors corporations even when musicians control their own rights, since licensing to advertising represents for some artists the only possibility of financial success. Neither artists who have sold their rights nor artists who cling to their rights can be viewed as powerful next to multinational companies.

The 1999 Volkswagen Cabrio commercial featuring late folksinger Nick Drake's "Pink Moon" received a comparably positive reaction. In Chapter 3 I consider how the negative critical and public reaction to music in advertising has at times been tempered by creatively successful ads, and how aesthetics play a mediating role in the negotiation between advertiser, musician, and fan. Volkswagen's award-winning spot featuring little-known folkie Nick Drake's heartrending song is often credited with driving the practice to its current state of omnipresence, suggesting that the treatment of commercials as artistic works in and of themselves has opened up advertising as a more suitable vehicle for the placement of licensed music. If commercial art can be deemed art, why not commercials? As Thomas Frank documents in *The Conquest of Cool* (1996), there have been artistic visionaries working in advertising since the late 1950s, figures who didn't simply co-opt qualities from the counterculture movement, but helped to actively constitute the movement. Commercials that succeed as entertainment present advertising as a cultural-commercial hybrid in a way that less creative ads do not. Savan writes, "It's the *subtlety* of the sell that corporate-sponsored rock stars are increasingly judged by, not the fact that they're selling at all" (1993: 90). This is why a case like the Volkswagen "Pink Moon" commercial was a challenge to traditional notions of selling out and boundaries between art and commerce; the ad was beautiful and poignant.

Chapter 4 considers the changes in the radio and music industries that have boosted advertising as an alternative source of exposure and revenue. In terms of music in advertising, 2000 was the year of Moby; the electronic artist became a star after licensing all 18 tracks off his 1999 album *Play*. The success of *Play* is credited almost entirely to the artist's extensive licensing of its tracks, leading both to massive record sales as well as commercial radio play, both of which had previously eluded the artist. Especially as commercial radio becomes a less viable option for many musicians and as record sales are at least perceived to be threatened by illegal downloading, licensing to commercials becomes an attractive alternative source of revenue. I examine whether the benefit to a band can compensate for commercial taint, and whether the promotional benefit of being featured in an ad outweighs any perceived art versus commerce conflict.

Related to the issue of potential benefit to the performer is the question of whether the act of licensing music to advertisers can be viewed as a subversive one.

That is, licensing to advertisers may not only provide financially, but if spun well could be a boost to integrity as well. Some musicians, including Moby, have reportedly donated the compensation they received for commercial placements in clever and arguably subversive ways. But do these acts really countervail the benefits reaped by the advertiser using the song? The impossibility of quantifying this scale keeps the subject open to deliberation and in Chapter 4 the rationalizations offered in favor of licensing to advertising are weighed.

The type of product or service promoted by an advertisement presents another element of the debate surrounding popular music's use in advertising; in this way, the powerful illusion of branding is highlighted. In Chapter 5 I look at how the use of popular music in advertising presents potential consequences related to branding. Through the cool cachet invoked by the brand, companies like Volkswagen appear to be less of a threat to popular music. Further, the particular selection of music for an ad campaign may serve to increase a company's perceived cool. Though distinctions between one type of product and another based on branding are usually misleading, if effective, constructions, the use of popular music as a tactic in this regard is common.

Coke and Pepsi have perhaps the longest history with advertising of any consumer brands; their campaigns, old and new, provide an entry to understanding the use of music for branding. By emphasizing the entertainment qualities of their campaigns, and by applying characteristics of rock music to the promotion of their products, Coke and Pepsi have elided traditional debates about the dangers and consequences of commercial affiliation. The balance of power often brought into play by the art versus commerce debate—where the artist is weak and the corporation predatory—is thus obscured. By portraying the colas as involved in a genuine and close relationship with popular music, the cola companies accentuate the commonalities between popular music and advertising. Chapter 5 demonstrates how music is used as a shortcut towards branding as false consciousness.

Chapter 6 deals with one of the most impassioned discussions surrounding the use of music in advertising: whether the use is reverent to the perceived spirit or original meaning of the song. In the case of well-known pieces of music, the meaning previously associated with the song is, the advertiser hopes, transferred onto the product or service being advertised. Sometimes the ad does the work of transferal for the viewer, changing the lyrics to suit the item being promoted. The strategy of bricolage that may empower consumers to produce meaning through "making do" (de Certeau 1984) with the media available is employed by advertisers as well. By selecting specific sections of songs, rearranging and changing lyrics, and combining music with visuals, advertisers construct convenient preferred meanings.

Television commercials that have paired songs with apparently incompatible products or services have often been subject to greater attention and censure. I look at Wrangler's use of Creedence Clearwater Revival's "Fortunate Son" and Royal Caribbean Cruise Lines' use of Iggy Pop's "Lust for Life" to examine advertising's capacity to restructure popular music texts. Wrangler's use of "Fortunate Son" truncated the track so that it was reduced to a patriotic soundbite: the song was cut after the lines "Some folks are born to wave the flag/ ooh the red, white, and blue," conspicuously omitting the refrain "But it ain't me, it ain't me." For years now, Royal Caribbean Cruises has used Iggy Pop's "Lust for Life" in its ads. The song is notoriously about the singer's heroin use and, before the cruise line licensed it, the track's most famous placement was in the film *Trainspotting*, an adaptation of Irvine Welsh's novel about Scottish junkies. If the fear is that commercial use of popular music poses a threat to the song by completely recontextualizing it, these two cases provide prime examples. Huron argued that "it is the overt knowledge of objectives and the consequent desire to control and handle the tools of musical meaning which make advertising such a compelling object of musical study" (1989: 572). In other words, the fact that decisions in advertising are so calculated and purposive makes advertising an especially rich place to explore the use of popular music.

Chapter 7 revisits some of the underlying tensions that were outlined in previous chapters, exploring how, for many artists, the practice of licensing music to television commercials is neither completely stigma-free nor totally out of the question. For lesser-known artists, licensing music to commercials is increasingly being used as a means to an end. While advertising may not be the ideal vehicle for exposure, some artists have licensed a song or two to advertisers just until their names are on the map and record sales pick up. I assess the current state of popular music in advertising through the case of indie-rock group the Shins licensing "New Slang" to a McDonald's ad. The Shins licensed the track to McDonald's despite a general ambivalence towards the practice. Since then, the band has seen an increase in record sales and offers for licensing in less contentious arenas, such as television and film. Frontman James Mercer says that he does not regret licensing the song to McDonald's but thinks "it's the kind of thing that, you know, you do once, and then you don't have to do it again. We're certainly less inclined to do something like that now, since we're actually making money off the record" (LeMay 2004). With an eye to the future, this spot serves as a reminder of the complexities of advertising's affair with popular music.

Many of the musicians I spoke with were neither proud nor ashamed of their decision to license music to commercials; all of them talked about the difficulty of making a living through music, and the dearth of options and opportunities to be heard and get paid. Yet even as this cloud of resignation hangs in the air, there are still musicians, both well-known and lesser-known, unwilling to enter into the exchange, and Chapter 7 considers their perspectives as well.

This investigation into the practice of song licensing in television commercials provides a direct entry into issues specific to commercialism, like branding and profitability, and also into broader issues that are central to the popular arts, such as copyright and control over the text. The continuing debate over music in advertising can seem at times selfish, where the opposition often appears to be saying little more than "This is *my* music and I don't want it shared." And contesting the use of music in advertising can appear a trifling battle: it is *just* music, after all, so what's the big deal? However, disapproval of the practice is also evidence that many critics are not content with the modern environment of hypercommercialism, or the unencumbered unification of creative work and marketing. Scholars of media policy are concerned by the lack of information and involvement on the part of citizens in legislating communication yet, insofar as the practice's ubiquity is essentially a result of advertisers taking advantage of the wobbly radio and music industries, the persistence with which some musicians and fans condemn commercial licensing of popular music is an unwitting vocalization of discontent with media policy.

This book addresses a number of questions prompted by the use of popular music in advertising: how does media legislation sometimes clash with ideologies of music culture? In what ways do old debates involving the tension between artistic and commercial goals re-emerge within changing media environments? Why is the practice of licensing to commercials viewed as appropriate to some people in some cases and reprehensible by other people in other cases? By unpacking the practice of music licensing in advertising through a variety of case studies, this book also seeks to illuminate theoretical issues regarding art, popular music, commercialism, and media regulation. Popular music in advertising continues to be an unresolved debate—neither unanimously approved of nor unanimously dismissed as debasing—because popular music itself is unresolved: it is at once art and commerce, to varying extents and in different proportions.

Studying the Use of Popular Music in Advertising

This study utilizes a combination of media analysis and interviews to explore the issues surrounding the use of popular music in advertising as a means of addressing broader questions about interactions between cultural and commercial objectives. In order to examine the discourse and debate around the practice of licensing popular music to advertisers, I analyzed popular and trade press coverage of the practice and conducted in-depth interviews with 29 cultural producers related to the practice of music licensing.

The decision to include both popular and trade press in this analysis allows for a multiperspectival consideration of the processes and issues involved in the practice of song licensing. The popular press is where discussions of music in advertising have been most frequent and most articulate. While fan message boards sometimes contain well-reasoned analyses of the practice, much fan discourse consists of simply emotional cries of "sell-out." Coverage of the practice in the popular press tends to be more critical, applying classic critiques involving the distinctions between artistic and commercial goals. Consequently, music and cultural critics bring a sense of professionalism and clarity to the issue, while often also displaying the concern of a true fan. On the other hand, both the music and advertising trade press tend to examine the practice as it relates to potential benefits to musicians and advertisers. Ethical and aesthetic issues are often elided in favor of business and logistical matters.

Through an analysis of the popular and trade press coverage of this practice, I explore whether and how the general reaction to the practice has shifted over time, what have been identified as the problems and opportunities associated with the practice, and how popular musicians have partnered with advertisers to various results. While some of the popular press coverage includes quotes from musicians and advertisers involved in the practice of song licensing, the space and form of newspaper and magazine reportage do not allow for a very deep or nuanced conversation about the various pros and cons, causes and consequences. To compensate for this lack, I conducted in-depth interviews with various parties related to the practice of song licensing for commercial use, including musicians, music supervisors, advertising creatives, licensing managers, and record label owners and employees.

I interviewed musicians who had licensed tracks to advertisers, as well as a few who turned down offers to license tracks. Some of the musicians also composed music for commercials. The companies to which informants had licensed or composed music represent some of the most prominent names in advertising, such as Nike, Kleenex, Volkswagen, Saturn, Citibank, Sears, and Calvin Klein. I spoke with music supervisors about the process of mediating between musicians and the agency/client. Some of the music supervisors work at independent music houses, which handle both licensing and composition, that are hired by ad agencies. Others are full-time in-house music supervisors, working only for their agencies, though sometimes collaborating with music houses on projects.

My group of informants also included a number of advertising creatives, including copywriters, art directors, and creative directors. Most ad agencies do not employ full-time in-house music supervisors and, when outside agencies are not commissioned to suggest music, ad creatives will pitch and select music themselves. All of the advertising workers I spoke with have dealt with the music selection for at least one major ad campaign.

I spoke with a few people who manage licensing for labels and publishing groups, large and small. For smaller labels, that may not do enough licensing to warrant a devoted position to such transactions, often the owner manages licensing offers. In some cases indie labels hire an autonomous pitchman to promote their bands for TV, film, and advertising placement. One of my informants ran a company that represents the catalogs of hundreds of independent artists for various labels. Larger independents usually have at least one employee solely devoted to licensing, and major labels have entire departments. A few of my informants were more tangentially related to the practice of music licensing in advertising, including a journalist who has written about the practice for over a decade, the music promotions director of a large retail chain, and an account manager of one of the largest library catalogs used for licensing (music composed specifically for placement in moving-visual media). (See Appendix for more detailed information on informants and method.)

Together, the themes developed through interviews and press analysis elucidate the modern reality of the practice, the industrial changes that have provided a foundation for the increased use of popular music in advertising, and the unresolved tensions surrounding media alliances that explicitly blur cultural ambitions with commercial objectives. The intellectual and historical context against which this practice must be considered is charted in Chapter 1.

Chapter 1

As Heard on TV: The Marriage of Popular Music and Advertising

Art versus Commerce, Revisited

The presence of popular music in television commercials continues to be met with concern from fans, critics, and musicians worried about the meaning of "selling-out" and the potential consequences of tearing down the wall, however porous and poorly defined, between artistic and commercial interests. Even as individuals who formerly opposed the practice have started to relent and reconsider the practice on a case-by-case basis, most people would not want their favorite song used to sell a product or service. The protectiveness with which popular music as a popular art is guarded can be understood as a result of the combination of the ambiguity of art-ness as an attribute and the upward battle that popular music, as a form that relies on mass-production, -distribution and -consumption, has faced in being legitimated as art. The use of popular music in advertising thus engages with old debates about the status of popular music as art, the status of art as commodity, and the tensions between artistic and commercial endeavors.

The disapproval with which popular music in advertising is sometimes met seems like a classic result of art and commerce clashing, yet popular music's position within this debate is complicated. Firstly, there is the question of how relevant this dichotomy is for any discussion of culture; I recognize the distinctions between art and commerce as flexible and subject to the whims of other cultural changes. I also recognize that both popular music and advertising are shaped by cultural and commercial objectives, that both are cultural-commercial hybrids: commerce makes art possible, just as art encourages commerce. I therefore do not refer to the division as a stable reality, but as a social construction; "the objectivity of the institutional world, however massive it may appear to the individual, is a humanly produced, constructed objectivity" (Berger and Luckmann 1966: 60). The continuing employment of the culture versus commerce construct both inside and outside of art worlds speaks to our shared cultural values regarding the definition and autonomy of art, and the explicit impingement of corporate interest on artistic realms. What we experience as reality is created through our shared and shifting understandings. Accordingly, that the division between culture and commerce is constructed does not make it any less significant as an indicative and useful analytical tool for studying popular music, advertising, or interactions between the two.

Secondly, there remains the question of how mass-produced popular culture fits into the construction; the belief expressed by critics that popular music can be corrupted by commercial intent relies on the assertion that popular music, though situated within a commercial realm, is, or derives from, art. Insofar as other popular arts, including film and television, are distinguished from the fine arts by possessing mass media qualities, the tensions present in the popular music world reflect larger tensions at work in the production of culture more generally.

Before popular music could attempt to engage in a battle with commercialism, popular culture had to engage in a battle with high art over status. While popular culture has always in a sense been taken seriously, if only for the potential harm it may cause to society, it has followed a long and arduous path in its quest to be taken seriously from an aesthetic perspective. Modern public debates, such as those initiated by groups like the Parents Music Resource Center, continue to echo much earlier arguments about the detrimental effects of popular culture. Contemporary critiques of popular culture still draw on the same presumptions that propelled detractors in previous eras.

One of the earliest attacks on material popular culture came from F.R. and Q.D. Leavis who, along with their followers, bemoaned the presumed negative effects of mass-produced and mass-consumed media. Reacting to the cultural crisis of the 1930s, the Leavisites adopted Matthew Arnold's mid-nineteenth-century "Culture and Civilization" claim that culture has always been in minority keeping and that the refusal of the masses to submit to the authority of the intellectual and cultural elite would inevitably lead to chaos. Where Arnold railed against the working-class lived culture of post-industrial Britain, the Leavisites directed their ire towards mass media, including popular film and advertising.

In the same period, the Frankfurt School, whose settlement in the United States spurred numerous treatises concerned with the drug-like nature of popular culture, worried that the consumption of popular culture by "cultural dupes" would lead to a blind submission to authority and, ultimately, a fascist state. From popular culture's inception, the qualities associated with the form—its mass-production and -consumption, its commodity status, its tendency towards standardization— were associated with passive consumers, uncultured and easily influenced zombies. Theodor Adorno singled out popular music, in particular, for falling far short of the standards set by serious music. To Adorno, the "fundamental characteristic of popular music" is standardization, such that "the composition hears for the listener" (1990/1941: 302). Further, various groups and genres in popular music are only pseudo-individualized. Consumers believe they are making a choice between one band and another, or one type of music and another, but really popular music is little more than a "multiple-choice questionnaire" (1990: 306); the choices are limited, and the ramifications of choosing one over another are few.

In the post-World War II years, elites began to accept that popular culture was here to stay. The right wing of the mass culture war relaxed, confident that an anarchic uprising was not imminent, and the left wing threw up its arms—and, in some cases, moved out of the United States—convinced that submission to totalitarianism was inevitable. Attention turned from the political and social impact of popular culture on its consumers to popular culture's impact on high culture. Dwight Macdonald's critique of masscult, later redirected towards midcult—the "debased, trivial culture" (1983: 71) that masquerades as high art while maintaining all the unpleasant qualities of mass culture—exemplifies the fear that popular culture will suck the life out of and eventually destroy high culture. Through the 1940s and 1950s, literary figures and art critics continued to carp about the debasement of high culture in the popular realm.

The Centre for Contemporary Cultural Studies at the University of Birmingham is generally recognized as legitimating popular culture as a site of academic study, yet its founding members held an ambivalent attitude towards popular culture. Although scholars associated with the Centre emphasized the active agency of the audience, they did not necessarily champion the popular culture consumed by the audience. If anything, the Birmingham School began as a restrained celebration of popular culture. For instance, Richard Hoggart (1957), one of the earliest supporters of working-class culture, was hardly a fan of the American rock music being disseminated by the milk-bar nickelodeons. As Hall and Whannel's (1964) assessment of the popular arts concluded, although some examples within a popular form possess culturally and aesthetically valuable traits, not all cases of the form are of equal quality by the criterion of art-ness. On the topic of music, Hall and Whannel's proposal meant moving from the conventional aesthetic position, which ranked classical music as clearly more aesthetically valuable than pop music, to a comparatively progressive position where jazz became the category understood to be clearly more valuable than pop music.

Within the realm of popular music, distinctions are consistently made between more and less artistic genres, often around variables already involved in the discourses of cultural difference, such as race, gender, and class. In the 1960s, as "rock musicians drew on artistic ideology to legitimize and make sense of their movement," black music was excluded from the definition of art as "self-consciously *thought*" by its classification as "body music": natural, rhythmic, good for dancing (Frith 1981: 20–21). On the one hand, a genre like blues is seen as "too natural to be art" and, on the other, less "natural" genres, including 1960s soul and later disco, are often subject to the opposite accusation that they are "too artificial" (Frith 1981: 21).

Likewise, the assessment of popular music as art has also been bound up with assumptions about gender. Not only are female musicians perceived as generally less artistic than male musicians, but male musicians with mainly female audiences are also positioned lower in the popular music hierarchy. This distinction is partly because rock, often considered the authentic to pop's inauthentic, is male-dominated. Female musicians are pressured into blandness and "have rarely been able to make their own musical versions of the oppositional rebellious hard edges that male rock can embody" (Frith and McRobbie 1990: 377).

The role of class in the assessment of art-ness was identified by Gans, who expected "Bob Dylan to be more popular with 'higher' taste publics; an action-oriented 'belter' like the late Janis Joplin, with 'lower' publics" (1999: 124). Similar to the distinction around race, the implication is that true art comes from the mind; that which comes from the heart or soul fails to meet this criterion. Action-oriented belters are perhaps more closely aligned with folk art than with the high arts. Hall and Whannel's suggestion that in evaluating popular culture distinctions must be made within the category—a proposition that has played out around race, gender, and class, among other categories of analysis—indicates that at least some forms of popular culture transitioned from being a challenge to "real" art to being considered art themselves.

In his attempt to define literature, Eagleton wrote that "one can think of literature less as some inherent quality or set of qualities displayed by certain kinds of writing ... than as a number of ways in which people *relate themselves* to writing" (1983: 9). Likewise, the shift from mere entertainment to art that popular music, and other popular arts, experienced can be identified less through internal qualities than through the presence of related activities and classificatory practices. The treatment of a cultural form by external institutions, such as the academy and the press, can be used as a measure of the form's placement in the arts hierarchy. Baumann (2001) argued that the American film industry underwent a shift from entertainment to art as a result of a number of key factors, including the establishment of competitive film festivals, ties to universities, the transition from studio- to director-centered production, and the intellectualizing discourse of critics. Popular music has benefited from many of the same factors: there are prizes awarded to popular musicians, such as the Grammys and the Mercury Prize, university departments and academic journals devoted to the subject, and popular music critics employed by newspapers and magazines the world over. Similar to the studio-to-director shift in film, the shift from performing standards and other musicians' compositions to writing one's own material marks an artistic shift in a musician's career, and it is a criterion used to distinguish popular musicians as artists from popular musicians as entertainers (recall the Beatles' transition from entertaining moptops to artistic visionaries).

In the high arts, not every work will meet the demands of the art world's shared aesthetic standards. A work can be accused of being inauthentic, commercial, unoriginal, or simply bad; even Adorno admitted that there is "bad serious music which may be as rigid and mechanical as popular music" (1990: 304). But at least there *exist* shared, if constantly changing, aesthetic standards against which judgments are passed. The category of popular music does not adhere to a single set of aesthetic values. To be sure, many of Adorno's critiques of popular music— its standardization, its pre-digested nature—continue to be articulated as critiques against charting groups. In addition, even among popular music genres where aesthetic values such as authenticity are prized, not all have the same relationship to commercialism that rock does and, consequently, commercial entanglements are not necessarily strained. Certainly authenticity is a salient characteristic of hip-hop discourse, but tends to be tied more to street credibility than to commercial affiliation; "keeping it real" does not preclude partnerships with sneaker or beverage companies. Qualities present in some types of popular music—acquiescence to market trends, easy entry into commercial relationships—are thus carried around as baggage by musicians opposed to those same traits. That varying and sometimes oppositional philosophies co-exist under the broad banner of "popular music" is a reminder that, like other examples of popular culture, the category of popular music is both fluid and internally contradictory, which presents an obstacle to the creation of and devotion to rules that might assert popular music more clearly as art. Because commercial affiliation and corporate sponsorship are difficult issues to negotiate for some artists but free of tension for others, there is no consistent rule by which the use of popular music in advertising can be judged.

One reason why popular music that considers itself art becomes easily conflated with popular music that has no such ambitions is that both involve similar, if not identical, modes of production, distribution, and consumption. The most artistic popular music and the most commercial popular music circulate in the same form and system. The form of popular music is an intrinsic obstacle to its artistic legitimation; like other mass-produced and -distributed media, the sheer magnitude of the form can seem counter to art-ness, where the "aura" of uniqueness once dominated as an aesthetic standard (Benjamin 1968). By 1900, the age of mechanical reproduction problematized the concept of the aura and rendered uniqueness no longer a requisite standard of art. With reproducibility accepted as a characteristic of new arts such as photography, the stage was set for other reproducible forms to enter the art world. However, even as the aura faded, the concern over whether art was pure (art for art's sake) persisted. In creative form, popular music had siblings in the legitimated art world, but in function it stood out as commodity.

Being denied artistic legitimation in part because of popular music's status as commodity creates the false impression that "real" art in capitalist democracies resides somehow outside of market commodification. This is hardly the case. As Becker pointed out, the popular arts are not alone in being treated as commodities: "Many, but not all, societies treat art as a commodity which can be bought and sold like any other commodity" (1982: 167). In the United States, there is no art that is produced and consumed outside of the commodity system: "popular culture is distributed by profit-seeking firms that try to maximize the audience, but then so is much of high culture, at least in America, where government subsidies and rich patrons are few" (Gans 1999: 31). Though the arts are created within a commodity system, not all commodities begin life equally; there is a "clash between the commodity status of art and the status of commodities" (Bogart 1995: 8). For the popular arts, entrenched as they are in a commercial system, value tends to be assessed in terms of profitability. As Caves (2000) highlighted, the economist's view of cultural output as mere commodity fails to take into account the "art for art's sake" property of creative work.

Production is not the only stage that unites aesthetically diverse types of popular music; all varieties also share distribution and consumption practices, albeit to different degrees. Compact discs are produced in part to be played on radio, often commercial, and music videos are created to be played on commercial television. While most musicians may never receive exposure by either medium, few, if any, would object to being played on the grounds that it is a commercial system. That is, even though some musicians adopt a stance of anti-commercialism with relation to the creative process of music-making, functioning within an intrinsically commercial system is not seen as a contradiction. In terms of distribution, too, both ends of the popular music spectrum receive similar treatment, sold through offline and online record stores, be they large chains or small independents. Ultimately, aesthetic and philosophical differences within the category of popular music can get lost behind the seeming monolith presented by shared modes of production, distribution, and consumption.

While it is true that not every musical performer adheres to the same artistic standards and boundaries, measured by its related practices, the popular music industry as a whole has achieved the shift "from a form of entertainment to a cultural genre that could properly be appreciated as art" (Baumann 2001: 404). With this shift comes the opportunity for individuals involved in the production and consumption of popular music to participate in the debates surrounding associations between popular music and advertising. When it comes to the use of music in advertising, old divides resurface in a way that differentiates popular music from classical music. Classical music is viewed as clearly being degraded by commercial interest, while the impact on popular music is less clear.

The tension between artists and advertisers existed in the fine art world long before the popular arts were recognized as potentially subject to similar artistic standards. The position that popular musicians find themselves in today was occupied at the turn of the twentieth century by fine artists who hoped to attain visibility and financial stability through illustrating print advertisements; charges of commercialism soon followed (Bogart 1995). "Commercial arts," explained Becker, "use more or less the same skills and materials as fine arts but deliberately put them to uses no one regards as artistic, uses which find their meaning and justification in a world organized around some activity other than art" (1982: 296).

In the case of popular music licensing, Becker's definition of the commercial arts becomes complicated. Commercial use was probably not what the artist intended at creation, but the introduction of popular music into a world organized around commerce can eclipse the originally intended use. The concern being expressed by "sell out" discourse is that commercial affiliation might devalue as mere commerce what fans and musicians believe to be art. Despite popular music's different intentional origin, its relatively new relationship to advertising nonetheless mirrors the long-standing tension between fine art and advertising, "a century of uncertain courtship between artist and advertiser," in which artists are "eager to enter the agency, make a fast buck, and depart with independence intact" (Lears 1987: 133). Similarly, negative responses to the practice of song licensing in advertising parallel early-twentieth-century critiques of commercial art wherein "many observers perceived the forces of commerce to be adversely affecting the intents and practices of artists and to be encroaching inappropriately into realms of experience once deemed private" (Bogart 1995: 4).

Since the popular arts are already considered in many ways "commercial"—because they are openly distributed in commodified forms and through commercial media industries—as opposed to the high arts, popular artists are always already involved in the creation of work that is both cultural and commercial. As a consequence, popular artists must remain aware of the decisions that could result in being perceived as excessively commercial. By situating themselves in opposition to commerce's goals and activities, even while reaping commerce's rewards, popular musicians can stake a claim to artistic integrity.

As Frith put it, "The belief in a continuing struggle between music and commerce is the core of rock ideology" (1981: 41). Because popular music is promoted as an art, the music industry has an interest in preserving this ideology. To compensate for popular music's position within a commercial system, commodity culture and capitalism are sometimes stridently scorned by musicians for fundamentally valuing the bottom-line over aesthetics. Stratton argued that the economic structure of the music industry "requires the apparent conflict between art and capitalism for its preservation" (1983: 153). For Stratton, a reliance on an ideology of art allows consumers to see beyond the commodity form of records. He asserted that the "distancing of the music from its originator, the artist, is a matter not only of its assumption of commodity form but also one of societal positioning. The music is not only commodified; in the process it is also distanced, alienated, from the artist, and becomes an object which is understood to exist in its own right" (Stratton 1983: 148). Romantic ideology distracts consumers from the process of commodification, and the record company's success is tied to its ability to achieve this connection between artist and consumer. The connection between artist and consumer is by no means steady and impervious to harm; the life that popular music leads, particularly as it is appropriated within other media, can be a reminder of popular music's non-aesthetic properties, such as its willingness to adapt to external commercial settings.

Popular music has long been adopted for use within art and entertainment settings, such as film, television, and sports events, and recycled within popular music itself. Frith considered the relationship between popular music and other industries: "Individual consumption is not records' only fate as commodities; they are also used as the 'inputs' for other media. This is most obviously true for radio … but even when the media are not so closely joined, the record industry can be a means to further profits" (1981: 127). The institutional settings that adopt popular music in order to sell services and products provide one of the current battlegrounds on which the struggle between cultural and commercial interests takes place. Grossberg recognized neo-conservatism as the most insidious attack on rock for the way it "celebrates (at least certain forms of) rock, but only by significantly reconstructing its very meanings and significance" (1992: 7). The use of popular music in advertising presents similarly discomfiting situations, in which the embrace of music presents the risk of transmogrification: the musical text "is modified when its use radically changes in ways that the original author could never have imagined" (Tota 2001: 116).

Acknowledging the integration of rock into the mainstream as paradoxical to contemporary attacks on rock, Grossberg wrote that rock "is omnipresent (providing the background music for advertising, television, films and even shopping). And it is not only the classics or oldies but contemporary songs and sounds that are used. Whether or not it has become 'establishment culture,' it does seem that rock is losing its power to encapsulate and articulate resistance and opposition" (1992: 9). What potential to empower can a song retain after an advertiser has used its power to promote a product or service?

Mundy noted that "the relationship between popular music and the screen is a long one and that debates about the relationship between image and sound are not new, even though they may have taken on an urgency and significance which characterizes contemporary concern with the politics of the cultural" (1999: 4). Today, "The dominant use of music on television, one might conclude, is to sell things" (Frith 2002: 281). The tension that exists between popular music and advertising, as expressed by fans and critics, is related to television's already strained relationship to music. Frith mapped out the reasons why the ideology of rock is anti-television: that rock 'n' roll was associated with the radio and, thus, defined against television; that television appealed to a family (not youth) audience; that it accommodated commercial pop against which rock was distinguished (2002: 283). Yet at the same time, it was through television that potential audiences were exposed to rock, and it "could be argued that the visual conventions of rock performance were shaped by television" (Frith 2002: 283). In the same way, while popular music, especially rock music, is by principle anti-commercial, some groups have benefited in record sales and an increase in fanbase through exposure in advertisements. But advertising remains a suspicious partner to music for the same reason that television fails to foster trust: "The very voraciousness with which television consumes all kinds of music suggests that it has little concern for music as music at all" (Frith 2002: 287). It should be no surprise that the most commercial aspect of television (the television commercial) is especially met with suspicion when it forges a relationship with popular music. The debate around the use of popular music in advertising often hinges on what advertising is doing with and doing to music.

Prior debates about the status of popular music as art, current aesthetic distinctions at work within popular music, and ongoing tensions with commercial interests all play a role in the discourse surrounding the practice of song licensing to television commercials. As a result, despite its lengthy history, popular music's relationship to advertising has never been free of critique and apprehension. On the other hand, there is some indication that critical responses to interactions between popular music and advertising are beginning to recede. In the absence of critical monitors, commercial interests would be free to reign over cultural production, a vital reminder that the role of advertising in popular music culture requires constant assessment and scrutiny.

The Evolution of Music in Advertising

Even prior to the industrialization of music and before the advent of television, marketers utilized music as a commercial appeal. In the early twentieth century, radio series featured corporately sponsored music groups, such as the Browning King Orchestra and the Kodak Chorus (Barnouw 1978: 17), and music in retail stores "was more than a lively testimony to the expansion of American concert life. It was part of a new and wider phenomenon in American culture: art in the service of consumer capitalism, art appropriated for and subjected to the interests of commerce" (Tyler 1992: 76). In examining the various uses of music in department stores, from concerts and background music to employee groups, Tyler illustrated that the alliance between music and marketing was never without its critics; early department store concerts "created a mild stir in the press, indicative of both the novelty of such a grand musical fete within a department store and the uneasiness harbored by some about the growing ties between music and commerce" (1992: 81). Critics at the time voiced concern that "music in the service of consumption hollowed out music as an art, robbed it of its integrity, and reduced it to an ugly commodity" (Tyler 1992: 111), an opinion that could just as easily come from the mouths of modern critics commenting on the use of popular music in advertising.

The fears of critics are not without warrant. Music's use in department stores did not simply influence marketing strategies, but also influenced the structure of music. In the department store environment, musical pieces were shortened and modified "to fit commercial needs," a trend that reached into the recording and radio industries too (Tyler 1992: 105). In 2005, McDonald's offered to pay rappers for approved mentions of its Big Mac in songs, perhaps the most extreme contemporary equivalent of this phenomenon (Graser 2005).

As an art, music was not alone in its linkage to commerce; twentieth-century America saw increasing commercialization across the arts. "In the stores music became increasingly bound up with the consumer culture, both as a commodity itself and as an agent for selling other goods. In this, music shared the fate of other art" as evidenced, for example, by the use of poetry in greeting cards (Tyler 1992: 110). The use of music in retail environments continues today, and not without censure; critics charge commercial establishments with "purchasing music so as to consume listeners' responses to it" (Sterne 1997: 25–6). Major chain stores select music meant to be reflective of the brand and to assist in providing the continuity, regardless of geography, offered by chains. Many companies hire employees whose job is solely to attend to the music-related decisions; the clothing chain Urban Outfitters, for example, has a Music Promotions Director who selects the music that is played in the stores and manages Urban Outfitters' sponsorship of live music events. In some cases, a line between the commercial goals of musicians and advertisers is not recognized at all: musicians submit breakfast-themed songs to be played in Waffle House jukeboxes, and Starbucks is releasing high-profile artists on its own record label. Popular music has a prominent role across contemporary marketing, but the most direct use of music in order to sell a product or service is its placement in advertisements.

To Tyler, the modern use of music in commercials is a direct consequence of the early-twentieth-century employment of music in department stores: "Perhaps today's most prominent embodiment of their efforts, reflecting both the power and paradox of the alliance, is the use of music in television commercials" (1992: 112–113). The presence of music in retail environments is a clear predecessor to the practice of licensing music for advertisements, though the history of popular music is in fact replete with relationships to commercial enterprise, all of which can be viewed as overtures to the current licensing mania. The past two decades have witnessed more widespread and conspicuous examples of commercial affiliation in popular music, but the association has in fact existed since the dawn of rock 'n' roll: in 1954 the King himself, Elvis Presley, loaned his voice to a radio jingle for Southern-Maid Donuts (Tayler 2003). In *No Logo*, Klein contended, "The branding of music is not a story of innocence lost," noting that musicians "have been singing ad jingles and signing sponsorship deals since radio's early days, as well as having their songs played on commercial radio stations and signing deals with multinational record companies" (2000: 46). But if historical examples reveal a deep-rooted relationship between musicians and advertisers, these predecessors in corporate affiliation also differ in significant ways from the use of popular music in television commercials.

Commercial radio, the main channel of music distribution, is perhaps the most obvious but least interrogated example of popular music's association with advertising. Discourse surrounding the use of music in television commercials has rarely drawn a parallel between this practice and the commercial radio system, yet in both cases advertising is relied upon to deliver the music to listeners and possibly compel listeners to then purchase records and concert tickets.

The popular music industry has relied on advertising not only to pay for the delivery of music by radio, but also in order to promote its own products. Music marketing ranges from advertisements for albums to the proliferation of artist-related merchandise. In the 1960s there was barely a product category that did not contain goods featuring the Beatles' names and faces. Ads for music have the same self-contained quality as music videos: it is still advertising, but both are primarily selling the music itself. On the other hand, licensing an image for use on a cereal box is similar to licensing a song to a cereal commercial. The primary product being sold is the cereal, and the connection between musician and cereal is an arbitrary one.

Popular musicians have also forged relationships with advertisers through endorsements and sponsorships. Before it became common practice to license music for advertisements, which suggests an implicit endorsement, musicians could be seen and heard lending support for products and services. During the 1980s, concert sponsorships became progressively more common; perfume company Jovan's sponsorship of the Rolling Stones' 1981 tour is considered a defining moment. Though sponsorships can be understood as inverted endorsements—here the company is endorsing the artist—the implied backing works both ways. A band allowing itself to be endorsed by a product suggests an endorsement in return. Plus, with endorsements and sponsorships alike, the companies pay the musicians, an indication of which party is being asked to compromise and which is expected to reap the long-term benefits of the exchange.

Where music licensing diverges from these other examples of interactions with advertising is in the degree to which pre-existing music overlaps with the commercial matter. On commercial radio, music is played between advertising appeals but not during them. Merchandise often features the names and images of the musicians but, aside from jingles composed for spots featuring the products, rarely their music. Endorsements and sponsorships likewise juxtapose images and activities of musicians with slogans and products. When music is played in commercials, however, the artistic and marketing messages are delivered in tandem. The music supports the visuals of the spot, and the visuals of the spot add an additional layer to the music. Sterne's assessment of the purpose of music in commercial spaces rings true for music in advertising as well: "the sound is like another layer of packaging laid over commodities," which "contains the real instructions for use" (1997: 38). Since the 1980s, and in widespread fashion since the mid-1990s, popular song licensing has become pervasive in all moving-visual media industries, but the upsurge has been most dramatic in advertising. *Entertainment Weekly*'s "What's That Song" feature identifies tracks used in ads and TV shows, and both *Advertising Age* and *Creativity* regularly devote space to the trend. Prior to the adoption of popular music in advertising, classical music was used in commercials for its status-marking ability and because it is "the least disliked of all types of music by most sectors of the population" (Thornton 1996: 13). While critics have acknowledged that the use of classical music might attract new listeners to the genre, the practice has been primarily treated as an obvious case of debasement, a sad commentary on modern cultural values that one of the only mass media venues playing classical music is simultaneously abusing it (see, for example, Oestreich 2002). The use of popular music has evoked similar claims, yet the overwhelming presence of popular music in advertising and its more complicated relationship to commercialism have also induced more carefully measured pros and cons.

Evaluations of the practice of song licensing in advertising vary widely depending on the perspective and field of the source. For instance, approaching the practice from a legal standpoint, Miles claimed that, while "musicians have traditionally avoided exploitation by the corporate world, lest they diminish their artistic integrity and become sellouts," now well-respected artists license their music to advertisers and "these artists have not only retained credibility in the music industry, but the exposure in television commercials has boosted their lagging record sales" (2003: 121). In her assessment, Miles devoted little attention to the industry circumstances surrounding licensing to advertisers and the potential consequences of advertising's role in music culture, instead uncritically championing a practice that remains infused with tension and uneasiness. Likewise, Al Kohn, a former vice president of licensing for Warner/Chappell Music and author of the definitive book on music licensing, deemed the hesitance of certain artists to license their music to commercial advertising "a mystery" and concluded, "Modern artists who find their popularity on the wane will soon regret their decision to withhold their approval of licensing their music for commercial purposes" (1996: 1039). Notions of artistic integrity and autonomy never enter into the debate from these perspectives. Taylor's recent piece on the entry of electronica music into television commercials (2007), joins the project of this book by beginning to consider the larger industrial context in which licensing to advertising sits, but is ultimately celebratory of a practice which he sees as clearly beneficial to artists and no longer stigmatized. More critical and cultural voices are needed to insist that the partnership between artists and advertisers does not simply provide evidence of a stigma being lifted; advertisers may feel that by providing an additional venue for popular music they are doing musicians a service, but the relationship often appears more parasitic than philanthropic.

If, as Grossberg has suggested, the fear of co-option by the political right is that rock loses its resistive and oppositional force, song licensing in advertising is more than just proof of rock's place within the establishment: it represents an analogous threat. As Tota explained, the secondhand use of music in advertising may "contaminate some subsequent experiences of listening" (2001: 116). Yet there is a growing chorus of voices (not least, and expectedly, in the advertising industry) that join Miles and Kohn in suggesting that the practice is no longer perceived as a threat, and that the stigma once attached to "selling out" is diminished or gone. In July 2003, "The Music Issue" of *Creativity* proclaimed, "Remember Nike's bold and controversial use of the Beatles' 'Revolution?' At the time, some purists screamed 'Heresy!' Now it's no big deal" (2003: 6). Later in the issue, a headline calls music licensing by advertisers "what used to be called selling out" (2003: 26). Reporting on the practice, the *New York Times* suggested, "The stigma of selling out has begun to wane" (Hanson 1999) and the *New York Daily News* took it a step further, stating, "After decades in which musicians would sooner part with their firstborn than relinquish their songs to the ad industry, suddenly serenading clothes and cars has become the hallmark of cool" (Farber 2001: 12).

Despite the presence of these opinions in the press and in legal and business fields, opposing views continue to circulate. Among these critical voices are musicians, both established and relatively unknown (or, in other words, both financially secure and insecure). There remains a shrinking, but vehement, group of artists who have said they would never license a song to a commercial, including Bruce Springsteen, REM, Paul Simon, and U2 (though U2's involvement in the iPod campaign, promoting the U2 iPod, illustrates the line's fuzziness). Even a few formerly prominent, but now penniless artists refuse to license songs for commercial use; despite living in a motel, Pat MacDonald has turned down numerous six-figure offers for his hit "The Future's So Bright I Gotta Wear Shades," concerned "that his own songs would be ruined for him, as Lou Reed's 'Walk on the Wild Side' was for MacDonald, by its use in a Honda commercial" (Marks 1998: 51).

Finally, a glance at online message boards and letter-to-the-editor sections in music magazines illustrates that, contrary to the claims in *Creativity*, many people still consider Nike's use of "Revolution" to be heresy and still label song licensing to advertising "selling out," at least some of the time.

Recording artists who license their music for use in advertising risk losing credibility with fans and critics, the same audience relied on for career longevity. A song's use in an ad campaign may also reduce the chance that other, potentially more artistic venues such as film will license the track (though, on the other hand, advertising may also help return a track to popular consciousness, increasing the chance it will be licensed again). Whether the song licensing alienates fans or turns off other potential purchasers, the same concern is being articulated: that affiliation with a product or service sullies the emotional resonance of a song. Frith wrote, "Numerous fragments of classical music have had an unexpected second life as advertising tracks, their emotional meaning defined by products and sales talk rather than by composers and conductors" (2002: 281). This statement increasingly applies to popular music, where, in some cases, songs have a *first* life in advertising. Far from being a settled debate, the discussion surrounding the use of popular music in advertising goes on, and with it the call for closer examination.

Chapter 2

Selling Revolution: The Role of Authorship in Music Licensing

The debate over music in advertising often revolves around who has permission to grant the use of a song in a commercial. This chapter considers the role of authorship in music licensing through an examination of the 1987 watershed event that saw the Beatles' "Revolution" licensed to Nike by Michael Jackson, owner of the publishing rights to the group's song catalog. The system of music copyright complicates the assumed link between authorship and ownership such that the songwriter does not necessarily own or control the licensing rights. The use of "Revolution" by Nike is a tale of old notions of authorship struggling to survive under a modern system of copyright, and, as the earliest prominent case of music licensing in a commercial, it is an apt starting point for the analysis of this practice and the larger issues invoked by interactions between popular music and advertising. This case and others like it suggest that popular music does not receive the same type of moral consideration as the fine arts, where the creator is legally protected from uses of the work that may threaten his or her reputation, even after the work has been sold. In the absence of a legally-backed system of authorship ethics, the entry of unguarded commercial interest into the realm of culture is facilitated.

Authorship and Copyright

Different types of creative works throughout different eras have been subject to various conceptions of authorship, and sometimes none at all. Prior to the seventeenth century, scientific texts demanded recognition of the author, while literary works were often anonymously attributed. Stories passed down through oral tradition found no reason for holding on to an original source; the author, like the story, changed hands with each telling. Acknowledgement of the author in scientific texts served the purpose of crediting and holding accountable those that put forth theories. It was not until the seventeenth or eighteenth century that this example was reversed, such that science was accepted as a coherent system that no longer required author verification, while the author became an important figure in literary work in terms of assessing meaning and value, resulting in the modern foregrounding of the author in literary analysis (Foucault 1977).

Fifteenth-century painting in Italy had no room for the notions of originality and autonomy that later came into play with the Romantic conception of authorship; as Baxandall wrote, "in the fifteenth century painting was still too important to be left to the painters" (1972: 3). While surviving works from this era may be among the most prized lining the walls of museums today, the price of these paintings at the time was based as much if not more on the market price of the materials used—gold and aquamarine, in particular—than on the name of the artist who wielded the brush. Over four centuries later holes continued to be poked into presumptions about authorship in the fine art world; Dadaists like Michel Duchamp, for example, complicated and mocked the notion of authorship with their presentation of readymades and use of pseudonyms.

In the literary world, the elusive and highly contested concept of authorial intention has often taken center stage (Foucault 1977). Nineteenth- and twentieth-century literary debates alternately affirmed and questioned the role of the author in determining the meaning of the text. From the 1920s, New Criticism devoted itself to close readings of texts, and decidedly rejected materials outside of the text, especially biographical information about the author. Poststructuralists took this line of thinking to its natural extreme, questioning the presence of the author in readings of the text altogether, and turning years of attention to intentionality on its head by empowering each reader as the real locus of meaning.

As these changes over time suggest, the relative importance of authorship as a category of serious consequence for understanding works has been variable, both for determining financial compensation and as a sign of respect for the creative process. In the contemporary era, discussions of authorship are often linked to discussions of ownership. With mass mediated art, such as film or popular music, the power to make money from and exert control over works is directly tied to copyright, and copyright law has had a significant impact on the cultural understanding of authorship. As Rose explained, "No institutional embodiment of the author-work relation, however, is more fundamental than copyright, which not only makes possible the profitable manufacture and distribution of books, films, and other commodities but also, by endowing it with legal reality, helps to produce and affirm the very identity of author as author" (1993: 1–2). Yet historically copyright is not necessarily owned or controlled by the creator of a work. With popular music, even when the composers are first copyright owners, they are hardly left in a powerful position: "In order to get any financial return from their work, they have to cede many of their rights in it to management companies, publishers, and record labels. To put this another way, the history of music is a history of composers and artists, as well as their rights, being exploited" (Frith and Marshall 2004: 11).

The reason that copyright law "remains unchanged—despite the contradictions between the Romanticist assumptions about authorship and the very real practices of cultural production—is because the law, as it is currently constituted, works to the advantage of wealthy copyright owners" (McLeod 2001: 25–6). Additionally, with popular arts there are so many hands in the pot that the determination of authorship and ownership becomes particularly complicated. Just as with fine arts, the popular arts require an art world inhabited by numerous individuals in various positions to move the work from production to distribution to consumption (Becker 1982). Popular music includes composers, musicians, engineers, producers, and labels in the creative process. While Foucault asserted that "we can easily imagine a culture where discourse would circulate without any need for an author" (1977: 138), this culture becomes less imaginable when the discourse in question is part of a capitalist industry, as it is with popular music.

There is an obvious motivation for artists to maintain this powerful and deified position of authority: modern authorship, or "the ideology of 'authorship'," is inextricably linked to copyright and ownership in Western culture (Jaszi 1994: 31). Privileging the author in this way (which simultaneously grants the author ownership of "meaning") is a profitable business. However, the music industry's copyright system confuses this connection between authorship and ownership. Because music copyright can be bought and sold, individuals outside the creative process may also occupy an ownership position. Major label contracts tend to require the artist to concede at least some copyright ownership to the record company. When the term is up, some artists cannot afford to purchase the rights and instead end up at the mercy of another less artistically invested owner. Even when the band featured in a commercial is well-known and successful, that does not guarantee that the artists agreed to license the song. As a consequence, the hands that control popular music may not belong to individuals with an interest in preserving the integrity of the artist or catalog. This was the situation when Nike licensed the Beatles' "Revolution" for its 1987 ad campaign.

The system of music copyright comprises multiple rights that address all the various ways that songs can be reproduced and, in the eyes of those in the industry, exploited. In order to license a track for placement in a moving-visual medium, a synchronization license must be purchased, allowing the licensee to set the music to visuals (Kohn and Kohn 1996: 429). A synchronization license comprises two sets of rights: publishing and master use. Publishing rights refer to the written composition and come built-in to authorship of a song; songwriters automatically own their publishing. In this way, publishing rights are most closely tied to authorship and the creative origin, except that these rights can be bought, sold, and shared. Many artists enter into publishing deals, where a percentage of publishing rights are ceded in exchange for a cash advance from a music publisher. Music publishers also provide services to the artist, managing copyrights, licensing music, and collecting royalties, which are split between publisher and composer according to contract. Publishing deals, like all legal contracts, can range from the reasonable to the unscrupulous. If an artist made a deal that resulted in a loss of control over the publishing, then a licensee would not need to seek the artist's approval to use the composition, but rather the third party who has purchased or been assigned the rights.

If a licensee wants to use the original version of a song in an ad, as opposed to a cover version, master use rights must also be secured. Master use rights are generally owned and controlled by whoever paid for the sound recording. In some cases this might be the musician, but usually the master use is controlled by a record label, whether independent or major. There are infinite combinations of publishing and master use rights, involving any number of parties and many types of profit splits. Jack McFadden, owner of independent March Records in New York City, described his standard agreement with bands on his label:

> Typically for an independent label, I can't speak for everybody's record contracts, but I give my bands control of their publishing, especially if they already have a publishing deal with someone. On the copyright stuff I have an exclusive license, but in all my contracts these synch things that come up are a mutual agreement. (personal communication, 2005)

McFadden, as well as other independent label heads and employees I spoke with, stressed the importance of fair contracts and good relationships, an indication that morality is used as a distinguishing marker of the independent music world. Even in the absence of a legal imperative, independent labels try to adhere to an unwritten moral code. Major labels, many were quick to point out, may not have the same emotional investment in or concern for any single artist on the roster, resulting in a less egalitarian or less sensitive split of rights.

Typically, the cost of a commercial synchronization license is a flat fee, determined by the renown of the artist and whether the song has been licensed previously. If the advertiser wants to extend the length of time or the territory in which the song will be used, additional fees are negotiated (Kohn and Kohn 1996: 1038). In addition to master use and publishing rights, music copyright encompasses mechanical rights, which protect the mechanical reproduction of music as through music boxes or, most commonly today, compact discs. Performance rights ensure that the copyright owner is compensated for other musicians' public performances of their work, and print rights require the purchase of a license for reproducing sheet music or lyrics. With every use of music comes a connected right (Kohn and Kohn's 1996 music licensing tome trounces *Ulysses* in heft). "The bottom line is that there is a lot of money to be made from the use of a song in a commercial— through the purchase of a synchronization license from the copyright holder in the song, through the performance royalties paid to the copyright holder in a song and through the licensing of a master for the use of an original song" (Miles 2003: 126).

Depending on the distribution of rights, record labels, publishing companies, and any number of third party investors stand to profit from the commercial exploitation of copyright. Advertising presents one of the most profitable vehicles for copyright exploitation, generally demanding fees much higher than would be required to license to film or television programs. Where the creators of music may be concerned that commercial affiliation could negatively impact the reputation of the song or artist, the other parties might only acknowledge this concern insofar as an association with a product or company could limit future use. Because copyright generates income for parties aside from the music's creator, the exploitation of copyright does not necessarily consider the musician's best interest, either financially or artistically.

For all the rights that are connected to popular music, there is one type that is conspicuously missing: moral rights. Most Western countries have adopted some version of France's *droit moral* as a non-economic complement to copyright, in place to protect the artist even in the absence of control over other rights. *Droit moral* are inalienable and grant protection to the work in situations where the integrity or reputation of the artist may be affected, even when the artist no longer owns the copyrights. In the UK, moral rights are in principle acknowledged, but are secondary to economically translatable rights. In the US, negligible recognition of moral rights is limited to the visual arts, and there is no equivalent for music; in fact, the refusal of the US to sign on to international copyright laws has at times been a direct result of a moral rights inclusion. Without moral rights, musicians have no inalienable protection against potentially offensive licensing. Musicians who have for one reason or another assigned publishing rights without a right to refusal, or sold publishing rights altogether, can no longer control the exploitation of their music. That the limited moral laws applied to the visual arts are not extended to popular music implies that popular music is a lesser culture, undeserving of the same protections. As a result, popular music is made vulnerable to commercial interests, creating an environment in which the power in interactions between popular music and advertising resides almost entirely in the advertiser's wallet. This amoral system of music copyright has resulted in some of the more outrageous licensing deals. If American copyright incorporated *droit moral*, the Beatles could have prevented Nike from using "Revolution."

Modern critiques of copyright often argue that copyright is too restrictive, limiting through exorbitant fees artistic uses of copyrighted works, such as sampling in music. Cases like Nike's use of "Revolution" demonstrate how the system of copyright can also negatively impact artists by downplaying or neglecting the moral aspect of artistic creation. Both of these dilemmas illustrate music copyright's blindness to non-economic goals and refusal to afford popular music the same cultural guidelines present in the fine arts. Advertising's relationship to popular music is not legally monitored in the same way as advertising's relationship to the fine arts, allowing distinctions between cultural and commercial goals to be more readily collapsed.

"Revolution" Rights

In 1963, in order to minimize their tax losses, the Beatles were advised to convert their revenue into primarily capital gains rather than income; investing in a publicly held company was one method. The Beatles assigned their publishing rights to manager Brian Epstein's Northern Songs company, and the day that Northern Songs went public laid the groundwork for one of the most notorious cases of music in advertising. Six years after the assignment of the publishing rights, the company's share controllers sold Northern Songs and its assets to the highest bidder, Associated Television Corporation (ATV), and in 1985 ATV sold the catalog once again. Though Yoko Ono and Paul McCartney, never the closest of friends, joined forces in an attempt to purchase the rights, the pair was outbid by Michael Jackson, who bought the catalog for a reported $47.5 million. While the songwriters and their estates continued to collect royalties, they retained no control over licensing decisions. Soon after Jackson's purchase, covers of Beatles songs began appearing in moving visual media, including television commercials, and it was only a matter of time before an original recording made its way into advertising.

In 1987, it was reported that Nike had purchased the rights to use the master recording of "Revolution" in a campaign for their Nike Air, with the message "Nike Air is not a shoe … it's a revolution." This case represented the first time that an original Beatles track would be put to use as a commercial theme song, and the resulting public dialogue between the artists and advertisers presents a microcosm of the dichotomy formed by the two major perspectives that have historically dominated copyright battles: copyright as protecting authorial propriety, on the one side, and copyright as protecting authorial property on the other. The history of copyright is filled with cases that address the "mingling of propriety and property" (Rose 1993: 82).

The living Beatles and Yoko Ono responded to the ad with a lawsuit, claiming that it was written into their contract with Capitol-EMI that their work not be used in commercials. More powerful than the legal charge, which proved tenuous at best, was the claim that such a use of a Beatles song was simply immoral. As Leonard Marks, attorney for Apple Corps. Ltd and Apple Records Inc., explained, "The Beatles don't sing jingles to peddle sneakers, beer, pantyhose or any other commercial product … The Beatles want to stop advertisers from jumping on the bandwagon by trying to sell their products by associating with the Beatles and their music" (Potts 1987: F1).

While the lawsuit presented the four plaintiffs as a cohesive front, the truth is less clear, particularly with regard to whether the objection to the ad was motivated by potential loss of reputation or revenue. Yoko Ono's position was especially ambiguous and wobbly. She endorsed the use in *Time* (Pareles 1987), then sided with the Beatles for the lawsuit, and later sold Lennon's "Instant Karma" to Nike. Much was made of the fact that the fees paid by Nike to license "Instant Karma" through Lennon Music were donated to the United Negro College Fund to endow the John Lennon Scholarship (Farhi 1992). Yoko Ono lent the name of her late husband to Nike yet again in 2004, when *Hello!* reported that she had inked a deal with Nike to produce shoes featuring Lennon's image ("Odds and Ends" 2004). Ono's willingness to license Lennon's music and image not only to advertisers, but to Nike specifically, suggests that her involvement with the lawsuit probably had more to do either with the fact that Lennon's estate would not have received full compensation from the deal or because preventing a united front would have only further alienated her from the surviving Beatles, with whom she had a history of publicly aired battles. Likely, it was a combination of the two; Ono had little to gain, financially or socially, by dissenting.

Paul McCartney, too, has sent mixed messages over the years about his attitude towards commercial affiliation, calling into question the claimed motivation of the lawsuit. Certainly McCartney's post-Beatles career has not been free from commercial affiliation. In 1990, when McCartney scheduled a meeting with Michael Jackson to discuss the commercial placements of Beatles songs, the *Independent* questioned "what arguments McCartney will be using to support his claim that commercial usage demeans the songs" ("Sleeve Notes" 1990: 15) since his tour the previous year had been sponsored by Visa. Some of the advertising and music industry workers I talked to had a similar outlook, viewing all sorts of commercial involvement as similarly compromising, and questioning how licensing to advertising is any different or worse than other corporate relationships. Co-founder and General Manager of spinART records Jeff Price wondered why a musician who had signed to a major label (as corporate an entity as other advertisers), played at venues that sold Budweiser, or worked at a Kohl's would feel conflicted about licensing to a commercial (p.c., 2005). It is true that certain types of commercial affiliation, whether because they are less visible or more deeply ingrained, have been less subject to scrutiny or critique, but it is also true that not all commercial deals affect music and music culture equally. Signs of corporate sponsorship at a concert may be unsavory, but are unlikely to mar the musical content of the show in the way that advertisements have been accused of devaluing licensed music. Commercial affiliation should not be regarded as an all-or-nothing proposition; the use of music in advertising presents unique tensions and consequences.

Some early reports claimed that both Ono and McCartney initially approved of Nike's use of "Revolution" (Battaglio 1987b), yet publicly McCartney disapproved. In an interview in *Rolling Stone*, he expressed the source of his displeasure with the Nike ad: "We were offered Disney, Coca-Cola and the hugest deals in Christendom and beyond," he said. "And we never took them, because we thought, 'Nah, kind of cheapens it.' It cheapens you to go on a commercial, I think" (Magiera 1987: 3). However, based on his involvement with other licensing deals, it seems that McCartney does not hold the same respect for non-Beatles music being used in this manner. Having invested in publishing himself, McCartney was no stranger to licensing music for advertising; he licensed Buddy Holly's "Oh Boy" to Buick (the "Oh Buick!" campaign), for instance. In 2005, McCartney licensed the Wings song "Band on the Run" to Fidelity Investments and agreed to license his single "Fine Line" to Lexus. The Lexus commercial featured the car company's new hybrid, a product arguably in line with McCartney's environmental philosophies. But purity is difficult to maintain when partnering with any large corporation: the *Boston Globe* noted that McCartney's statement claiming that he and Fidelity "have a lot in common—a commitment to helping people, a dedication to the arts, and a belief that you should never stop doing what you love doing" (qtd. in Abelson 2005: F1), came amidst allegations that the company's traders had accepted inappropriate gifts from brokers.

For all of the questions raised by Ono and McCartney's equivocations and later actions, the statements attached to the lawsuit resonated with the press and the public; the perspective that Beatles songs, though legally the property of Capitol-EMI and Michael Jackson, were in fact a part of something much larger and non-economic (propriety) struck a powerful chord and left an indelible mark on the ongoing music licensing conversation.

From the perspective of Nike, the moral component of this battle was simple: the use was legal and therefore they had done no wrong. Nike insisted that whatever problem might exist, it was between the Beatles and their record company ("EMI Calls" 1987). Head of Nike Phil Knight explained, "We negotiated and paid for all legal rights from Capitol-E.M.I., which has the licensing rights to all the Beatles' original recordings, and S.B.K., which represents Michael Jackson's interests as owner of the publishing rights … Any implication that we did anything improper or disrespectful to the Beatles is untrue in our opinion" (qtd. in Pareles 1987: 23). Knight's perspective is consistent with the copyright-as-property argument, where impropriety and disrespect are linked only with the legality of use. Of course, in the copyright world, as in the real world, it is indeed possible to be disrespectful without breaking a law. Capitol-EMI, too, was unapologetic in its insistence that the agreement was legal: one journalist reported that an EMI spokesperson "insisted Capitol had the right to license the use of the song and denied that the spot was an endorsement of Nike by the Beatles. 'We have the right to license the music as we have,' she said. 'We forbade any endorsement [by the Beatles] to Nike'" (Battaglio 1987a: 1). Again, in legal terms the spokesperson's claims were correct, but it is undeniable that the use of this famous track in a commercial represents at least an implicit endorsement of the product, whether or not the Beatles themselves appear in the commercial sporting sneakers and displaying their thumbs up. Part of the appeal of poaching culture is that advertisers can, through such exploitation, attach their products to the cultural moments and figures represented by the music.

Nike representatives went on to suggest that the lawsuit was a strategic attempt by the Beatles to grab headlines; as spokesperson Kevin Brown put it, "It's pretty apparent you can get more press attention if you say, 'Nike rips off the Beatles,' than if you say, 'Apple files another in a series of lawsuits'" (qtd. in Battaglio 1987b). When the company decided not to renew the licensing agreement for a second year, Nike insisted that the decision was unrelated to the lawsuit or public reaction. Any doubt over Nike's claim was ultimately put to rest by the courts, who agreed that the use was a legal one. The absence of *droit moral*, which would have provided the Beatles with a morally-based legal defense, in US copyright law is thus crucial to this decision; "the legal concept of copyright has been shaped by music industry practice and, in particular, by the distribution of music industry power, as much as it has shaped them" (Frith and Marshall 2004: 14). If the Beatles were able to prevent placements, they would *de facto* be blocking revenue streams to other involved parties, including the publishing and master use rights owners (in this instance, Michael Jackson and Capitol-EMI).

Interestingly, the advertising world recognized that the idea of an improper or disrespectful use of "Revolution" could not simply be reduced to a legal argument. But rather than focusing on the wants of the musicians, the perspective of the ad world considered the spot itself, arguing that the ad was a high-quality one and had positive results for company, agency, and artist. *Adweek* credits the spot with not simply benefiting the ad agency, but pushing the advertising world towards art: "Wieden & Kennedy exploded onto the national scene in 1987 with a spot featuring The Beatles' 'Revolution,' a controversial move to introduce Nike's Air technology that showcased their bravery, creativity and ability to push advertising into the realm of art" (Parpis 1999). Indeed, with this campaign, Nike developed a positive reputation within the advertising world that persists today and was reflected in the discussions I had with ad creatives, even if they did not approve of the use of "Revolution": Dan Neri, a creative at Tierney Communications, remarked, "If you look at it back when it ran it was sort of a breakthrough. In the '80s advertising was such a different beast; you can't judge it against what's done today. I don't think popular music was really used like that" (p.c., 2005).

An artistically effective spot could, suggested the ad world's reaction, offset the potentially devaluing impact of licensing a well-known piece of music (an element of music's use in advertising to be examined more deeply in Chapter 3). *Adweek*'s Barbara Lippert defended the use: "it's the late 1980s, a time of appropriation of old ideas, style, irony and of Ringo Starr standing beside a man in a polar bear suit in wine cooler commercials … In any case, Lennon's music is wonderful, and it's great to hear it again … In Revolution, he sang, 'You know it's gonna be all right,' and, indeed in the hands of this agency, it is" (Lippert 1987). Would the advertising world have sung a different tune had the spot been poorly executed?

Echoing Ono's rationalizations regarding commercial use of the Beatles' or Lennon's work, the advertising side has also claimed that licensing music to commercials allows the songs to be heard by a new generation. Whether the Beatles actually need the publicity (they are, after all, the most famous band worldwide), there has been some evidence that viewers have responded to these uses as predicted. When "Instant Karma" was used by Nike, for instance, the "company started getting calls on its 800 number from teens who liked the song (new to them) and wanted to know who sang it so they could find it at the record store" ("So Who Are Those Guys" 1992). Yet before singing the praises of advertising as the optimum channel of music distribution, it should be noted that the Beatles' album *1*, a compilation of the group's number one singles released in 2000, climbed the charts without the aid of a commercial placement. In the case of Nike licensing "Revolution," it seems clear that the advertiser benefited from the exchange far more than the band, whose name and music had already blanketed the globe.

The final perspective that bears consideration is that of the publishing rights' owner, Michael Jackson. Jackson's purchase of the catalog followed two successful collaborations with Paul McCartney, on 1982's "The Girl is Mine" and 1983's "Say, Say, Say" (Johnson 1995: 4). When Jackson purchased the Beatles' publishing rights, the collaboration and friendship ended, and the licensing of

"Revolution" for commercial placement added insult to injury. In 1990, the story of Nike and "Revolution" was revived when Paul McCartney traced Michael Jackson's purchase of the Beatles' publishing to a conversation that he himself had with Jackson about the benefits of investing in music rights. During his friendship with the young pop star, McCartney advised Jackson to invest in publishing, to which Jackson responded, jokingly thought McCartney, that he would buy Paul's publishing ("Michael Jackson Fooled" 1990: 3A).

In the end, Jackson reported feeling guilty about the deal, and the excessive commercialization of the Beatles' work, confessing, "I've cried over this, Paul" (qtd. in Rush and Molloy 1995: 19). But however heavily this guilt has weighed on Jackson, it has not stopped him from continuing to exploit the catalog commercially. George Harrison expressed concern over the continued licensing: "Unless we do something about it, every Beatles song is going to end up advertising bras and pork pies" (Johnson 1995: 4). At the same time, Jackson has insisted that he "sees himself as a custodian of the great recordings of the 1960s," presenting as evidence that he "recently blocked a rap album of Beatles' songs" (Johnson 1995: 4). Although Jackson does seem to exercise some sort of propriety rule in licensing the rights, it is telling that Jackson would see it suitable to license to advertisers but prevent the presumably artistic use of Beatles songs by other musicians. Jackson's line between appropriate and inappropriate uses does not use commercialism as its moral compass.

The significance of authorship to understanding relationships between popular music and advertising is highlighted by the emphasis on property by those individuals in the greatest positions of power and profit. It is not in the interest of copyright owners who are not the original creators to recognize the moral rights of authors or to cede control to authors. Michael Jackson may view himself as custodian, but by refusing to acknowledge the authors' desires, he plants himself firmly on the side of commercial goals. The contractual negotiations involved in licensing are thus mediated by a partial party, resulting in a potentially disastrous situation for cultural works. Imagine if the director of a film had no control over the products placed into his or her work, or if a cultural venue was forced to post the name of a corporate sponsor it did not support in its lobby. The persistent lack of attentiveness towards interactions between popular music and advertising widens the door to this reality.

The Wake of a Cultural Zeitgeist

Although Ono and McCartney's motivations for the lawsuit were ambiguous, and legally Nike was not at fault, many fans and journalists bought into the lawsuit's moral claim that this was a matter of reputation, not money. Today, this early case of popular music being licensed for an advertisement continues to be referenced as the classic example of a television commercial exploiting and devaluing a socially significant song. In terms of interactions between popular music and advertising, this case and others like it illustrate the apparent callousness with which commercial enterprise can sometimes approach and exploit popular music and suggests that advertisers cannot necessarily be trusted to handle popular music with a fan's sensitivity. While the system of music copyright refuses to monitor the morality of associations between popular music and advertising, the public has at times punished companies through vocal disapproval.

When the Nike deal first surfaced, the op-ed pages became populated with angry critics and fans who were devastated by what was largely seen as a defining moment in the commercialization of music. As Chris Morris, the *Los Angeles Reader*'s rock critic, explained, "When 'Revolution' came out in 1968 I was getting teargassed in the streets of Madison. That song is part of the sound track of my political life. It bugs the hell out of me that it has been turned into a shoe ad" (Wiener 1987: 18). Many of the pieces decrying Nike's use of "Revolution" wondered what sacrilegious move would follow. A *New Republic* writer mockingly suggested "Happiness is a Warm Gun" for use by the National Rifle Association (Wiener 1987: 18). The *Washington Post*'s Paul Farhi noted that Nike's use of "Revolution" "kicked up fan protests and a lawsuit" and worried that advertisers "have been grafting popular songs onto ad campaigns for so long that no one complains," before presenting a tongue-in-cheek list of potential appropriations by Madison Avenue, including "Give Pizza a Chance" for Domino's (Farhi 1992: G1). A spokesman for Nike said the company "had received about 150 to 200 letters from people objecting to Nike's use of the song" (Wollenberg 1988).

The advertising trade press responded to the outcry by insisting that fans are merely sensitive about *everything*. *Advertising Age*'s assessment refused to distinguish between fan objection to a political statement (or lack thereof) versus commercial affiliation, a conflation that is unsophisticated: "Remember that a lot of young people were offended when 'Revolution' was released in 1968 because Mr. Lennon's lyrics were saying 'count me out,' and scorned those on the New Left with 'minds that hate'" ("Beatles Still Mean Business" 1987: 16). The *Wall Street Journal* published a parodic report of the "Revolution" story, poking fun at the seriousness with which people responded, and comparing the licensing deal to world political crises:

> The dirty capitalists. Have they no shame? Where is Alex Cockburn when we need him? Mr. Cockburn, a connoisseur of old cars and older ideas, has spent his summer in the Journal huffing and puffing about Singapore and Nicaragua while the summer's biggest mini-story lies untended – the battle over "Revolution." ...
>
> You could bomb Mecca, blow up St. Peter's, dynamite the Washington Monument, wash your car with the American flag, burn the Magna Carta, sack Jerusalem, throw eggs at Graceland and (maybe) admit publicly that you prefer Julian to John Lennon. But sell sneakers with "Revolution"? This is *sacrilege*! ("Review & Outlook: Sacrilege!" 1987: 14)

For all of the joking, the press coverage did recognize Nike's use of "Revolution" as marking an important moment in advertising history: *Brandweek* reported, "Revolution started the revolution; that is, Nike's use of the Beatles' rock anthem to peddle its product pioneered today's endlessly proliferating use of pop music in ads" (Shanahan 2003).

Two decades later, the case of Nike licensing "Revolution" continues to be referenced as an example and omen. Stories of recent examples of music licensing in advertising often mention the case of Nike and "Revolution," in order to show how reaction to the practice has changed over time or as a reminder of why this event mattered, and still does. A *New York Times* fashion review traces the devaluing of the 1960s to the Nike ad: "As readers of op-ed pages may remember, many Americans—baby boomers, to be exact—did not take warmly to the use of a sacrosanct pop cultural product to sell a less mythologized synthetic-soled consumer one" (Bellafante 2001: 8). Other current press references include personal accounts, such as this recollection in the *Toronto Star*:

> As a card-carrying baby boomer, I think I can pinpoint the moment when movie music began to shock and appall my generation.
>
> It was in 1987, the year the Nike shoe company thought it would be cool to use the Beatles' "Revolution" to promote their footwear.
>
> I remember sitting in a movie theatre that year, hearing loud boos from the audience as the Nike ad played. Moviegoers at the time were still fighting commercials in cinemas, a battle long since lost, but they were particularly incensed by the use of "Revolution" as a sales tool. ...
>
> What was most upsetting about Nike's "Revolution" ad, I think, was the incongruity of the message. The song isn't empty pop gibberish; it's a serious protest about the futility of violent uprisings: "When you talk about destruction/ Don't you know that you can count me out." (Howell 2005: D01)

Many people for whom Nike's use of "Revolution" was not of great importance later reflected on this case when the advertising world used other songs. One *Creativity* writer described being unaffected by Nike's use of "Revolution," but confessed that "in the past few months my heart has been crushed by TV commercials that abuse the music from my teenage years, the mid- to late 1970s" (Stockler 2000: 22). Another journalist, who had not even been conceived when the Beatles washed ashore, was not bothered by Nike's use, noting it was "not my generation, after all," but was appalled that Modern English's "Melt with You" was being used to hawk hamburgers for Burger King (Platt 1996: 1).

For people who work in music and advertising, the controversy over Nike using "Revolution" is a significant cultural memory. The informants I spoke with—musicians, music supervisors, licensing managers, and advertising creatives alike—had memories of and opinions about this case. Advertising creative Dan Neri drew inspiration from Nike's "Revolution" campaign when, following the reports that Nike used sweatshop labor, he produced an anti-Nike ad (2005). The spot borrowed the aesthetic of the original ads, inserting shots of child labor into the athletic narrative. Crucial to the power of the spot, explained Neri, was the use of "Revolution," which highlighted the incongruity between Nike's practices and claims. Although the ad was pulled almost as soon as it aired (among other legal issues, the song had not been licensed), it went on to win industry awards. Public showings of the spot elicited polarized reactions; Nike was a beloved client for creatives, respected for its willingness to take artistic risks. While some colleagues praised Neri's work, others saw it as an attack on an industry favorite.

Tim Barnes, music supervisor and sound designer at Lost Planet, who worked as a music supervisor for a Nike campaign in the mid-1990s, recalled seeing the "Revolution" ad:

> I was in college and I wasn't a massive Beatles fan at that point in my musical life, so I don't know if I really thought much of it. I remember being surprised that Nike was so powerful that they were able to do something like that. I guess it resonated with me because I do remember seeing that commercial for the first time. (p.c., 2005)

When Barnes had the opportunity to select music for a Nike ad, he made his decisions based on what he felt would be truly revolutionary: rather than exploiting the fame and social significance of well-known bands, he convinced the company to license tracks by German rock group Faust and experimental indie group Rachel's. The Verve's "Bitter Sweet Symphony" replaced the tracks on later airings, but Barnes was still pleased with what he saw as a subversive choice: "It was so awesome to hear Faust, this fucked up German rock band … on this commercial for Nike, blast into fucking millions of homes across America and worldwide" (Barnes, p.c., 2005).

For musicians who license music to advertising, it would be near impossible to avoid the case of "Revolution" in the decision-making process. Kurt Heasley of Lilys, who licensed a track to a Nike campaign that ran during the 1998 Olympics, was well aware of Nike's position in the history of music licensing: "Oh absolutely, the whole 'Revolution' argument. Everyone wanted to feel like they had the special product, and this is what the new marketing strategy became," he explained, comparing the use of popular music in advertising to what jingles were to the 1970s (p.c., 2005).

This instance of music licensing, while not the first, was significant because it was the Beatles, whose treatment as sacred and untouchable has never been matched by another group. Thus, as BBH's Hegarty put it, "Using a real Beatles track in an ad is crossing a final barrier I suppose" (qtd. in Matthews 1987). Tom Petty, who has refused to license his own music to advertisements, explained, "I hate to see these Beatle songs selling sneakers and stuff. Because the music always meant more to me" (qtd. in Swenson 1987). Not only is the Beatles' music historically and culturally important in and of itself, it is also representative of the 1960s and 1960s values, presenting another reason why this particular case drew so much criticism. The use of the Beatles by Nike is viewed in this way as devaluing not only the Beatles but also an entire era. *New York Times* journalist Frank Rich questioned whether the 1960s died on "the day the Beatles' 'Revolution' popped up in a Nike TV ad" (1999: A15). A writer for the *Ottawa Citizen* proclaimed Nike's use of "Revolution" to be a generation's "icon of misappropriation by the advertising industry" (Dee 1999: A15).

Especially for those unfamiliar with the details of copyright law (which, by my count, is most of us) this use of music, set against the background of artist disapproval, seemed unjust. The lawsuit's moral claims resonated with much of the public, which was moved by the statement of lawyer Marks that the "use of their names, their recording and their goodwill in connection with the Nike commercial and the surrounding ad campaign was completely unauthorized by them" (Potts 1987: F1). A greater knowledge of music copyright than is possessed by the general public would be required to ask the follow-up question of the complainants: Was the use theirs to authorize? At the same time, the gut reaction of the press and public, in defense of the musicians, reveals that music copyright law fails to reflect cultural intuition. Even some advertisers agree that, whatever the legal procedure, the approval of the artists is important to the integrity of a licensing deal. In 1998, when Volkswagen was considering using a Beatles song in an ad campaign, the company, familiar with the Nike debacle, sought to clear the use with the authors before negotiating a fee with the rights owners (Bowley and Rawsthorn 1998).

In light of the power imbalance inherent to interactions between popular music and advertising, where the latter controls the financial viability of the former, sensitivity towards the tradition of authorship is necessary. By linking copyright solely to ownership, morality becomes removed from the equation and the ability to monitor advertising's cultural role. Music copyright law should incorporate the attitude of the public, which, in this case, regards the desires of creators as important, even in the absence of legal ownership. After all, when popular music and advertising meet, it is the cultural interests, not the commercial interests, that need protection.

Music supervisors, who select the music used in commercials, are in a unique position to weigh in on the debate over the importance of authorship to music licensing. Many of the music supervisors I interviewed, whether in-house at advertising agencies or at music supervision companies, came to their positions from a music, not advertising, background first. Josh Rabinowitz of Grey Worldwide, Dan Burt of JWT, and Tim Barnes of Lost Planet have all toured and recorded with bands. Tricia Halloran from HUM continues to DJ on Los Angeles's KCRW. With their love of and experience with music comes a real sensitivity towards the uphill battles that musicians face. However, because of their work in advertising, music supervisors also have a comprehensive understanding of the laws of copyright. If the musician side favors the propriety argument, and the advertising side the property argument, then music supervisors, who straddle the fence between both sides, must confront an internal conflict that replicates the propriety/property tension.

On the one hand, there exists a "they made their bed" mentality. When I asked Ten Music's Sarah Gavigan whether she feels conflicted dealing with rights that she knows are not controlled by the author, she explained,

> I can't be responsible for them selling their rights or not selling their rights. It would be like feeling responsible for somebody selling their stock. They may have made a bad choice, but it was their choice. But, you know, they should know that when they sell their publishing that that's possible. (p.c., 2005)

Perhaps it is ultimately the author's responsibility to maintain some control over copyrights in order to avoid the situation faced by the Beatles. However, most of the artists who have no control over the rights to their music negotiated such deals long before the use of popular music in advertising became standard practice and, therefore, could not have predicted this type of exploitation.

If there is a bright side to this high profile case, it is that through the discourse surrounding Nike's controversial use of "Revolution" many music supervisors and ad creatives who deal with music placement have been sensitized to the concerns about authorship and ownership. Fred Kovey, a copywriter at Walrus, a small creative agency in New York, recalled working on a spot for Atkins that nearly used one of his favorite Zombies songs. For Kovey, that the song was not ultimately used was a relief both because it was saved from overexposure and because, as he discovered, the authors did not control the rights:

> I guess my personal feeling is certainly I would never feel weird about going to a band and saying, "Do you want to use this song for an ad?" because I think it's a great source of money for no extra work. But there's something weirder about it to me when the person who wrote the song doesn't even get to make the call. I mean granted maybe they shouldn't have sold the rights to it but ....
> (p.c., 2005)

Kovey's explanation makes clear that even for individuals familiar with the laws of music copyright, the cases involving a complete lack of power on the part of the author continue to cause discomfort.

However sympathetic advertising creatives and music supervisors may be to the artist's position, their ability to prevent the use of a track for moral reasons is limited in the advertising industry. As this analysis has suggested, the advertising world's attention to moral issues of authorship tends to go no further than ensuring that the use of material is legal. And if the ad industry were truly to turn its focus to morality then surely the issue of authorship in music licensing would be but one item on a long list. Individuals who work for agencies are ultimately bound to serve their bosses and clients, even if this means crossing their own moral lines.

Arnold creative director Chris Carl admitted he "would have a pretty tough time" if he were put in the position of licensing a track that was not controlled by the author, but he reasoned that "at the end of the day I have a job. And I'm trying to actually sell the product and if that's the song and that's what works and I can use it, I guess I'd probably, to be honest, I'd probably do it anyway" (p.c., 2005).

Although they must concede to the desires of the client, the music supervisors I talked to attempted to take the artist's perspective into consideration in the choices they made. Tricia Halloran from the HUM Agency, a music house hired by ad agencies, explained, "I would not consciously pitch things if I knew the artist would hate the idea of it," and, while she acknowledged that she would ultimately serve the client, she also hoped to "put some sensitivity to what the artist wants. It's definitely a balance between the artist and what the client wants" (p.c., 2005).

It is relatively rare today for artists to have absolutely no control over their publishing rights, partly because they have benefited from the hard lessons learned from rock's first generation of musicians to run into copyright woes. But the situation and issues relevant to the case of the Beatles and Nike have been revived with other artists from the same era and in the same powerless rights position. Two similar cases that have provoked a more muted response are Applebee's use of the Turtles' "Happy Together" and Wrangler's use of Creedence Clearwater Revival's "Fortunate Son." In the former example, the publishing rights were licensed and the lyrics changed from "Imagine me and you, or you and me" to "Imagine steak and shrimp, or shrimp and steak", prompting one journalist to resolve, "Whoever pimped 'Happy Together' to Applebee's and turned it into a pitch for meat and seafood must be strangled" (Segal 2004: C01). The songwriter, who does not hold the licensing rights and was unaware that the lyrics could be changed without his permission, was understandably upset by the usage. Wrangler used the original recording of "Fortunate Son," also not controlled by the composer, and edited the track into the ad in a way that undermined the anti-Vietnam sentiment and instead presented the song as a patriotic anthem, upsetting the songwriter and countless fans. Nike's use of "Revolution," as well as these related instances, offers a straightforward plea that easily garners sympathy: what is being dealt with is not sterile copyrighted material, but art, and deserves to be treated as such. The wishes of the artists, whatever their legal right to the music as property, should be respected as an immutable moral component of interactions with advertisers.

In part because musicians have become more familiar with the intricacies of copyright and publishing, and the potentially devastating results of giving up control, there are unlikely to be many more cases that are as clear in their power dynamics and morality as these. However, even if the particularities of this case are rare, it still serves to highlight the discrepancy in power between musicians and corporations (whether those corporations are in the music or sneaker industry).

Licensing deals inevitably revolve around issues of power, regardless of who controls what rights and to what extent. Artists are relying on licensing more and more as a means of gaining revenue and exposure, both of which have become increasingly difficult to come by through traditional avenues. Licensing music is a negligible exercise of power by individuals in the least powerful position in this practice. Defenders of the use of music in advertising claim "it's their choice" as their mantra, but "choice" suggests multiple and equivalent options. Like other cultural debates that respond to questions of obvious power imbalances with claims of choice—discussions of globalization and cultural imperialism, for example—this defense is oversimplified and unfair.

In his essay "Music and Media," Frith considered the relationship between copyright and "the most significant aspect of the twentieth-century technological revolution in the popular music trade: songs and melodies (musical 'works') became an essential component of all forms of mediated entertainment, from the cinema to the mobile phone" (2004: 172). Unfortunately, this licensing bonanza pays little heed to the musician's desires when the musician does not own the rights. Music copyright, with its amoral stance towards authorship, allows cultural creators to thus become unwitting partners to advertisers.

Information about copyright ownership, such that the audience was provided through the high-profile case of Nike licensing "Revolution," can simplify an otherwise complicated practice; there is an overwhelmingly disapproving ethical response to art being used in a way that is inconsistent with the artist's wishes, evidence that copyright law is not aligned with cultural logic. Even when musicians do control their own copyrights, the balance of power more generally still favors corporations in most cases, where multinational companies manage the routes by which musicians may generate revenue. In other words, if licensing to advertising represents the only way that certain musicians might reasonably support themselves through their music, they possess little more power than musicians who sold their rights in similarly desperate situations. The conversation about music in advertising is necessarily a conversation about power, even in contemporary cases where the asymmetry of power is less extreme than in this revolutionary one.

Chapter 3
Commercial Art: Advertising as an Artistic Vehicle for Music Placement

The tension intrinsic to partnerships between popular music and advertising can be partially relieved by melding the intent and characteristics of the advertiser with an artistic form, and consequently emphasizing the similarities between the cultural goals of popular music and the cultural goals of advertising. Sponsorships or product placements are less offensive to fans and critics when they are "done tastefully" and, likewise, advertisements that can be viewed as artistic forms in and of themselves raise fewer concerns about whether they are destroying the music licensed within. In this regard, artistic commercials present what appears to be a more developed blending of commercial and cultural interests.

The use of popular music in advertising can be seen as another example of the modern blurring between entertainment and commercialism; "Today we stand on the threshold of a qualitative breakthrough in the commercialization of our media: the traditional distinction between editorial or creative work and advertising—the separation of church and state—is being toppled by commercial pressures" (McChesney 2004: 138). As cultural-commercial hybrids, both popular music and advertising are open to charges of commercialism, but also to validation as art. McAllister (2003) examined the modern fusion of commercial culture and popular culture, explaining, for instance, that Super Bowl commercials are treated by viewers and the media as popular cultural texts. Popular culture waxes nostalgic about ads from days of yore, ads from foreign lands, and award-winning ads, repackaging traditionally between-program content as entertainment programs. The cable channel TV Land, which re-runs classic television programs, also airs ads from past television eras. How is it that the cultural aspects of some advertising have managed to outweigh and outlive commercial objectives? The television commercials that make this transition are not simply conveying information or selling products, but dressing up the marketing pitch in a decidedly artistic package.

The notion of advertising as art is not new, but as the quality and quantity of creative ads has risen, so too has the acknowledgement of advertising's status as art by individuals outside the industry, including the viewers expected to watch them and the musicians asked to license to them. This chapter considers the history of advertising as art, the role of music supervisors and ad creatives in establishing this perception, and the impact of this characterization on music licensing. It asks whether there remains a rationale for distinguishing commercial from cultural objectives in an era when commercial pitches are presented as art and culture boasts of its own commercial success.

Advertising as Art

From the earliest days of advertising, the concept of advertising as art was promoted within the industry. *The Art Directors Club: Annuals of Advertising Art* has been published since the late 1920s, collecting the year's most thought-provoking and lauded ads alongside commentary. Placed in such a forum the customary goal of advertising, to sell, is no longer the primary goal. Instead, advertising is considered as an artistic form. In the same early period, some cultural critics identified ad creatives as among the most brilliant artists of the time. Shi considered the commentary, positive and negative, of literary intellectuals on advertising in the 1920s; while many wrote about advertising as crass and manipulative, others focused on the artistic innovations and Machine Age spirit of copywriters (Shi 1979). Proponents of mass advertising concluded that the sorry state of modern literature was because the true creative geniuses were working in advertising (Shi 1979).

By the start of the twentieth century, explained Ewen, industrial designers had already recognized the importance of aesthetics to sales, emphasizing the style, rather than mere functionality, of products: "Partly as a response to unprecedented marketing needs; partly to establish a uniform and easily recognizable corporate identity; partly in response to avant-garde tendencies in the arts, giant industrial corporations began to develop multipurpose styling divisions in the first decades of the twentieth century" (1988: 41–2). That products were being pitched and sold based on their style opened a clear entry for advertising, too, to capitalize on the public's presumed response to aesthetically-minded design. The famed ad man Earnest Elmo Calkins described how it was necessary that the products featured in the ads were artistically designed and packaged lest they ruin the stylish ad into which they were thrust. In this way, the changes in industrial design are inextricably linked to the changes in advertising design. "By 1915, the marriage between business planning and aesthetics had already shaped the visible aspect of commerce," and advertising was one realm in which these results could be witnessed (Ewen 1988: 43).

The artistic merit of advertising began to be significantly recognized outside of the industry in the 1960s with the ascent of well-known creative agencies and the subsequent image overhaul of creative workers. In his analysis of advertising's relationship to the 1960s counterculture movement, Frank described how, despite the conservative view of the counterculture as treasonous, "rebel youth culture remains the cultural mode of the corporate moment, used to promote not only specific products but the general idea of life in the cyber-revolution. Commercial fantasies of rebellion, liberation, and outright 'revolution' against the stultifying demands of mass society are commonplace almost to the point of invisibility in advertising, movies, and television programming" (1997: 4). Through his analysis, he complicated the notion of co-optation, "the process by which [co-opters] make rebel subcultures their own" (1997: 8–9), by beginning with the assumption that members of the American corporate world did not simply seek to tap the youth market but identified with the struggles of the counterculture. In the standard countercultural narrative hip is opposed to business, and there is little attention paid to changes in corporate culture (Frank 1997: 18), but, in fact, "Business concern over the creativity crisis roughly paralleled the larger culture's worries about conformity" (Frank 1997: 22).

In this era and as a result of the creative work presented in print advertising, the traditional image of advertising workers entered a period of refitting. Instead of the Man in the Gray Flannel Suit, ad creatives could be imagined as free-thinkers, untamed artists behind some of the most critical visual imagery of the time. With the championing of ad creatives came other activities and institutions that stressed the artistry of advertising. In Chapter 1, the role of external factors in legitimating popular music as art was discussed. Similarly, legitimating forces have contributed to the acceptance of at least some examples of advertising as art. Magazines like *Advertising Age*'s offshoot *Creativity*, which is dedicated to the consideration of advertising's design elements, are a reminder that "effectiveness" in advertising does not only suggest the movement of units; it also has an emotional connotation. An ad may be very effective as an *objet d'art* but may fail to increase sales of the product or brand advertised.

Perhaps the most obvious force in legitimating advertising as art is the presence of organizations that distribute awards for creatively successful commercials. There are dozens of national and international award events in advertising; probably best known is the Clio Awards, which, in 2008, was in its 49th year. The purpose of the Clio Awards is described by the organization in terms of recognizing creativity in advertising: "Founded in 1959 to celebrate creative excellence and innovation in advertising, the Clios inspire and pay tribute to one of the most interesting and influential art forms in modern culture" ("Clio Awards Press Releases" 2006). Awards festivals like this one treat advertising more like artistic visual media such as film, in part because, over time, advertising has become closer to film in quality and visual intent. The broadcasting of some of the awards shows on television also indicates the recognition of advertising as a cultural form.

Among the most significant shifts in the aesthetic history of advertising are the shifts "from explicit statements of value to implicit values and lifestyle images" and from textual material to visual images (Jhally 1987: 22). Both of these shifts allowed advertising to imitate film in terms of aesthetics through the incorporation of more subtle narratives. Less often recognized but no less important to the evolution of advertising is the changing role of sound and music. Sound design in advertising can be of film quality, and the presence of popular music in advertising is more akin to movie soundtracks than to the jingles of yore. The increased use of pre-existing popular music is a natural extension of the 1960s trend that saw advertising creatives replicating the hip chart sounds for use in campaigns. Frank noted, "Admen in the 1960s loved rock'n'roll, or at least claimed they did" (1997: 113). One way they displayed their hipness and youthfulness was through incorporating the sights and sounds of rock music in their work.

As television commercials approach the aesthetic quality of other arts, both visually and aurally, distinguishing markers between the two forms recede in relevance. Even the most common critiques railed against advertising—that it was manipulative and exaggerative—were argued by some to be more analogous to other arts than critics would admit. Surveying the characteristics shared by art and advertising, in 1970 Levitt wrote, "Both are rhetorical, and both are literally false; both expound an emotional reality deeper than the 'real'; both pretend to 'higher' purposes, although different ones; and the excellence of each is judged by its effect on its audiences—its pervasiveness, in short" (1970: 89). Decades later, the distinction between art and advertising is more nebulous than ever, as creative advertising and commercial entertainment vie for the attention of viewers.

Volkswagen and Nick Drake

Conversations about the use of music in advertising often involve distinctions between more and less artistic spots. Volkswagen's 1999 "Milky Way" spot, which featured folksinger Nick Drake's "Pink Moon," is commonly referenced for its artistry among ads featuring licensed music. As a commercial whose artistic power arguably outweighed its selling power, "Milky Way" represents a critical moment in the relationship between popular music and advertising.

At the release of "Milky Way," Volkswagen had behind it a long history of creative innovation in advertising. As Frank (1997) described, advertising creative Bill Bernbach and specifically the Doyle Dane Bernbach agency's Volkswagen campaign started and epitomized advertising's Creative Revolution in the 1960s. Over the course of a decade, VW's image swung from that of a Nazi car company to one of the hippest companies competing in the marketplace. In the mid-1990s, the same aesthetic that was hailed as groundbreaking in the 1960s was again utilized in Volkswagen's ad campaigns, although this time in television commercials as well as print. All white backgrounds and spare visuals (often just the VW vehicle) underlined the campaign's theme: VW was an honest, reliable car that did not need to distract the customer with flash. Arnold's Chris Carl described the 1990s campaign: "They just took what Bernbach did and they modernized it, but they kept its integrity" (Carl, personal communication, 2005). By 1999, Volkswagen had experienced a resurgence in recognition of its creativity in advertising, and by this time the incorporation of music into the company's campaigns was understood as part of its creative strategy: already the company had released ads featuring lesser-known bands like Spiritualized, Luna, Stereolab, and Velocity Girl. Indeed, in 1995, when Velocity Girl was asked to license a song to a VW ad, the artistry of the current campaign played a role in the decision-making process. Velocity Girl's Archie Moore recalled, "I remember thinking then—and even before we were in negotiations—thinking that the 'Drivers Wanted' series of ads was a relatively cool one and we were hoping that our song would end up in one that we liked. And I remember being, not ambivalent, but I wasn't disappointed by it at all. It wasn't a bad commercial" (p.c., 2005).

"Milky Way" continued the tradition of using relatively obscure music, but broke with the spare aesthetic. The 60-second version of the spot opens with a bird's-eye shot sweeping along a river and a VW Cabrio driving across a bridge at night. In the shots that follow, the ad introduces the four young protagonists sitting in the car, sometimes looking up towards the stars in the sky. Halfway through the ad, the car pulls up to a party at a house decorated with festive lanterns and filled with partygoers; the stereotypical drunken college fete is embodied by a fist-pumping attendee emitting, "Woo!" The foursome in the car survey the scene, and look at one another, telepathically agreeing whether to stay or not. In the next shot, the car's lights are turned back on and they return to the road, content to spend the night driving in each other's company over attending the party. The soft strumming of Nick Drake's heartrending "Pink Moon" plays in the background, its lyrics confirming the galactic power that apparently overwhelmed them en route to the party: "I saw it written and I saw it say/ Pink moon is on its way/ And none of you stand so tall/ Pink moon gonna get you all/ It's a pink moon/ It's a pink, pink, pink, pink, pink moon." In the final shot, the VW logo stands in for the moon in the sky, as the tagline "The Cabrio" changes into the company's campaign theme "Drivers Wanted."

The spot gained an almost immediate place in the cultural zeitgeist, with discussions invariably turning to the music. Nick Drake was a British singer-songwriter who released three albums in the late 1960s/early 1970s to little fanfare; the album *Pink Moon* came out in 1972. In 1974, Drake died of an overdose of antidepressants, which was deemed a suicide at the time, a conclusion that continues to be the subject of speculation among fans. After his death, it seemed doubtful that Drake's gentle, moving voice and skillful finger-picking would ever find a wide audience, but over the years his legacy was bolstered by famous fans who cited him as an influence. By the time Boston's Arnold placed "Pink Moon" in the "Milky Way" ad, Drake had achieved cult status, yet only sold a small number of records each year. As a direct result of the ad, Nick Drake and "Pink Moon" were catapulted into popular consciousness. Calvin Johnson, founder of K records, identified Drake as "far ahead of his time" and noted that the VW commercial "struck a chord with people. It was the right time, and people were like, 'Wait, this music speaks to me.' ... and that might not have happened if he wasn't in this commercial" (p.c., 2006). The ad swept the year's awards festivals, and sales of Nick Drake CDs, aided by "as featured in the VW ad" stickers, multiplied. SoundScan figures showed that "year-to-year sales of Drake's album increased nearly 600% during the first 10 weeks of 2000" with *Pink Moon* selling "more than 4,700 units" in 2000 "compared with 815 in the same period in '99" (Morris 2000). The success of "Pink Moon" as a result of VW's campaign left an impression on musicians, established and budding. The youngest musicians I interviewed were members of the Spinto Band, most of who were in their early 20s. Unlike the older musicians I talked to, members of the Spinto Band barely remembered a time when popular music in commercials was rare, yet they still recognized "Milky Way" as a special case and critical event for its ability to bring recognition to an artist previously unknown. As we discussed the licensing of one of their songs to Sears, the Spinto Band's Jon Eaton recalled, "I think the Nick Drake ad actually made a lot of people find out about him. I remember when that came out and it was right around when Napster was happening and next thing I knew on the file sharing program in my school was all Nick Drake albums that everyone had that you could download" (p.c., 2005).

The role of "Pink Moon" in the success of this spot was interesting, in that it both added to the artistry of the commercial and was also protected by the visual artistry of the spot: because the ad "worked"—it was an aesthetic success—the usual negative discourse surrounding the use of popular music in advertising was, if not stopped, at least reduced and accompanied by positive appraisals. Reactions to the ad and its inclusion of the Drake song consistently mentioned the sheer beauty of the spot. One journalist wrote, "As television advertisements go, it is hauntingly beautiful" (Daniel 2000: F1). Another remarked, "Fast-forward a quarter-century, and Drake is all over the TV airwaves thanks to a phenomenally successful VW Cabrio commercial. The understated, beautifully filmed ad—in which the song Pink Moon provides the soundtrack for a night drive—has been airing for months, and is still in regular rotation" (Zivitz 2000: D14). Like the press at the time, advertising creatives were also attentive to the significance of "Milky Way," both for its aesthetic and its impact on Drake's music.

Josh Rabinowitz, director of music at Grey Worldwide, described the spot as "incredibly poignant," explaining, "You feel it. And that's why advertising is kind of cool because it is about ideas and the little sound bites or visual bites in that 30 seconds" (p.c., 2005). Many of the advertising creatives I interviewed referenced this VW ad as critical to the use of music in advertising. Fred Kovey, a copywriter at the small creative agency Walrus, observed, "I think that Nick Drake ad was definitely a big watershed in the ad industry. And that was actually kind of nicely done, I thought" (p.c., 2005). The linking together of the ad being a "watershed" and "nicely done" is no coincidence; it is because the ad was so well executed and so aesthetically successful that the industry and the public reassessed the use of music in advertising around this example. Dan Burt, music coordinator at JWT, pointed to the VW ad as one of the reasons why the attitude towards advertising's use of popular music has changed: "I mean when I started here, it was after that Nick Drake thing and a bunch of other stuff happened, so I don't think it's that big a deal [anymore]. I think a lot of people don't think it's that big a deal if there's a song in a commercial" (p.c., 2006).

While "Milky Way" confirmed for many that advertising and advertising's use of music can be both innovative and artistic, the response to the spot was not entirely positive. For individuals like Lost Planet's Tim Barnes, who was working as a music supervisor, placing pre-existing music into ads, the use of lyrics signaled a turn in the practice of licensing to advertising. From Barnes' perspective, the use of "Pink Moon" provoked questions about where to draw the line in licensing and when a use has a detrimental impact on a song.

I think that Volkswagen and Nick Drake was one of the first things that I was really ever aware of as a licensing thing, outside of "Revolution" and Nike, where someone was actually using lyrics. All the licensing I had done up to that point was all instrumental, it was always cutting around the vocals, using parts of the songs that were instrumental and where there weren't any vocals. You weren't selling—as far as the music goes—you weren't selling this car or Tylenol or whatever based on the lyrical content of a song. You were selling it on just the feeling of the music that was created and I don't think there's anything wrong with that. And I think when you start getting into just slapping up a song, where you're hearing the singing and all this other kind of stuff, that's when I think you really get kind of locked in to the sort of torture of "I can't listen to this song again," or the association becomes so strong. (p.c., 2005)

Likewise, although Dan Burt saw the ad as a tipping point in the use of music in advertising, he also confessed that the spot affected him negatively as a fan of Drake, which, in turn, has influenced the way he sees his job:

I don't know, that kind of ruined Nick Drake for me. Probably a lot of people. I think some of my job is ruining music [laughs]. Before that I had one Nick Drake album and I kind of wanted to get the other ones, and then it was just, like, there's something fun about how this obscure band that you like no one else likes it. While at the same time I'm sure the Nick Drake people are happy to get money because he never made any. (p.c., 2006)

Finally, many of the negative reactions revived the discourse about authorship that had marked the case of "Revolution" being used by Nike: the late Drake obviously was not available to grant permission. "There's nothing new about the corporate world exploiting songs for its own purpose," wrote one reporter. "But it's especially unsettling when singers rise from the dead to hawk wares – even more so when it's someone who never compromised their art" (Zivitz 2000: D14). Through these comments, it is clear that behind even the most lauded uses of music lie shadow dilemmas. Many fans, including those who work in advertising, feel that placing music within a commercial context has the potential to ruin it, whether through cementing a strong association with the product, or by making mainstream an artist that was previously held close by few, and that collaboration with a corporate entity should be a decision left to the artist.

If "Milky Way" can be viewed as legitimating advertising as an art and as a vessel for containing and sharing music, then the uncertainty articulated by those with the greatest stake (advertising's music supervisors) suggests that advertising remains complicated as an art. It is like film in some ways, such as its presentation, but unlike film in others, such as the specifics of its marketing objectives. This sort of concern over the use of music by visual media is almost non-existent with respect to film soundtracks. Still, the overall consensus around this VW spot, in the press coverage and among the individuals involved in music placement, is that the ad did more good than harm, both for pushing forward the concept of advertising as art and for Nick Drake's estate. One journalist noted, "In a running dialogue of posted messages on the Amazon.com site for 'Pink Moon,' those in praise of the advertisement outnumber those decrying its supposed exploitative nature by a ratio of 10-to-1" (Daniel 2000: F1). Unlike previous high-profile cases of popular music used in commercials, "Milky Way" prompted a reassessment of the practice; "It took a dead, obscure English songwriter to reveal a positive side to corporate America's relentless exploitation of rock 'n' roll as a selling tool" (Walker 2001).

Although the creators of "Milky Way" confessed to being surprised by the tremendous reaction to the ad, the actions taken in releasing the ad cast the spot as more than just a promotion for a car. The release of the ad on the internet prior to its distribution was an attempt to connect with consumers of Volkswagen *advertising*, not necessarily Volkswagen vehicles. VW's reputation for and history with featuring music played a key role in this strategy. Volkswagen's director of marketing/advertising explained,

> We're launching on the Internet primarily because we wanted to try something new. We hope it will create a fun and exciting buzz about the ad before it hits the airwaves. We know from our electronic dialogue with customers that there is a significant website audience who really connect with our advertising and the music we use in our ads. This is an easy way to give this group a special preview. (qtd. in "Milky Way" 1999)

The concept of "a special preview" is one typically applied to film, or other artistic forms, and its use in this campaign suggests an active strategy to frame VW advertising as art.

The suggestion that advertising is at times art implies that creative ad workers such as those involved in the decision to license popular music may be characterized as artists. The following section considers ad creatives as artists, examining this conception through the use of music in advertising. Just as the increased artistry in advertising makes commercials a more attractive vehicle for the placement of pre-existing music, popular music acts as a bridge between the competing interests of culture and commerce within advertising.

Artists in Advertising

Advertising agencies can be understood as divided into two distinct spheres: account service and creative. Much like the journalistic division between accounts and editorial, the two sides can at times clash, with the creatives sensitive to being told how to do their jobs. As Arnold's Chris Carl put it:

> It is not so much about what we want to do versus what we're allowed to do, but getting them to learn how to say "no" to a client. All too often account service,

and this does not include all of them, but very often, they are more concerned about pleasing people than doing what's right. (p.c., 2006)

While account service has an interest in pleasing the client, a goal that incidentally includes the success of a spot's artistry, it is the creative side that has the most direct stake in the aesthetic decisions.

Advertising creatives thus act as the connectors between advertising and art, applying creative design to products, services, and brands. They are the artists of advertising agencies. Part of the aesthetic design of commercials is the sound and music, whether composed for the spot or licensed to the spot. For individuals outside of agencies, such as music supervisors or licensing managers at labels, negative stereotypes of advertising workers are challenged by interactions with advertising creatives. Tricia Halloran, whose experience as a DJ for Los Angeles's public station KCRW preceded her joining music house HUM as a music supervisor, described her concern about entering into advertising through this role:

> I think I was a little leery about it in the beginning. I think I kind of viewed it as, like, well I'll go do this job and it'll be a way to earn a paycheck but it won't be that artistic or fulfilling. And the people will all be kind of slimy, but it turns out none of that is true actually. I love the job and the people that work at advertising agencies are all super creative. Most of them went to film school, and they're really into telling stories with their commercials. (p.c., 2005)

Comparisons of ad creatives to roles in the more legitimated arts, especially film, are common, suggesting that for music supervisors the placement of music into advertising and the placement of music into film are not as different as they might have been in a previous era, before advertising was as widely accepted as an aesthetic form. Some of the informants I interviewed referred to advertising creatives as "artists," narrowing the gap formed when art is produced for an explicitly commercial purpose. The director of film and television for Beggars Group, Jenn Lanchart, noted advertising's shift to a more artistic form as it relates to music placement:

> I think things have changed a lot. There's so many different artists working on advertising these days and trying to make commercials look better and sound better. ... There's so many cool people and I've been meeting them and they're really interesting and really into music, familiar with the catalog, and familiar with all sorts of music. And really great creative minds—and they want to get exposure and they want to help you to garner exposure for your artists. (p.c., 2005)

Calling advertising creatives artists may appear to be overstating their role; after all, it is the client who ultimately has the final word. However, as Halloran's mention of "film school" implied, many advertising creatives enter into the advertising world with arts backgrounds. The creatives I talked to hailed from backgrounds in the fine and popular arts, including music, reflecting changes in advertising that began during the Creative Revolution of the 1960s, when figures from the art world began to get involved in advertising as spokespeople and directors (Frank 1997: 138).

The artistic backgrounds described by the advertising creatives I interviewed ranged from fine art training to autodidactic experience with popular art forms. Movement into advertising was portrayed as financially motivated: For graduates of art and design programs, creative jobs in advertising are more available and financially rewarding than many other creative jobs. While working in advertising is not the ultimate goal for most art students, the harsh reality of how difficult it is to sustain oneself as an independent artist sets in at graduation. Jeff Hale found himself incidentally doing work for ad campaigns through a partnership between the design firm he worked for and an advertising agency. He explained:

> I think a lot of the ways that I got involved in advertising—I was a kid coming
> out of design school and I was so green and didn't do my homework enough that
> I kind of walked into a situation where I was involved a lot more in advertising
> than I thought I was. (p.c., 2005)

Hale, working as a freelance designer and painter when we spoke, found full-time advertising work ultimately unsatisfying and is selective about the freelance advertising jobs he picks up. Other creatives rationalized that their full-time jobs in advertising allowed them to afford to work on their own art in their free time. Dan Neri, a creative at Tierney Communications, came from an art background as well, rooted in his early experiences as a graffiti artist. He related his passage from graffiti to advertising:

> I'm from New York and I started doing graffiti on the trains, got caught, got into
> an anti-graffiti program, got into art, then went to Penn State and the University
> of the Arts and learned about everything from sculpture to poetry. The art
> program's pretty diverse which was kind of interesting because you didn't know
> what you were good at. You might be a great puppetmaker, God forbid. But
> you got to try everything. When I got into advertising I found that I really like
> selling, but in a creative way, not in a slimy way. But really using art to move
> people. (p.c., 2005)

The creatives I talked to had all been involved with campaigns that used popular music and/or musicians and, for this reason, it is perhaps not surprising that, in addition to fine art backgrounds, many also had experience as working musicians. Tim Barnes of Lost Planet was in the band Ditchcroaker in the early 1990s, and later became "a hired gun" for artists including the Essex Green, the Silver Jews, and Jim O'Rourke (p.c., 2005). JWT's Dan Burt was in a small band called Knodel, which, he jokingly related, "sold like one record. To a friend" (p.c., 2006). Fred Kovey was a member of the band Aden, which released records on indie label TeenBeat, and Chris Carl of Arnold was in the midst of releasing an album as The Artificial Hearts at the time of our interview. Josh Rabinowitz of Grey described his extensive background as a trained and touring musician:

> In terms of my educational background, I went to a music and art high school in New York. I'm a trombone player. I got a degree in music from Tufts University, went to the New England Conservatory of Music. Then I was a trombone player for many years and had a band that still exists that's been around for about 18 years. (p.c., 2005)

These types of advertising creatives, with their strong backgrounds in fine art and music, are indicative of a generational change in the ad world. In discussing why lesser-known music is used in advertising more often, Arnold's Chris Carl offered, "I think that's definitely a generation thing too. I think that people my age now are in positions where they're making decisions and everybody that I work with has great taste in music" (p.c., 2005). Obviously there have always been people the same age as Carl (mid- to late 30s) working in advertising, but creatives who are now in their 20s and 30s grew up in a different music environment, during the era of college rock and the rise of independent record labels. This generation of ad creatives, in addition to having stronger backgrounds in the arts and music, also displays a taste in music tending more to the underground, rather than the charts, opening up a wealth of music for placement that previously would have been ignored. The use of lesser-known music in advertising is a result of this younger creative generation's presence in advertising.

As much as their backgrounds, ad creatives' taste in music as consumers has an influence on the music suggested to be used in campaigns; a critical qualification for fulfilling the music supervisor role is being a serious music fan. Barnes explained his entry into the field of music supervision as largely a result of "being a fan of the music that I was trying to get used" (p.c., 2005). Carl's description of the role of music in his office makes his agency sound more like a record label or radio station:

> All the guys that work in the creative department have kick ass music collections. They're all completely into music and I don't think that was necessarily [the case before] … not this kind of music, not like music that no one really knew about as much. There's a lot of music lovers in advertising too. That's pretty standard. Everywhere I've ever worked one of the most fun things about it is sharing musical tastes with all the other people you work with. Everyone's trying to show you or expose you to something you might not know of and everyone's trying to outdo each other on what's more obscure. It's such a big part of people who are in the business. There's another reason it's being used, because I'm not sure if that was always the case. (p.c., 2005)

As Volkswagen's "Milky Way" spot illustrated, the artistry of advertising and the use of more obscure music can feed and reinforce each other. The senior vice president of UTV records suggested that the taste of ad creatives, combined with a more open attitude within advertising, is the reason why more obscure music is being used in ads: "They're reaching into their own personal grab bag. There's a lot more willingness on the part of ad agencies and clients to accept that kind of left-field thinking. Ten years ago if a copywriter came up with that idea, [the client would say] 'Yeah, but no one knows "Pink Moon." Let's get "Blue Moon""" (qtd. in Walker 2001). Indeed, this explanation describes exactly how the music for the "Milky Way" spot was selected; Arnold senior copywriter Shane Hutton explained, "I brought in some stuff from my record collection, and that song was one of them. As soon as I played the Nick Drake track for [creative director] Tim [Vaccarino], it was like, 'Done'" (qtd. in Morris 2000). The use of more obscure music is part of a creative shift in advertising. Michael Nieves, whose company Sugaroo! represents the catalogs of a number of independent labels available for placement in visual media, remarked,

> A lot of creatives in advertising agencies now they're into this idea of turning people on to music through their work. I think almost specifically in opposition to the more tried and true use of a recognizable song—I mean on one level using a recognizable song is easy, anybody can use a recognizable song if you have the budget for it. I think it takes a lot more creativity to go and turn people on to your thing by turning them on to a piece of music they've never heard before. (p.c., 2005)

Both experience in the arts and passion as music consumers help to inform the way that creatives approach and view their work in advertising, not merely as vehicles through which products are sold, but potentially as works of art. How advertising creatives understand their jobs, with respect to both artistic and commercial goals, suggests a sometimes tenuous position, and one not dissimilar to the position of musicians who license to advertising campaigns. The creative work performed by creative directors, artistic directors, and copywriters is, like licensed music, placed in the context of marketing; like musicians, ad creatives recognize this outlet for their artistry as ultimately controlled by the interests of the client, and, as such, distinct from the art they may create independently. The relationship between popular music and advertising is fraught even for individuals positioned occupationally within the advertising industry.

Straddling Culture and Commerce

Although advertising creatives do not possess the same independence and freedom that artists can boast, advertising is a space in which creatively fulfilling work can and does get produced. Dan Neri described advertising as one of few places where creativity is financially rewarding: "There's a lot of ways to be creative, but I don't know that there's a lot of ways to make the money you make in advertising [by] being creative and that's the trap" (p.c., 2005). Advertising offers the rare combination of being a financially sustaining career while providing "a place to be creative, and space to do something that would be fulfilling" (Barnes, p.c., 2005).

As discussed earlier, changes in the quality of and approach to advertising have made the medium closer in some ways to film, and this is an aspect of commercials recognized by all of the parties involved in music licensing, from the ad creatives and the licensing managers, to the musicians. In explaining why the use of popular music in advertising has become more common, the potential artistry and creativity of advertising consistently emerged as a mediating factor. Carianne Brown, director of film and television music for Universal Music Publishing, pointed to the quality and creativity of spots as responsible for the changing attitudes of musicians she represents:

> The quality of the spots are better. You don't have the cheesy commercials that you used to years ago. And I think people have a lot more pride in ads than they used to. The spots are just so much more creative. So that makes a huge difference. If we're talking about a really cheesy brand or product, that's one thing, but a lot of the car commercials in particular have done some really great spots. And alcohol [companies] have put together some really really great spots, so it's not as taboo to be part of it because the quality is better. (p.c., 2006)

For independent artists, too, the artistry of commercials has become an important factor in deciding whether or not to license to a campaign. The Beggars Group's Jenn Lanchart described the decision-making process of Chan Marshall (Cat Power) as being strongly influenced by the visuals of the spot: "Chan is very interested in working in all entities including advertising if it's the right thing. She's directly involved in any placement that I have her music in. I mean she wants me to pitch her music everywhere. If she believes in it, if she feels it's a good spot aesthetically, she'll do it" (p.c., 2005). Rather than dismissing advertising out of hand, the aesthetics are judged just as any other vehicle for music placement would be, a major shift from the days when commercial affiliation of any sort by musicians was necessarily a lightning rod for criticism.

The emergence of music videos as a cultural form has assisted in recontextualizing commercials, particularly those relying on a popular music soundtrack, as art. Music videos are themselves advertisements for records and, in form, commercials are sometimes indistinguishable from videos. Talking about the placement of an MIA song in a Honda campaign, Tricia Halloran, music supervisor at the HUM Agency, explained why the previously advertising-wary artist chose to license to this spot: "I think because these ads are so artistic and beautifully rendered and animated and they really don't look like ads at all, they look like music videos. This is a project that she felt like she could really see her music in" (p.c., 2005).

Jack McFadden, owner of March Records, summed up the perspective that has allowed advertising to emerge as a vehicle for popular music on par with film and television: "You have to sometimes see the commercial first. Is the commercial cute or not? Because commercials are art. I mean, they really are. I mean they're commercials, but in the end they can be pretty" (p.c., 2005). There is perhaps no greater evidence of advertising's movement into realms formerly occupied by more traditional arts than the emotional resonance experienced by viewers. McFadden recalled the emotional reaction provoked by an ad that featured one of the bands on his label: "When I saw the Hummer ad, honestly I knew nothing about Hummer and, like I said, I don't really like Hummer, but when I saw the ad I fucking cried. It was just pretty and cute" (p.c., 2005).

The involvement of directors and other creative workers from the film, television, and music video industries further demonstrates that at least some commercials can be viewed as art. The presence of directors who are known for their work outside of advertising helps to draw commercials into a more artistically legitimated position. Copywriter Kovey noted the fuzzy line between having a "Michel Gondry video for your song" and having "your song used in a commercial directed by Michel Gondry. There are definitely a lot of weird lines" (p.c., 2005). Tricia Halloran described how she included the involvement of directors when pitching commercial offers to bands:

> If you can't send the rough cut then you send a description of specifically what is going on in the ad, what is the product and as many quality creative names as you have, like who directed it, who's going to edit it, the kind of stuff that affects the end product. It's definitely about presenting the project in a way that bands understand it's going to be a quality piece of video. (p.c., 2005)

Likewise, musicians who had licensed songs to commercials relied on names of directors as an assurance that the final product would be creatively executed. The CitiBank ad that featured a Ladybug Transistor song, for instance, was directed by Errol Morris. The Ladybug Transistor's Gary Olson offered,

> That one was actually directed by Errol Morris, the documentary director, so it was a bit arty. And he had done I think four or five other spots of that series and it was cool because it just used the first 30 seconds of the song. It wasn't edited at all. It was an instrumental, but there was no voiceover on it or anything like that. The visual was a kid making faces and at the end a little CitiBank logo popped up for the last few seconds. (p.c., 2005)

In Olson's description of the ad, the spot's artistic characteristics and avoidance of more typical advertising strategies, like voiceover, are appreciated. Joe Pernice of the Pernice Brothers was also swayed by the involvement of director Errol Morris, when he licensed a song to a Southern Comfort ad in Europe (p.c., 2006). Likewise, Kurt Heasley of Lilys mentioned director Roman Coppola's involvement in the

Levi's campaign that used a Lilys song as a promise of good quality (p.c., 2005) and Warren Zanes described the Miller Beer commercial that featured the Del Fuegos as "like a mini-documentary" (p.c., 2006). Even when a big name director is not involved, the use of director names and film styles continue to be used as reference points and indicators of artistry, as when Heasley described the Nike ad featuring a Lilys song as "David Lynch-esque" (p.c., 2005).

Yet for all the characteristics that advertising shares with forms more traditionally considered to be art, ad creatives are keenly aware of the constraints imposed by the industry. In discussing the creative and artistic opportunities presented by working in advertising, the ad creatives I talked to were all quick to acknowledge that it was still just a job, and that ultimately the client's needs had to be served, even if that meant compromising the artistic vision. As Jeff Hale represented the balance between the creative side and the marketing imperative, "You kind of disembody, break into two individuals when you're working on some of this work" (p.c., 2005). Dan Neri also displayed an active awareness of the limitations:

> The funny thing is, advertising, it's a strange business in the sense that it's supposed to be a real creative industry, but it's a real corporate industry in the sense that most agencies act like accounting firms. So, yeah, we want you to be a non-conformist, a really interesting creative, walk around with your shoes off and then if you do it they look at you like, "What the hell?" I don't think there's many people in the industry that are really happy, because we're all frustrated in the sense of being held back creatively. (p.c., 2005)

Arnold's Chris Carl and Grey's Josh Rabinowitz both described the process by which ideas they were initially pleased with were changed through collaboration with the clients or other advertising workers. Although he acknowledged that compromise was sometimes tough, Rabinowitz reasoned, "I just roll with that, that's part of the process" and that, in the end, it's about "getting the work done" (p.c., 2005). Instead of offering constant creative fulfillment, such that the romantic conception of the artist might suggest, advertising provides the possibility of occasional and treasured satisfaction.

"Once a year," was Carl's estimate for how often he is in a position of fully realizing his vision for a spot. "So there's a lot of compromise and a lot of disappointment," he noted, adding, "The times that it goes well it's pretty awesome" (p.c., 2005). When ad creatives discuss the work that falls into this rare category, their language becomes similar to what would be expected from artists talking about sharing work. Tim Barnes described the feeling of seeing his work on television, notably using the word "art" rather than "work": "Something that I did is being transmitted into millions of living rooms and that's cool. Who wouldn't want that? Who wouldn't want some art that they did to get out there?" (p.c., 2005).

The use of music in advertising contains a constant reminder that, despite the similarities, advertising remains distinct from film: the licensing costs are much higher for television commercials than for film or TV program use. "Exploiting" is the term commonly used by those in the industry to describe the process of licensing music to visual media, but the word takes on a more explicitly damaging connotation when applied to advertising. Advertisers are expected to pay a fee that makes up for the damage to the copyright's value incurred by commercial use. That is, when popular music is used in moving-visual media, subsequent opportunities to license may be limited; a film or television producer, or another advertiser, may not want to license a track that is already associated with a particular company. Due to the frequency with which advertisements are broadcast, and their potential to reach a much larger audience than films or television, the association may be viewed as particularly strong to other potential licensees.

A Prettier World: But at What Cost?

As artists who have accepted a certain amount of compromise in order to make a living doing creative work, advertising creatives such as copywriters and music supervisors occupy a position parallel to that of musicians who license work to advertising. Like musicians, advertising creatives tolerate the compromises inherent to working in advertising in order to be able to sustain themselves through creative work. As a consequence, advertising creatives are both sympathetic to the perspectives of musicians and aware of the discomfort of commercial affiliation. "Milky Way" was described as "sensitive and well-executed" by one journalist, who concluded that it had "done Drake's legacy more good than harm" (Zivitz 2000: D14). To be sure, sensitivity was expressed by the spot's copywriter: "It was personally a somewhat difficult decision to change it in any way … It was [edited] to get all the sweetest bits in. It wasn't to mask [Drake's] demons" (Morris 2000).

At the same time, through their work ad creatives help to defuse some of the tensions built into commercial affiliation. An ad like "Milky Way" is one point along an ever-rising trajectory of creativity in advertising, borrowing from the Bernbach age as it ushers in a new age. Licensing music to advertising has been reconsidered by musicians and creatives not because the relationship to companies or products has necessarily changed, but because the relationship to advertising as an art has changed. Dan Neri used Nike as an example of a company that has conjured one reaction for its creativity and another for its business practice: "from an advertising standpoint, all creatives always wanted to work on Nike because that's a brand that sort of changed advertising. Design and advertising came together and everybody wanted to work on Nike," but then news of its sweatshops was released, "and you're in advertising and it was kind of weird" (p.c., 2005).

Advertising, as an art, becomes almost disconnected from the marketing goal for creatives and musicians. Many of those who praised "Milky Way" did so *despite* the product's presence: "Sporty automobiles aside, it's a perfect visual complement to this undeservedly obscure genius" (Greenwald 2000: G09). Instead of focusing on the commercial intent, ads are measured against other forms of art and entertainment. Chris Carl explained that he would disagree with the perspective that "art is art" and advertising is not:

> I think it's like anything else. You can go to a record store and 90 per cent of it is shit, you can go to a gallery and 90 per cent of it is shit, you can go to a book store and 90 per cent of it is shit, and you can watch TV and 90 per cent of it is shit. Advertising is an art form and it's a big part of culture, too (p.c., 2005)

The Spinto Band's Jon Eaton made a similar comparison when he noted a Spike Jonze ad was "a lot more artistic than a lot of the movies where they just use [Outkast's] 'Hey Ya!' while they wash cars or something" (p.c., 2005). In other words, ads that use more obscure songs creatively rank as more artistic than films that stick hit songs into soundtracks, presumably with an eye on sales rather than the creativity of the scene. Just as there is an unsuccessful way to use music in film, there is a successful way to use music in advertising. "I kind of am of the mind that I would like my world to be a little prettier," concluded March Records' Jack McFadden, "and if they're going to use music anyway I would rather them use a Luna song than a Creed song" (p.c., 2005).

Interactions between popular music and advertising are as much a consequence of artists working within commercial industries as they are a consequence of commercial industries seeking to incorporate cultural objects into their marketing pitch. The resulting products, like VW's "Milky Way" spot, are often more aesthetically successful, but may also hide the true relationship between the advertiser and the music incorporated into its campaign. Companies and products may appear to recede behind entertaining or artistic content, but their clear commercial goals persist. This is as much a reality for the advertising creatives producing the spots and the musicians licensing to them as for the viewers.

The swing towards more artistic presentations of advertising was not simply or innocently a result of ad creatives with artistic visions. Like all decisions in advertising, aesthetic changes were linked to what agencies and clients thought would be most effective. As Earnest Elmo Calkins once put it, beauty is the "new business tool" (qtd. in Ewen 1988: 45). Writing of trends in the 1930s, Ewen noted, "At a time when 'art for art's sake' was taking hold as a dominant faith among art critics, *art for control's sake* was becoming the dominant practice in the marketplace" (Ewen 1988: 50).

The use of popular music in advertising can be beneficial to ad creatives, insofar as the option to use pre-existing music opens up creative possibilities. It can also benefit musicians as a sometimes beautiful alternative avenue for exposure and revenue. But popular music's relationship to advertising is especially valuable to companies, and it is important that when weighing the issues involved in interactions between popular music and advertising, this reality is recognized.

In 1996, McAllister commented on "The Camouflage Strategy" of advertising, in which ads are disguised as content: "Frequently, ads combine the ad form with the media forms that surround the ads; like the anticipatory advertisement, they are becoming intertextual, depending upon the audience's knowledge of popular culture" (1996: 105). The use of popular music in advertising exemplifies this practice, and the current popularity of music licensing in advertising can be understood as one example of a larger trend whereby commercial interest is seeking to hide within more entertaining and artistic shells. Especially in the age of time-shifting, when it has become easier than ever for viewers to fast forward through commercials or access commercial-free versions of programming, as through paid downloading, the pressure on advertisers to produce campaigns that people will want to sit through has increased dramatically. This becomes a problem for interactions between popular music and advertising when viewers can no longer easily distinguish commercial from cultural objectives, potentially bestowing advertisers with a greater amount of power, and reducing popular music to a supporting act for advertising messages.

Chapter 4
"The New Radio": Music Licensing as a Response to Industry Woe

One of the biggest music stories of 2000 involved the sudden fame of electronic recording artist Moby who, having never achieved commercial radio play or significant record sales with previous releases, found his album *Play* on the pop charts following the placement of all 18 of its tracks. Snippets turned up in films and television shows, and, for a period of time, in what seemed like every other commercial spot in markets around the world. *Play* tracks were licensed to Nissan, Rolling Rock, Maxwell House, Volkswagen, Nordstrom, and American Express, among others. The licensing orgy around *Play* ultimately led to radio airplay that almost certainly would not have been conceivable otherwise, and record sales in the millions. While the case of Volkswagen licensing "Pink Moon" proved advertising capable of reviving the career of a dead folksinger, Moby's success validated advertising as a launching pad for lesser-known or new musicians in both the independent and major label music worlds, where suddenly licensing became seen as not simply an extra source of revenue, but a way to break an artist.

Since Moby's turn to licensing, similar stories have followed, including those involving artists who had barely cut their teeth when Madison Avenue offered a hand: another electronic act, Dirty Vegas, climbed the charts in 2002 after its infectious "Days Go By" was used in a Mitsubishi ad. The group was dubbed "the first new act to be launched by a 30-second sound byte of a song" (Farber 2002: 46). In 2005 British garage-rockers the Caesars saw a comparable effect after being featured in an iPod spot. Chatter about advertising as the new radio and a life preserver for the record industry became increasingly common in both the trade and popular press. Remarking on the release of Universal Music's CD compilation *As Seen on TV: Songs From Commercials*, one optimistic newspaper reported, "Seems everyone wins when pop music is used in commercials. Advertisers sell more products, and the artists sell more records" ("Pop Music in Ads" 2001: 5D). The compilation included both old, previously undiscovered gems (Nick Drake's "Pink Moon," Trio's "Da Da Da"), classic hits (Cat Stevens' "The Wind," T. Rex's "20th Century Boy"), and more recent tracks by relative unknowns (Badly Drawn Boy's "The Shining," Propellerheads' "History Repeating"), highlighting advertising's capacity to drum up interest for a range of musicians, but it is the capacity to bypass the normal methods of promotion for new artists that particularly captured the interest of record labels.

The use of newer and younger artists in commercials was largely a consequence of the changes in advertising mapped out in Chapter 3: by the mid-1990s music selection in spots began to reflect the advertising creative demographic, many of whom were young men with a passion for alternative and underground music. By the new millennium there had been a major shift in advertising music from the old soul often employed in the 1980s to new and unfamiliar tracks (Simpson 2000). But if the cause of the shift seems obvious, then the major consequences for at least some of the artists licensed were surprising. Conveniently and not by chance, the rising incidence of acts that have broken through advertising has occurred as the radio and music industries have undergone multiple and sometimes disastrous changes. As changes in the radio and music industries have resulted in narrower opportunities for a narrowing range of artists, the advertising industry gladly stepped in to offer musicians and labels large sums of money and potential widespread exposure. The sum of all of these shifts and changes creates a distinct environment for the production of music culture, and casts relationships between popular music and advertising in a new light, with advertisers playing hero to the damsel-in-distress of the struggling artist. Through this partnership, advertising's role in popular music culture became redefined; instead of a last resort for and admitted compromise to the creation and distribution of popular music, advertising was portrayed as a champion of music that might otherwise be unheard. However, celebration of the benefits of licensing to commercials must be weighed against the perceived damage presented by the relationship between music and advertising.

Industrial Context and the Production of Culture

An exploration of the various processes involved in the production of culture can help to provide an understanding of how organizational, legal, and technological factors constrain the creation and distribution of popular music, and why the music industry's interest in licensing to television commercials has risen significantly. Responding to theories of the culture-society relationship that have either formulated culture and society as two autonomous systems or as causally connected, research into the production of culture seeks an alternative approach by turning from the content of culture and "focusing instead on the processes by which elements of culture are fabricated in those milieux where symbol-system production is most self-consciously the center of activity" (Peterson 1976: 10). The increased use of popular music in advertising speaks not simply or necessarily to changes in the content of popular music, but to changes in the context through which popular music is created, distributed, and consumed.

One advantage of studying the processes involved in the production of culture is that, by looking across diverse areas of cultural production, we can "highlight communalities and parallels in the production of symbol systems" (Peterson 1976: 11). Yet this search for communalities has often been inhibited because "the range of work contexts in which culture is produced can be viewed as a continuum from the pure, basic, theoretical, esoteric, or fine, to applied, practical, mundane, or popular", where one type of culture (usually high) is recognized as superior to another (usually popular) (Peterson 1976: 13). In acknowledging the similar processes at work within high and popular culture realms, such as the necessary but strained relationship to commodification, we begin to move beyond the stifling "academic-commercial distinction" (Peterson 1976: 13) that has at times hindered the search for parallel processes. The use of popular music in advertising should not be dismissed as the simple joining of two commercial forms; within popular music, and within advertising, the same distinctions between superior and inferior, artistic and commercial, crop up. But such distinctions do not always predict what type of music is licensed for television commercials: both acts that are perceived as artistic and those that are perceived as commercial have been featured in ads, suggesting that there are other, external factors at work.

Further, by considering the entire cycle of a cultural product, the production of culture perspective helps to compensate for the structural determinism of political economy and the audience privileging of cultural studies. The economic structure is a factor that requires the consideration of cultural studies—and, indeed, "discussions of capitalism have always figured centrally in its work" (Grossberg 1995: 1)—yet it is one factor among many.

By attending to the underlying processes of production, the notion of production is complicated. Production is neither as simple as the creative work of the artist or the meaning-making work of the audience, nor as inhuman as the mechanized factory assembly line pressing compact discs. Like the fine arts, the production of popular culture "involves the joint activity of a number, often a large number, of people" (Becker 1982: 1). And yet because of its mass production, popular culture cannot afford to take the same risks that a painter might; decisions involving the nature of the content are thusly linked to the manufacturing processes. A broad audience appeal is required to support the structure of mass production, which means that, despite industry claims to "give the people what they want," audience *choice* tends to take a backseat to audience *purchase*.

The belief that audience choice is reflective of societal wants or values is challenged by examinations of the processes that limit the range of choices. Heterogeneous audiences, the target of most mass-produced goods, "receive more stereotyped and ideologically conventional products" (Crane 1992: 106), which limits both the range of choices to be made as well as the space available to negotiate (construct) meaning. Classes of variables that have been identified as constraining the production of culture include law, technology, market, industry structure, organizational structure, and occupational careers (Ryan 1985: 3). For example, Ryan (1985) explored the emergence of copyright law and the ASCAP-BMI conflict as these industry changes relate to market competition and diversity.

"The type of industrial structure," wrote Crane, "has important implications for the characteristics of culture in the cultural arena" (1992: 50). The growing presence of popular music in advertising takes place against a backdrop of significant organizational, legal, and technological changes in both the radio and music industries. Consideration of the impact of deregulation and "the digital revolution" on radio and music constructs a framework through which licensing of popular music, long favored by advertisers, became an appealing option for artists and record companies as well. Successful interactions between popular music and advertising require some degree of mutual interest and benefit, and cases like Moby's provide musicians and labels with a rationale for working with advertisers that previously did not exist.

Media Deregulation

The increased use of popular music within commercial settings can in part be attributed to the homogenization of radio that has resulted from increasing media conglomeration, which has locked many musicians out of traditional avenues of exposure. While most of the concern that has been expressed in policy debates is focused on the deteriorating connection between radio stations and their local community as it concerns news, the standardization that has resulted from deregulation is further evident in music playlists, which are also no longer dictated on a local level, but by national conglomerates and programming consultants. Where maximizing profits led to standardization and predictability within commercial radio stations (Rothenbuhler 1987: 81–2), the consolidation of radio has resulted in standardization and predictability between markets, such that artists who formerly may have been denied airplay on some stations and granted airplay on others are practically locked out of all. Just as it is important for citizens to have access to a variety of political voices, so too should a democratic media system offer a variety of cultural forms, popular music included: "The media system is not simply an economic category; it is responsible for transmitting culture, journalism and politically relevant information" (McChesney 2003: 130).

In the aftermath of the 1990s deregulatory acts, four radio groups—Chancellor Media Corporation, Clear Channel, Infinity Broadcasting, and Capstar—controlled 63 per cent of contemporary hit radio/top 40, and 56 per cent of country (Prindle 2003). The range of music played on commercial radio has narrowed as a result. The practice of "pay for play," a modern form of payola involving so-called independent record promoters, is a "glaring example of anti-competitive behavior enhanced by consolidation" (Prindle 2003: 307). And this is one of the more extreme ways that smaller artists and labels get shut out of radio. Regular, and legal, radio routines— not least the low-risk playlists expected from anti-competitive markets—also systematically exclude lesser-known artists. Programming that might be deemed risky is unlikely to make it on to a playlist and there has been speculation that groups unwilling to cooperate with media giants like Clear Channel for touring— Clear Channel also owns a huge number of music venues—are denied airplay as punishment. Multiple factors can be understood to have assisted in reducing the range of music on commercial radio: "Between payola and the conservatism built into large commercial organizations, the range of music getting extensive airplay in the United States has shrunk, and the notion of localism in music content has been nearly eliminated" (McChesney 2004: 232).

Not only has the range within radio stations been threatened by the control of conglomerates, but the range of radio stations within markets, too, has been reduced to only the most profitable. For example, with the purchase of Clear Channel-owned Y100 by Radio One, and the subsequent format change from modern rock to hip-hop, Philadelphia, one of the largest cities in the US, found itself suddenly without a commercial contemporary rock station in 2005. It becomes easy to view companies like Clear Channel and Radio One as the enemy, but, ultimately, it is the environment of excessive commercialism and the bottom-line culture that has resulted from the FCC's measures that is responsible. These are just two of many corporations ready and willing to take advantage of the legislation.

The Future of Music Coalition, a not-for-profit collective of musicians, public policy analysts, and intellectual property law scholars, was formed in 2000 specifically to address the impact of deregulation on music radio. By combining statistical analyses of changes within the radio industry, including ownership consolidation and playlist shortening, with public opinion polling, the Future of Music Coalition has linked the results of deregulation to public dissatisfaction with commercial radio. The organization's 2002 report (DiCola and Thomson) illustrated how format consolidation limits the opportunities of musicians to receive radio play, greater format diversity does not translate to diversity in programming, and radio's relationship with the recording industry leads to playlists dominated by bands signed to one of the five major label conglomerates. Results of their public opinion poll indicated that citizens are not satisfied with the consequences of deregulation; radio listeners prefer for radio stations to be independent and locally owned, and desire a wider range of music that includes local offerings and longer playlists (DiCola and Thomson 2002). The disconnect between the realities of the radio industry and the wants of radio listeners provides evidence that the FCC has failed in serving the public interest, not only with respect to news programming, but also with music.

The advertising world has happily stepped in to fill the void left by the consequences of deregulation, offering artists who might not have access to traditional channels of distribution the chance to have their music heard. The moderator of a panel on music and marketing at the 2004 American Advertising Federation conference makes this connection between radio and marketing explicit: "I think that more and more, as the music business gets dominated by gigantic radio station conglomerates, the artists are going to try to find ways to get around that. And I promise you, it's in marketing and advertising" (Loomis 2004). As an alternative to courting radio play, music licensing affords opportunities to labels big and small. Of the forms into which music is placed, advertising offers both the largest payments for music and the greatest number of potential listeners. For independent labels, commercial radio has always been difficult, if not impossible, to break into, and the consolidation that resulted from deregulation only solidified the exclusion. Jack McFadden, owner of March Records, described the paradox confronting independent labels and artists: "You're locked out of commercial radio, but you're not locked out of commercials. Which is hilarious" (personal communication, 2005). This is the case despite the fact that commercial radio stations are supported by the same corporate advertisers that license music for ad campaigns. "It is so hard to get your songs played on the radio on a regular basis," explained Jenn Lanchart of the Beggars Group. She described the independent label position on radio:

> From an independent artist's standpoint or someone who works at an independent label, I see it as, when they sign with us, they have to be realistic. We have two people working in our radio department. One that does non-commercial and college and one that does commercial radio and specialty, which falls under the commercial radio realm. And the manpower is not going to be as extensive as it is in a major label. We don't have the kind of budgets to pour into radio promotions companies and independent radio promoters to get [playlist] adds on radio stations and the money is a huge factor in that. So a band will be very happy to get a commercial spot and be paid all this money and then if a radio station sees it and they hear it and it makes sense to them and they get an add [to a playlist] from that, great. And that can happen. (p.c., 2005)

Licensing to advertising is seen as not only an alternative avenue for reaching the ears of potential buyers, but also a way to reach the ears of radio programmers. As closed off to risks as radio may be, tracks that create buzz through their use in television commercials can jump the line and be added to radio playlists. Major labels, too, have attempted to take advantage of music licensing with the hope that such exposure will lead to radio play. Particularly in the aftermath of payola scandals, major labels are turning to advertising as another method of promoting new releases. Tim Barnes, music supervisor and sound designer for Lost Planet, considered how the narrowing of radio resulted in labels looking instead towards licensing:

> There's so little room in what's called mass appeal possibilities. There seems to be very little space. Everyone wants the sure thing, that's why I think every U2 record gets launched into major radio stations everywhere. Record labels constantly fight to get into that limited space. And what has happened is that this music licensing thing has grown a second head for the possibilities of the record industry. You used to need a lot of money to go talk to anyone at a major label to license music. This is not a long time ago, this is less than five years ago, you needed to have a lot of money to talk to them because you'd have to talk to their publisher too. And publishers it's the same thing. You needed a lot of money. And then all of a sudden they're calling you. (p.c., 2005)

While the second head of licensing used to be secondary to more traditional music industry interests such as radio and sales, over the past decade its significance has increased, as can be seen both through the growth of music supervision for advertising as a discrete position and by the attention labels now pay to placing tracks in moving-visual media. Indeed, as JWT's Dan Burt notes, it has become common for labels to hire employees to pitch for licensing placements: "there are people at all the major record labels and at some indie ones, too, that if I'm looking for a song for a commercial they'll send us stuff" (p.c., 2006). Film and television placement has become more significant to the major labels and their respective publishing counterparts, explained Carianne Brown, the director of film and television music for Universal Music Publishing, adding that it is "almost like a new radio, because radio stations are a lot more limited now" (p.c., 2006). The view of advertising as the new radio is invoked by musicians, too; Joe Pernice, whose group the Pernice Brothers has licensed to ads for Southern Comfort in Europe and Sears in the United States, echoed Brown's sentiments: "It's almost like commercial and television placement are the new radio" (p.c., 2006). Sarah Gavigan established Ten Music in part to represent indie labels that did not have employees pitching for them. Of licensing to advertising, Gavigan explained, "I started to see that there was definitely something there and, more than that, there was no one representing independents. It was obvious that the majors were going to find their way there eventually, but there was no one representing the independents" (p.c., 2005). Larger independent labels today do have either in-house or outside people pitching their music for placement in film, television, and advertising, and there are a number of music houses that dedicate themselves to the licensing of smaller, independent artists.

Music supervisors often frame their work as similar to that of a radio DJ, suggesting that music licensing is being treated by those close to the practice as picking up the slack of commercial radio, giving listeners what radio is not. Tricia Halloran, a music supervisor at HUM, also works as a DJ for KCRW, and sees the two positions as a perfect fit:

> The reason it's such a good match is because what we try to bring to HUM, what we try to bring to our clients, is a real knowledge about trends in the music business and what's hot and what's upcoming and what's going to break next and where all the great undiscovered music is. That's exactly what I do at KCRW. The things that both a music supervisor and a DJ do are spend a ton of time listening to new music and kind of analyzing it and just having a great knowledge about music, so it's actually a really good fit. (p.c., 2005)

The music supervisors and ad creatives I spoke with described feeling proud to have helped introduce a band to listeners through a commercial placement. Particularly when placing artists that do not have access to commercial radio airplay, music supervisors understand their work as serving both the bands and the audience, much like radio DJs.

If radio is providing a disservice to listeners, its impact on musicians is even more severe. Within the increasingly consolidated media environment, licensing songs for use in television commercials has become a more attractive option to the many groups excluded from radio play as both a quick payday and an opportunity for broad exposure. Those who may have previously dismissed the licensing of songs for use in advertising as, on the whole, compromising, have been forced to reevaluate the option and generate more detailed criteria to apply to specific instances. Thus, while to many it may appear that the stigma attached to commercial affiliation has been lifted, an examination of music in advertising against changes resulting from deregulation suggests that some musicians are licensing not because they are indifferent, but because they are seeking alternative venues for their music. Success stories, like that of Moby, are evidence that licensing to commercials has the potential to triumph over radio and music industry systems that seem determined to exclude most artists from ever being heard on a wide scale.

When *Play* was released in 1999 Moby found himself in a position similar to most other musicians with respect to radio: essentially locked out. Not only was Moby on an independent label, but he also created within a genre of music that, at the time and still today, is given little attention on commercial radio: the *Ottawa Citizen* identified the "pragmatic reason that electronic music is making an instantaneous leap to commercials and soundtracks: No one else will play it" (Lynch 2000: I6). In 2005 Moby described the circumstances under which licensing became the main channel of distribution for *Play*:

> Radio is opening up a bit now, but when *Play* came out all the stations had been bought up by corporations and rigidly formatted to a point where you had four formats, and if you didn't fit into one, you wouldn't get played.
>
> The only people who seemed interested were music supervisors for movies, TV shows and ads. So I thought, well, I've made this record I really like and I want people to hear it, and it won't get played on radio or MTV, so I guess I'll go with people who are willing to take it and present it to the public. (qtd. in Dickie 2005: 46)

Moby has described his and his label's approach to licensing as "indiscriminate," reiterating that, at the time, radio and MTV play evaded him (Harris 2000: 9). For lesser-known artists who license to advertising, a similar indiscriminate approach is expected; the more desperate an artist is for exposure and revenue, the less room there is for moral qualms, either with the philosophies of specific corporations or with commercialism more generally. The public tends to be more understanding of struggling artists who license their work to advertising than of successful artists, who need neither the money nor the exposure. Even so, Moby's decision to license to commercials still drew criticism from fans and other musicians.

Charges of hypocrisy ran especially high when Moby songs started appearing in car commercials. For years, the artist had been an outspoken critic of automobiles, telling the Associated Press, "The automobile is responsible for many of the woes facing mankind today" (qtd. in James 2001: 29). When a soundalike version of his song "Go" was used in a Toyota ad, Moby took steps to ensure that his fans knew the track was not his, was not done with his permission, and that he "would not let his songs be used to sell cars" (qtd. in James 2001: 109). In 1996, and again in

1999 with *Play*, Moby changed his position, licensing to car commercials and then purportedly donating his portion of the compensation to charities.

In addition, Moby's claim that he acquiesced to the licensing deals partly because "I figured that they were going to make the commercial with or without my music, so why not let them use the track and in the process help out some worthwhile charities" (qtd. in James 2001: 109) recalled debates over appropriation that were concurrently being applied to samples on his album. *Play* sampled American roots music from the field recordings of Alan Lomax, raising questions as to whether Moby's use of African-American vocals was inappropriate or trendy. But conceding with the critic who concluded that "Moby's attitude toward his source material is reverent, even wise" (Rosen 2000: 36), the movement of these songs, and their samples, into television advertising opens up further inquiries. In response to the soundalike used by Toyota, Moby seemed appalled that a sound identified with him would be used to promote a commercial product without his consent, yet by licensing tracks from *Play* he puts the sampled musicians in the same position. The late musicians whose voices could be heard in advertisements were unable to give or deny consent and, consequently, are unwilling endorsers of the commercial products advertised. In his discussion of world music sampling, McLeod makes the point that "although financial compensation is important, the monetary protection of traditional musics may not be the most significant issue for many cultures whose music is appropriated" (2001: 49). He notes the significant power ascribed to music as restricting its use, and while he describes this as a clash between Western and traditional musics, certainly there is the same tension between roots music and contemporary music, where the former was not produced in a world or industry of licensing and, some would argue, does not belong there.

Criticisms notwithstanding, the impact of Moby's success can be seen in the sheer amount of new music being used in advertising and the growth of professional positions built around music licensing. Moby's was "a music industry success story that was written early on, largely without radio, defying the traditional view that airplay is key to making a music star" (Boucher 2000), and its result was an industrial reevaluation of that traditional view. Placing music in television commercials moved from a sometimes controversial and certainly unconventional marketing approach to another cog in the standard promotional machine, particularly for artists with no clear entry into commercial radio. A reporter for *Billboard* magazine concluded that, after successes like Moby's brought a new perspective to licensing, "placing music in TV commercials and TV shows has become a viable, as well as increasingly competitive, way to break, market and promote dance/electronic artists, particularly when there are less adventurous souls at radio and video networks willing to take a chance with the genre" (Paoletta 2003).

In fact, claims that the stigma attached to licensing to advertising has diminished or disappeared are almost always linked to the benefits to artists, from the compensation received for the use to the potential to be picked up by radio as a consequence of the exposure. A *Toronto Star* article on Moby traces the practice of licensing to advertising back to Nike's use of "Revolution":

> Providing a pop music backdrop for commercials was once controversial – remember the angst created by Nike's use of the Beatles' "Revolution"? Now it has become a brisk and accepted business. Recently, acts ranging from veteran heavyweights The Who to up-and-coming Gomez have their music hyping products. The crush of music heading into television commercials has changed the mindset of new acts hoping to follow Moby and break through in electronic and DJ- oriented genres. (Boucher 2000)

By providing an environment in which music success stories could take place, advertising received a boost in turn. Slowly, the old stigmas attached to selling out and commercial affiliation were replaced in the press with declarations of new marketing approaches and victories for musicians locked out of radio. Becoming "the sound of commerce" (Segal 2002: C01), as Moby did, was a badge of honor, not shame. Positive experiences like Moby's recontextualized the use of music in commercials for artists eager to be heard, but even more so for labels, worried about another industrial condition changing the way the music industry works: the so-called "digital revolution."

The Digital Revolution

With technological developments in digital music and faster internet access, the illegal downloading of music has caused a panic for the recording industry, which has traditionally relied heavily, though never fully, on record sales for profit. The actual threat to record sales posed by peer-to-peer platforms and piracy has been called into question by critics who point to other explanations for dips in sales, as well as various and inconsistent estimates of sales that do not suggest a simple, steady decline. At the same time, whether or not the threat is real, the anxiety felt by the music industry certainly is. As the industry seeks out legal and technological solutions to illegal downloading and piracy, it has simultaneously explored alternative revenue streams to record sales.

The internet's influence over the terms of music distribution has forced record companies to seek other ways to stay in business (Breen and Forde 2004: 81) and the licensing of performance and publishing rights is a particularly ripe area in this regard. Downloading will not necessarily replace physical formats of music, but the industry is becoming increasingly involved in legitimate downloading services and lawsuits to decrease the use of illegitimate services (Breen and Forde 2004: 84–5). Forde identified "how the music industry is reconfiguring to capitalize on developments" such as the sale of ringtones and "the immense revenues that synchronisation licensing departments (for music use in ads, in films, on TV and increasingly in computer games) bring in" (Breen and Forde 2004: 85). Likewise

Jones noted that the internet, by problematizing where and when the point-of-sale occurs, forced the music industry to shift its focus to music licensing and performance royalties, and that the focus on copyright has overshadowed other issues surrounding digital distribution, including its effect on social exchange (2002: 221).

To date, there is no consistent evidence that illegal downloading is damaging sales; "Despite the RIAA's [Recording Industry Association of America] claims that Napster-driven piracy was eating into profits, recorded music sales in US reached an all-time high of 785.1 million units in 2000, up 4 percent from 1999" (McCourt and Burkart 2003: 339). The digital revolution, then, can be interpreted as simply a convenient excuse for problems that very well may have surfaced even in the absence of the internet. McChesney highlights how the music industry has chosen to blame digitalization almost entirely for its woes, and has sought to maintain its control through restrictive legislation:

> The ease of copying and sharing digital music files has proven nightmarish for music industry executives. It is difficult to isolate and calculate how much of the music industry's financial troubles are due to the Internet, since the industry has proven so dreadful at generating compelling new artists and since radio variety has been flattened by corporate consolidation ... In a genuine democracy, policies would be crafted to structure a music industry that better served the public in light of the new technologies. But in the United States music firms can use their immense political and economic power to get technical standards changed, PR campaigns launched, and copyright laws altered so they can maintain control over the industry. (2004: 222)

However much the threat of digital music has been overstated, the recording industry has not wasted time in looking to other sources of revenue to counter dips, or potential dips, in record sales. It follows that synchronization rights have become an increasingly valuable resource to record companies. Michael Nieves, whose company Sugaroo! represents the catalogs of many independent labels, explained, "with all the obvious stuff, the file-sharing and the downloading and all the things that are causing record sales to plummet, licensing is doing nothing but going up" (p.c., 2005). The implicated consequences of the digital revolution, such as file-sharing, represent a complementary threat to the threat of narrowing radio, and licensing appears to present a solution to both. On the one hand, licensing offers the opportunity to compensate for the exposure lost by changes in radio, which have left most artists without a reliable outlet for being heard. On the other, licensing provides an alternative source of revenue to make up for that which is purportedly being lost to piracy and illegal downloading. But the antidotal potential of licensing is limited by the very fact that it exists as one of few viable alternatives and relies on partnerships with other bottom-line-focused industries. As the advertising world becomes more aware of the music industry's reliance on licensing as a source of exposure, the tradition of paying a fee for such placement may be reconsidered.

Paradoxically, as the music business has become increasingly reliant on license fees, it has simultaneously found it necessary to pay for media exposure or waive rights (Frith 2004: 179), which begs the question, when do the effects of promotion "outweigh the forfeited rights income"? (Frith 2004: 180). The suggestion that song licensing to television commercials can serve as an alternative source of revenue to record sales has provided a rationalization to musicians who are perceived to have crossed a line between cultural and commercial objectives. In reality, whether licensing popular music to advertising will solve the financial problems of musicians and labels in the long run remains in question.

Weighing Evils: Major Labels and MTV versus Advertising

As all labels set their sights on licensing to help keep them afloat through changing times, independent labels also started to view licensing as another way to circumvent the same major music corporations that they had originally sprung up in opposition to. Licensing to advertising provides an avenue that avoids corporate-owned and -operated commercial radio, which has never been kind to independents, but it also challenges the importance of major label record contracts and MTV, both additional signals of the dominance of corporate control in the music industry.

While on the surface it may seem contradictory for artists who have made the decision to work only with independent labels to then license their music to giant corporations, some independent label owners, employees, and musicians talked to me about music licensing as one way for artists to maintain their independent status while still making a living off of their work. Joe Pernice of the Pernice Brothers explained how licensing to advertising allowed him to more easily establish his own record label on which to release his music: "I walked away from a record deal. I wanted to have control over my career so I walked out of a record deal, and I had to pay for my own albums" (p.c., 2006). Sugaroo!'s Michael Nieves described the situation of "fiercely independent" artists who are

> incredibly talented, have gotten major label offers, seven figure major label offers that they've turned down, but then conversely have licensed their songs to commercials because that enables them to continue their indie lifestyle. That enables them to buy the equipment they need to buy. That enables them to make the records they want to make. So by taking the corporate dollars it keeps them out of the clutches of the music business corporate dollars. (p.c., 2005)

In conversations about licensing, it is somewhat startling that MTV is often referred to by musicians and independent label owners as the most egregious offender when it comes to taking advantage of artists' desire for exposure. After all, MTV was created as an outlet for promotional videos, for which artists were "paid" in exposure. Over the years, however, the network has replaced blocks of videos with original programming, which is where the griping about licensing emerges. As spinART's Jeff Price explained, when a video is submitted to MTV, MTV reserves the right to uncouple the music from the visual component and use it as a soundtrack to its shows. Artists are rarely credited—occasionally a credit is provided after the program or as a link on MTV's website—and the usual synchronization fees are not applied. Jack McFadden, owner of March Records, discourages bands on his labels from signing contracts with MTV: "I think MTV exploits [bands]. I never say yes to any MTV show. They don't pay, they prey on indie labels and why should I sign my rights over so that you can use this song in any of your crappy *Real World* shows? Just so I can hear it?" (p.c., 2005). SpinART's Jeff Price calls MTV and MTV's parent company, Viacom, "the most exploitive horrible entity out there":

> It's disgusting. And it's the only entity out there that does this and it cheapens the music and it takes advantage of the situation and it shouldn't be done. And the problem is that a lot of people get stars in their eyes when MTV calls. "Oh great, we're going to be on *Road Rules*!" And they don't really realize what the hell they're doing. Particularly for the younger indie bands, when they authorize the rights and MTV just gets away with it and gets away with it and gets away with it. (p.c., 2005)

In the end, it could be claimed that by licensing music to advertisers, independent artists and labels are snubbing the major music corporations by running into the arms of other, and arguably more malevolent, corporations. How could aligning oneself with Coca-Cola, or Nike, or Sears, through the implicit endorsement of licensing, challenge the fundamental problems associated with the big music companies, when all of these corporations in essence share the same economic blinders that privilege the obvious and obviously profitable over the riskier but culturally progressive? Like all of the choices artistic parties must face when involved in partnerships with advertisers, distinctions become ever more complex, and individual cases a series of weighing pros and cons. Calvin Johnson, founder of K Records, recognized the importance and intricacy of the distinctions, and the extent to which the decision to license to advertising becomes particular to a specific artist and situation as a result: "When those offers come in, I just pass it along and it's entirely up to the band. I personally wouldn't do it because I just feel like it's a line I don't feel comfortable crossing, but I think it's a personal decision and every artist has to decide those things for themselves" (p.c., 2006).

Many artists have taken steps to tip the balance in favor of licensing music to advertising over working with major labels or MTV. Firstly, artists do not blindly enter into a licensing deal with any company or for any product. Although most of the artists I talked to admitted that a product or company would have to be particularly heinous for them to turn down a large sum of money, there have been many reported cases of musicians refusing offers for ethical reasons. A number of independent artists have turned down licensing offers from Hummer, for example. As the guitarist of Trans Am, who turned down an offer of $180,000 from the company, explained, "We figured it was almost like giving music to the Army, or Exxon" (qtd. in Hart 2006). Individuals who represent catalogs keep track of the guiding principles to which their artists adhere. Universal Music Publishing's Carianne Brown explained that it's her job "to know the sensibility" of bands, "to understand what they're going to be okay with and not" (p.c., 2006). Even Moby, who was reported to license to anybody and everybody, refused to cross certain lines, turning down some car commercials and, because of his stance on animal rights and cruelty, ads for cosmetics companies (Harris 2000).

In some cases, artists have atoned for the sin of taking money from corporations by redirecting some or all of the compensation in debatably subversive ways. The anarchist dance-punk group Chumbawamba, who had already received a fair amount of criticism for releasing a major label album, was approached by many advertisers to license their work after the single from that album, "Tubthumping," became a chart hit. Though they turned down what they perceived as especially repulsive offers (Nike, General Electric), Chumbawamba accepted other offers they received and donated the compensation to activists, some of whom scrutinized the behavior of those same companies (Rowan 2002). Their fee of almost $200,000 from General Motors, for use of the track "Pass it Along" in a commercial, went to two global justice organizations (Peterson 2002). Likewise, Moby similarly redirected his fee when he licensed a song to a car commercial in 1996, claiming, "There's something perversely satisfying about taking money from a car company and giving it to organizations which work to protect the environment" (qtd. in James 2001: 109). Ultimately, artists can circumvent commercial radio, major labels, MTV, or any combination thereof, and compensate for dropping record sales at the same time, by licensing to advertising. By redirecting the money paid for the license, artists can then deflect criticism about selling out and possibly contribute to a positive cause. But can any charitable donation even start to compare to the benefit that companies receive through their association with a song and a musician?

Pros and Cons of Licensing as an Alternative

There is no denying that this is an era which calls for alternatives, and from multiple perspectives and for varying reasons, licensing music for use in commercials has presented itself as an attractive alternative. Warren Zanes, former guitarist for the Del Fuegos, while not an unabashed advocate of licensing to commercials (his own band's experience resulted in an unpleasant backlash in the mid-1980s), emphasized, "if you want to be a part of the next phase of the industry you remain elastic ... you remain open to a multitude of options" (p.c., 2006). However, just as licensing to television commercials appears to offer a solution to radio and music industry woes, it simultaneously contributes to the problem of hypercommercialism, and raises important questions about the role of advertising in popular music culture. Further, insofar as they can be measured, the celebrated benefits of licensing to advertising versus radio play and record sales are neither reliable nor guaranteed.

The current state of the radio and music industries leaves much to be desired, and it is no surprise that many entertainment journalists and cultural commentators have expressed a need for new music gatekeepers, whether they be podcasters, music bloggers, or music supervisors. As a writer for the *Guardian* suggested (the problem of conservative radio and MTV programmers is no longer simply an American one),

> If we are to have our records chosen for us, perhaps they're better coming from a hip young ad exec or TV researcher than an industry-soaked Radio 1 producer. Daytime Radio 1 is dominated by R&B, boy bands and the business's hot projects. TV is less predictable. Sky, for example, have championed Flaming Lips and Six By Seven. They haven't made them hits, but as Sky becomes more mainstream it might be just a matter of time. The more power that can be removed from Radio 1 and MTV, the better it will be for consumer choice. (Simpson 2000: 14)

One of the presumed benefits of licensing is that ad creatives are more willing to take risks and provide exposure for bands neglected by traditional avenues, such as commercial radio. The suggestion that exposure can lead to hits relies on the expectation that, through licensing, artists will see an increase in record sales, ticket sales, other licensing opportunities, and radio play. These expectations appear to be validated by the success stories and claims such as this one from Steve Smith, singer of Dirty Vegas: "If we hadn't had the ad behind us, we wouldn't have gotten the song on the radio, and people would never have heard us. It sped up the whole process" (qtd. in Farber 2002: 46). But the truth is that licensing to advertising does not guarantee any of these benefits, and, more often than not, artists see little to no change in record sales and radio play. Even for the artists and genres that did break into radio through advertising, the response was not permanent: "Yes, Moby and Fatboy Slim and the Crystal Method have received some station exposure, but they're hardly in heavy rotation" (Lynch 2000: I6).

Two of the musicians I interviewed saw a substantial increase in record sales after a song was licensed to a commercial. The majority of record sales for the Walkmen album that featured a song licensed to a Saturn commercial occurred after the ad began airing, suggesting that the ad had a strong impact (Green, p.c., 2005). Isaac Green, owner of StarTime International, the Walkmen's then label, told me, "The record sales directly correlated to the exact number of times the ad played. The ad played more, the record sales went up. If it played less, the record sales went down. It was a phenomenon. But most advertisements don't work that well. Some do and some don't" (p.c., 2005). Green also saw the ad as helpful in getting the band commercial radio play, although Hamilton Leithauser, singer of the Walkmen, minimized the impact of the ad, and hesitated making that connection to later radio play: "It definitely made a lot more people aware of who we were. But I don't know, we weren't played on the radio until we had another song that really deserved or sounded more radio. And … the only reason we got on the radio is, I think, because of that song" (p.c., 2005). Similarly, though the Miller Beer commercial provided the Del Fuegos with a "higher level of visibility," Warren Zanes noted, "we kind of felt like it might have taken us longer, but we probably could have gotten there without it" (p.c., 2006).

In order to maximize the potential benefits of licensing to advertising, artists need the right combination of variables in place and a great deal of luck. In the ideal situation, the ad is released around the same time as the record, the artist is touring in support of the record, and the artist is credited in some way, through the spot, the company's website, or press coverage. Moby's success was not due simply to a licensing gimmick: he simultaneously toured and promoted the record for over a year (Boucher 2000). In the end, if the music does not connect with the audience, no amount of promotion or non-traditional marketing will work. Richard Sanders, president of V2 records, which released *Play*, noted, "We could have done all the same things with another record, with a different artist, and it might not have worked. This one struck a chord. We knew we had to go outside traditional, mainstream channels to find success for it, but from there the music is what made it connect" (qtd. in Boucher 2000). But there is no reliable winning combination. For each artist that has seen a commercial placement translate into record sales and radio play, there are hundreds, if not thousands, of others whose experience is anti-climactic in comparison.

The only guaranteed benefit of licensing to advertising is the synchronization fee. In Moby's case, the *Play* licensing bonanza earned a substantial amount of money for the artist and also for the label: "his record company, Mute, has earned a gargantuan amount of money (in the eight-figure ballpark, according to those in the know)" (Harris 2000: 9). This is an extreme case in which an album was fully and repeatedly exploited for commercial placement; most bands would be lucky to have one track licensed to an advertisement. Major labels and their complementary publishing houses employ entire departments of individuals whose job is, as Universal Music Publishing's Carianne Brown (p.c., 2006) put it, "to get as much out of these copyrights as I can," ensuring that the stream from licensing is steady. For independent labels, placements may be infrequent, but still very important. Jeff Price, owner of spinART records, said, "We'll usually have at least one phenomenal monetary compensation, one placement that yields a large master license fee each year. Every year there's something—and it's just that one placement, it's just huge. And it makes a tremendous difference to the artists we work with as well" (p.c., 2005). Although licensing has become a more significant source of revenue for indies, it is hardly a dependable source of income. Jack McFadden of March Records described licensing opportunities as a "lottery ticket": "It's not something you can count on. When you're selling and marketing records the traditional way you can kind of give a rough estimate and you can kind of make sure that you're not going to lose too much money, but you can never predict when someone's going to call you from Kmart" (p.c., 2005). Since the research for this book was conducted, both spinART and March Records have ceased operating, highlighting the unreliability of licensing income.

The irony is that the artists and labels that could use the additional revenue the most are often paid the least. The Rolling Stones and the Who can demand seven figure fees to license their work, while lesser-known artists might settle for one per cent of those fees. Plus, as the stigma attached to licensing has been lifted and as advertisers have begun to recognize the powerful position they are in with respect to music distribution, synchronization fees appear to be steadily decreasing. To StarTime International owner Isaac Green, the reason the fees are decreasing is because the debate over selling out has changed; it used to be that "the ad agency was compensating the band for the damage they would be doing to their career. No one feels that way anymore. Mitsubishi had this Dirty Vegas song and on the strength of it Capitol sold half a million records. And I'm sure Mitsubishi was like, 'Oh, Capitol would do this for free. We just did them a huge favor'" (p.c., 2005). Certainly cases like this prompt important questions: For how much longer will advertisers be willing to pay for music? Will there come a time when labels will pay to have songs placed in advertisements? If the synchronization fee is the only guaranteed benefit of licensing to advertising, the risk of it disappearing is noteworthy. For now, music supervisors try to ensure that artists are being fairly compensated. JWT music supervisor Dan Burt described negotiating a fair fee for artists as his responsibility: "part of what people at my job here are supposed to do is when people come to me with crazy ideas like that, we'd say, 'No, not only is that really low, but it's kind of demeaning.' Can we use your song and give you a Twizzler?" (p.c., 2006).

Licensing to advertising has had an undeniable impact for some artists in terms of getting added to radio playlists and selling records, and Moby represents the ideal scenario. Moby's success story has forever changed the way music in advertising is looked at; in 2002 the *Glasgow Herald* celebrated the latest Moby release by remembering "The Music that Launched a Thousand Products," a list topped by Moby himself ("The List" 2002: 6). At the same time, it is short-sighted to celebrate music licensing as an alternative at the expense of scrutinizing the industry changes that have created an environment in which licensing has taken on a new significance. The opportunities presented by licensing do not relieve us of the responsibility we have to examine and repair the radio and music industries.

That we can hear music in other places does not mean that commercial radio is no longer relevant. Even in this age of digital radio, internet radio, and music licensing, when new music can be heard in a number of new places and ways, commercial radio remains the source through which most people are exposed to new music. There is also a need to scrutinize the practices of the major record companies. *DIG!*, a documentary recounting the friendship and competition between the Dandy Warhols and the Brian Jonestown Massacre, offered a cautionary tale in its illustration of the pitfalls of major label contracts. In the film, TVT Records'

A&R representative Adam Shore commented on the typical success ratio of major labels: "I don't think there's another business in the world where you can have a 90 per cent failure rate and still say you're successful. It's crazy. You should be able to make money off every record. You just have to spend accordingly" (*DIG!*, 2004). (The Dandy Warhols, notably, found success in Europe through a song licensed to Vodafone.) This model would be less problematic if labels continued to offer support to the losing 90 per cent, but those acts instead tend to be dropped or, worse, neglected while still being held under contract. The major label system, driven only by profits, discourages art and encourages standardization. The recent surge in independent record sales is a heartening development, but, again, should not absolve us of our responsibility to monitor industry practices.

For bands that do not get commercial radio play, or the support of major labels and MTV, advertising provides a distribution channel to millions of potential listeners. For independent bands especially, licensing fees can be far greater than the profits earned from record sales or touring. But it is not an ideal alternative. To begin with, television commercials hardly provide an optimum environment in which to hear music. Unless the television is connected to a sound system, television audio does no justice to complex stereo recordings. In addition, typically only thirty seconds or less of a song is included in a television ad, and there is rarely indication that the music comes from an actual recording artist, crediting of the artist, or information about how the music might be procured. Lastly, the more significant a role played by advertising in distributing music, the more likely advertising will become like major labels, in terms of power and problems. The relationship between music and companies does not stop at licensing for commercials; more and more, corporations are partnering with music companies for expansive music tie-ins, such as streaming radio stations and promotional CDs (Garrity 2001).

To understand the production of culture, it is imperative that we also understand the factors that have the potential to change the process of production. In this case, legal, technological, and organizational transformations have all influenced the way that music is being distributed. The changes in law that resulted from mid-1990s deregulation legislation paved the way for widespread organizational changes in radio, and specifically for a small number of owners to control almost all commercial radio stations. Technological developments, from the digitization of music to peer-to-peer networks, have forced record companies to consider sources of revenue outside of record sales. Finally, as the number of major record labels has decreased, independent labels are answering this organizational shift by asserting themselves as a viable alternative to the corporate environment of the majors that gets blamed for a lack of quality control. Music licensing, of which advertising placement is, per individual case, more lucrative than film or TV placement, promises to solve the problems of exposure and revenue presented by the radio and music industries. In this way, the defense of licensing to advertising that points to industry woe acts to further endorse these types of interaction between popular music and advertising. Advertisers are characterized as almost heroic in their ability to support and break bands that the traditional routes overlooked.

But advertising's newfound role in distributing and financially supporting popular music is not simply the consequence of a variety of causes; it becomes a variable in the production of culture as well. Josh Rabinowitz, director of music at Grey Worldwide, is optimistic that in the near future the advertising world will go beyond licensing music to actually recording and creating hit music. Rabinowitz, who contributed an editorial to *Billboard* on the subject, told me, "essentially we don't need the middleman, you don't need the labels. A lot of people would prefer to associate themselves with a big corporation instead of a big label corporation" (p.c., 2005). Advertising could conceivably cut out the record companies, but it is not removing a middleman: it is replacing a middleman and with real ramifications. The greatest fear is that the success of artists through licensing to advertising will lead to commercialism infiltrating the creative process. *Rolling Stone*'s Rob Sheffield reflected on Moby's success: "You had to worry that the sequel would beat the formula into the ground, turning ancient spirituals into ad jingles: 'Nobody Knows the Arby's I've Seen,' 'Nike's Blood Never Failed Me Yet,' 'Colonel Sanders Gonna Make Up My Dying Bed' or 'Oh, Lawdy, I'm Not Gonna Pay a Lot for This Muffler'" (2002: 77). The growing trend of companies like Seagram's and McDonald's paying rappers to mention their products corroborates such concerns, but the apocalypse is hardly imminent: unprofitable and non-mainstream music cultures will always proliferate in some form, if only through word-of-mouth distribution. Although advertising may not destroy music culture, it is easy to imagine this channel of distribution being as limited or more limited than commercial radio and the major record label system.

The type of music used in television commercials tends to exclude some genres, or subgenres entirely. Hesmondhalgh described how the "atmospheric worldless aesthetics of dance music make it particularly suitable for use on film and TV soundtracks" (1998: 247); it is no accident that many of the artists that have broken through advertising create dance or electronic music. Electronic music is used a great deal in advertising, in part because it tends to be non- or minimally lyrical. In the typical dance music listening experience, listening is not the sole or main activity and, likewise, in advertising the music takes a backseat to the primary message being conveyed. Dance music also shares some characteristics with classical, another genre favored by advertisers. As one journalist put it, "electronic music is a modern orchestral score, fusing the sweeping and emotive qualities of classical movements with the energy of dance tracks. It's a hip way not to hire John Williams or sample Ride of the Valkyries for the millionth time" (Lynch 2000: I6). Advertising's penchant for dance music is good for electronic music, which has long been marginalized by radio and labels, but other types of popular music, as well as more experimental dance music, would likely be deemed less suitable for this practice. Music that does not lend itself to "easy" listening, and music that addresses heavy or political subject matters would be risky placements. Even if advertising did utilize a broad range of music, to rely on it as a main channel of support and distribution would lock out artists that do not choose to be associated with brands.

Against the myriad troubles facing the radio and music industries, licensing to advertising has offered itself as an uncompromising DJ and a generous patron of musicians. But as a major gateway, television commercials provide a channel that, like contemporary commercial radio, is necessarily narrow and, for the musicians who do license to spots, not a guaranteed career booster. Licensing to television commercials does not provide a solution to radio and music industry problems. At best, it provides different problems. At worst, the turn to licensing removes focus from the radio and music industries, both of which require overhauling in order to fulfill the reputed goal of regulatory bodies such as the FCC to serve the public interest through the diffusion of a wide variety of culture, not just the most profitable.

Chapter 5

In Perfect Harmony: Popular Music and Cola Advertising

Prior to the significant organizational, legal, and technological changes in both the radio and music industries that have produced an environment in which licensing to advertising is more common, music already represented an important weapon in the cola wars' arsenal. From Coke's classic 1971 commercial featuring hundreds of young people gathered on a hilltop to sing "I'd Like to Buy the World a Coke," to the more recent iTunes and Pepsi cross-promotion, music and cola, both products targeted primarily at a youth demographic, have endured a lengthy association. Through the case of the colas, this chapter examines how product type informs the licensing process and how music provides a shortcut to branding for products with no natural connection to music.

Bands for Brands

Where relationships between popular musicians and advertisers have often been uneasy, reigniting high art debates about the consequences of commercial affiliation, Coke and Pepsi have positioned themselves as having a more genuine connection to music culture as enthusiasts, champions, and partners. The two companies pursued this goal by creating advertising campaigns that were as much entertainment as sales pitch. In addition, the cola corporations have borrowed characteristics of rock music, such as authenticity and anti-authoritarianism, and applied them to their products, obscuring the archetype of preyed upon artist and malevolent commercial interest often activated in the art versus commerce debate. The cola companies and popular music may appear to be in perfect harmony, but such relationships raise serious questions about the role of advertising in cultural production. Through its use of popular music to advance commercial aims, cola advertising contributes to an increasingly hypercommercialistic media environment in the United States and abroad.

As the use of music and musicians in advertising has increased, a debate that was once reductive and obsessed with "selling out" has become more nuanced and concerned with the details of a commercial campaign. The decision of artists to be involved with a commercial campaign can be viewed as a comment on the particularities of the campaign as well as on the artist. One element of the discussion surrounding popular music's use in advertising involves the type of product or service being advanced, where some products and companies provoke an extremely negative reaction for their use of music, while others are met with ambivalence or approval. Many of the musicians, music supervisors, licensing managers, and ad creatives I spoke with suggested that the use of licensed music was more suitable for some products and services over others. Certainly there are some products for which licensed music or musical spokespeople are logical components of conveying information. The specific selection of music or musician may still reflect marketing objectives, but, at a very basic level, it makes sense that a digital music-playing device like iPod would include licensed music in its television campaign. The practical fit between music and music-related products is one reason why a director of film and television for a collection of independent labels told me that she chose to pitch an especially picky band for an iPod campaign, despite the band's history of rejecting offers to license to advertising (Lanchart, personal communication, 2005).

Further, even products more tangentially involved in our musical experiences have a sound reason to license music for use in advertising campaigns. For example, a product category that consistently licenses pre-existing music for its television commercials is automobiles, and for many consumers the car is where the majority of music listening occurs. But while automobiles may have a more apparent connection to music than, say, vacuum cleaners, the reputation of the company and product also intervenes in the artist's decision-making process. That is, within the category of automobiles, various other distinctions are considered, some real and others a result of branding. Tricia Halloran, music supervisor at HUM Music + Sound Design, explained that one of the bands she has worked with will license music to hybrid vehicles, but not to traditional gasoline-powered vehicles. In this example, there is a real difference, in terms of impact on the environment, between the products that this band will license to and those they would refuse. Some of the musicians I talked with described being more at ease licensing music to companies which they personally supported as consumers. Archie Moore of Velocity Girl rationalized that he was thinking about buying a VW bug when the group was approached to license "Sorry Again" to the company. Nick Krill of the Spinto Band, who licensed their song "Oh Mandy" to a Sears commercial said, "I get my tools there just the same as everyone else," but then jokingly acknowledged the absurdity of an indie-rock group endorsing hardware: "Although I would've probably got my tools at Tru-Valu. Plug plug! I just got $100 to say that" (p.c., 2005).

In other cases, the difference between products that do or do not fit with music licensing may be less easy to pin down. Brands that carry a cool cachet may appear to be less threatening in their use of popular music, and the "cool" of licensed music may seem a suitable match for the "cool" of the product. Continuing with the use of automobiles as example, it is notable that Volkswagen is regularly mentioned, in the press and in interviews I've conducted, as a company that, like Apple, has proven itself a good fit with music licensing. But whether Volkswagen as a company has values that are distinct in some real way from those of Pontiac or Cadillac is unclear; rather, Volkswagen's history of creative and innovative advertising has molded its positive reputation in the eyes of other creatives, in advertising and in music. Velocity Girl's Archie Moore admitted, "I feel kind of stupid for making the distinction, but we all agreed ... I think it was a company that we didn't have any problems with" (p.c., 2005). The music selected for a campaign may then increase the product or service's perceived hip character; that credible bands such as Stereolab and Luna had already licensed to Volkswagen also influenced Velocity Girl's decision. In cases where the positive reputation of the company is not as clearly attached to the content of the product—Volkswagen was known as the Nazi car prior to its 1959 image overhaul courtesy of the Doyle Dane Bernbach agency's classic campaign—there was a time before cool, when the product was known only for its utility: a time before branding.

The colas fall squarely into this category, where the relationship between product and music culture is one based entirely on construction. Let us not forget that Coke began its life as a patent medicine: hence, even the relationship between cola and "beverage" is a result of marketing, not *kismet*. The use of music culture to advertise a non-music related product relies on the illusion of branding and the capability of advertising to construct a certain personality around a product.

It is in this way that branding serves as an architect of false consciousness, constructing a link that appears natural, but in fact has no natural basis. In orthodox Marxist thought, false consciousness explains why a dominated class of people does not engage in social revolution, despite this being the only potential escape from class-determined submissiveness (see Lukács 1971/1923). Applying this notion to branding, false consciousness allows consumers to perceive the personality of a product or service that results from branding as natural and indisputable, preventing consumers from closer examination of marketing practices. As a dominant ideology of capitalist societies, commodity fetishism encourages false consciousness, and in particular the belief that relations to things can replace relations to people. As a consequence, things are thus invested with the same values and characteristics as people. Cordoned off from political implications, the impact of such marketing practices on cultural production and media policy are set aside as another, barely existent, conversation.

Yet, as willing as subjects may be to accept the fruits of branding as natural and always already there, consumers are also capable of stepping back, recognizing the relationship for what it is. The process of branding may attempt to hide the capitalist logic that guides it, but commercial viewers are not simply or always passive dupes embracing any claim of personality that advertising throws their way, and advertisers have responded to consumer cynicism by raising the branding bar, encouraging our willingness to be duped, however temporarily, by marketing practices.

In describing advertising as a magic system, Williams identified a cultural pattern in which the object itself is not enough to sell it; it must also be linked to some sort of personal meaning (1962), the very essence of branding. Williams also described how advertising acknowledges and, indeed, applauds our skepticism, responding to critiques of advertising's false claims with a wink to the audience. Advertising strikes a careful balance between fooling the viewer and assuring the viewer that he or she is no fool. Branding strategies, which transform in reaction to viewer shrewdness, ensure that gut reactions persist despite a knowledge of intent; the result is an era of a cynical dominant ideology and cynical subjects, Sloterdijk's condition of "enlightened false consciousness," where, as Žižek put it, "one knows the falsehood very well, one is well aware of a particular interest hidden behind an ideological universality, but still one does not renounce it" (1989: 29). There is a joy in allowing oneself to be taken for the branding ride that discourages renunciation and prevents a lucid and commonsensical response for even the quickest of viewers. Viewers may not necessarily or even often follow their viewing experience with a buying experience, but that does not stop them from experiencing the emotional manipulation aspired to by advertisers.

Indeed, ad creatives themselves, whose very job it is to construct the personality around brands, and who, as a consequence, should have a greater awareness of the constructed nature of relationships between brands and personality traits, fall prey to the same illusions. A creative director I talked with related watching a commercial that used a song by indie group the Pernice Brothers, and hoping that the ad was for Target, which has successfully branded itself as the cool alternative to more square department stores, relying in part on popular music to achieve this end. Instead the commercial was produced for the decidedly less hip store Sears, the realization of which bothered the creative director, though he ultimately caught himself buying in to branding techniques: "I guess if I got the Sears account I might try to do the same thing, which is kind of funny … I guess I have gut reactions … Target's a pure example of just how advertising can completely change your opinion of a company" (Carl, p.c., 2005). Like the Spinto Band, singer Joe Pernice reasoned that he already supported Sears as a consumer: "I like to build things, so I've bought a lot of Sears wrenches. I could honestly say I didn't have a problem with it" (p.c., 2006).

Articulation—meaning both an expression and a joining together—provides an entry point to understanding the process of branding, where the unity formed by articulation "is always, necessarily, a 'complex structure': a structure in which things are related, as much through their differences as their similarities" (Hall 2002: 44). Like McLeod's implementation of the term, I am interested in the use of articulation theory as a way "to understand the transformations of *cultural* production," and to examine "*how* connections are made, and *why* they are important" (2001: 14). The joining of music culture, through either a licensed track or the appearance of an artist, with a product or service in a commercial brings new connotations to both artist and company while naturalizing the relationship between the two. The value of articulating popular music to a product can be seen as especially important to advertisers competing with products similar, if not identical, in use-value, as is the case with cola.

Pepsi and Coke are examples of "parity products," where "marginally different products compete very closely, for the most part avoiding factual logical claims and relying on image management" (Huron 1989: 568); a close association with a style of popular music overrides the physical make-up of the product as the distinguishing mark. In presenting a product or service as engaged in a relationship with music culture, the distinction between popular music and advertising, and the lack of distinction between one brand and another, can both be hidden from view. One of the key foundations of the cola wars is that the products are very similar and not basic necessities, so that image through advertising became essential to selling the products; advertising is not about what the product does but who the consumer is (Frank 1997: 170). In part because both companies needed to move outside of the qualities of the products themselves to establish difference, Coke and Pepsi have perhaps the longest and most consistent relationship to popular music culture of any consumer products. As a result, an analysis of their histories with and strategies involving the use of popular music provides a revealing case study of how music is exploited for branding purposes.

Cola and Music Duets

Coke transferred its advertising account to McCann Erickson in 1956 and popular music was immediately a part of the equation, with some of the earliest campaigns featuring performers like Connie Francis and the McGuire Sisters. These were hardly the trendiest performers available during these first days of rock 'n' roll, but the early emphasis on popular music and musicians as sales pitch is notable. In 1963, Coke began its "Things Go Better with Coke" campaign and while the original theme was performed by the Limeliters, the company soon invited dozens of popular musicians, including some at the time more controversial rock artists, to pen and perform a version of the "Things Go Better with Coke" theme song. Artists from the Troggs to Otis Redding, the Left Banke to Lulu, put their own mark on the song. Clocking in at ninety seconds apiece and sounding thematically and aesthetically very much like the artists' known work, with the exception of the recognizable chorus, these ads could easily be mistaken for chart hits.

The event that arguably sealed Coke's relationship to popular music was the 1971 campaign featuring a group of wide-eyed multicultural young adults singing, "I'd like to teach the world to sing in perfect harmony/ I'd like to buy the world a Coke and keep it company." Two de-Coked versions, one by the Hillside Singers and the other by the New Seekers, went on to become chart hits. This was not the first time in the history of advertising that a song that began life as a jingle was reborn on the pop charts, but it may be the case that has been most deeply lodged in our collective memory, not least by Coke itself, which has returned to the campaign multiple times since.

Before "I'd Like to Teach the World to Sing" became a hit, Pepsi witnessed one of its ad themes also cross over into the radio charts. The theme to 1966's "Girlwatchers," Pepsi's Diet Coke campaign, became a top 40 hit for the Bob Crewe Generation as "Music to Watch Girls By." Compared to Coke, Pepsi was slow to use actual pop musicians, though its campaigns did utilize youthful music. In the 1980s, Pepsi made its affiliation to popular music more explicit, hiring some of the most famous entertainers of the time, including Michael Jackson and Madonna, to star in their commercials. These were two of the first spots for which the premieres were treated not as advertising, but as must-see programming. Over the next twenty years, artists ranging from Ray Charles to Shakira joined the promotional crusade. Perhaps making up for their late start in hiring actual artists, a 2002 Pepsi ad featured Britney Spears traveling through Pepsi ads from the late 1950s to the present, performing era-appropriate styles of music. Both companies have made music such a focus of their advertising campaigns that pop music history has to some extent been documented by the companies' marketing histories.

The turn to music for marketing purposes in these two cases served the purpose of reaching a desired market, since both popular music and colas share a similar demographic. While both Coke and Pepsi have long stressed youthfulness as a quality possessed by their consuming demographic, in the past the companies denied that their advertising was specifically directed at youth. Of Pepsi's 1984 Michael Jackson campaign, one journalist wrote, "the second of the two spots clearly shows several preteen boys and girls, holding caffeine-laden Pepsi cans, an apparent break with a company policy that had kept kids out of Pepsi television spots" (Brown 1984: C3), to which Pepsi's senior vice president of creative services countered that the ad was meant to attract their parents. By the 1990s, the colas were more honest about their target demographic and tactics to reach them, a signal that concerns over and fears about marketing directly to children have decreased dramatically in the US. In 1991, an article in *Advertising Age* reported that Coke "said a music tie-in is a natural fit for Coca-Cola since music appeals to the youth market, the primary target for soft drinks and for No. 1 brand Coca-Cola Classic in particular" (Fahey 1991: 1).

As Pepsi and Coke advertising has spread to other countries around the world, both companies have continued to use music as a means of branding across all promotions. Corporate sponsorship of music acts in the UK started to grow in popularity about a decade after the approach became common in the US, and Pepsi and Coke were early takers. In television advertising, too, the colas extended their approach to non-U.S. markets. Because these brands have relied so heavily on the globally-recognized language of Western-style popular music, in many cases the same ads that are shown in the US are broadcast internationally, with little or no adaptation. When spots have been created outside of the US, music remains the focus and international broadcasting takes on new meaning; for instance, Pepsi's 1989 "Glasnost" spot, which featured Soviet scenes paired with a score by Soviet rock group Pogo, was shown in the Soviet Union, but also during the Superbowl in the US, and later around the world ("Debut Set for Pepsi's" 1989: 5A). Through the campaign, Soviet and non-Soviet viewers alike discover that, despite other cultural differences, there are at least two universals: rock music and cola, preferably consumed together. Not only is the articulation between popular music and cola activated, but it is also shown to be immune to national and cultural boundaries.

Casting Doubt on the Perfect Harmony

In a lament of contemporary music Bob Dylan once noted, "You know things go better with Coke because Aretha Franklin told you so ... The corporate world, when they figured out what [rock 'n' roll] was and how to use it they snuffed the breath out of it and killed it" (Dylan 1985). (It remains unclear whether his decision to later license "The Times They Are a-Changin'" to a Bank of Montreal ad and "Love Sick" to a Victoria's Secret ad was a sign of submission or indifference.) The use of music and musicians in advertising draws out tensions that have long been part of larger cultural discourses involving perceived divisions between art and commerce. Julien Temple, director of Neil Young's video for "This Note's For You," a mocking critique of commercial tie-ins, explained,

> The best pop music is the truth of someone singing powerfully about what they feel. If that's owned by a conglomerate of soft drink, it's like having an invisible Pepsi sign engraved on your forehead.
>
> That's definitely part of the process of how pop music is being killed. It becomes useless because it's incorporated. Lots of record companies are chaining music down to where it's not very interesting and nobody can do anything different with it. This song is a piece of integrity, and the drink companies want to own it! (qtd. in Reed 1988: 19)

The relationships between corporations and musicians have ranged from sponsorships of tours and music programs, to the use of popular songs in ads, to, in some cases, the offer to pay artists for approved lyrical mentions of products, with each of these methods raising eyebrows to varying degrees in different markets. In 2003, the BBC's decision to allow Coca-Cola to sponsor its Radio 1 and *Top of the Pops* charts was met with disapproval. An article in the *Guardian* expressed the main questions: "Was it politically astute for the BBC to allow the mainstays of its youth programming to be associated with a product, as Chrysalis chief executive Phil Riley puts it, that 'rots kids' teeth'? Or for the BBC to be linked so closely with a multibillion-dollar corporate giant?" (Wells 2003: 8). This story would not have received any attention in the US, where not only is the top-rated *American Idol* sponsored by Coke, but the contestants prepare to perform in a Coke-themed lounge and appear in mini within-program commercials for Coke. Even in the absence of program sponsorship, however, the association between pop music, youth, and Coca-Cola already exists the world over, thanks to consistent articulation through advertising.

In the US, the association is not simply commonplace and accepted, but is often argued to be a sensible extension of standard capitalist practice. Common to the argument that relationships between companies and musicians are both positive and natural, are claims that popular music is, after all, produced within a commercial system and bought and sold as a commodity. Press coverage often treats licensing to commercials as a sensible branching off of other types of commercial affiliation, such as tour sponsorship. Some of the musicians, music supervisors, and licensing managers I spoke with made comments that similarly suggested that it is hypocritical to be against licensing to advertising when tours are so often sponsored or when bands and band members are implicitly lending an endorsement to products they use. When I asked Jeff Price, co-founder and general manager of spinART Records, whether he would discourage bands from licensing to a more controversial product, like alcohol, he responded, "Do I have a problem if one of our bands is serving beer at a bar? No. So why would I have a problem with their music being used in those commercials?" (p.c., 2005). Such a position conflates all commercial affiliation, when in fact there are many types and grades of commercial affiliation confronting musicians; as one journalist put it, "At every level there is a constant battle between the pride of the artist and the lure of Mammon" (Thorncroft 1986: I20). For each artist who is vocally anti-corporate, like Fugazi, or entirely incorporated, like Britney Spears, there are many more in between constantly negotiating their comfort zone within the commercial arena.

Buying a bottle of Coke and buying a compact disc may be similar experiences, but drinking cola and listening to music are not. When the experience with a product, as opposed to simply the purchase of a product, is taken into account, divisions between artistic and commercial goals, though in many ways unstable and blurred, are also based on real perceptual and emotional differences. As it becomes more natural to hear, experience, and be exposed to music through advertising, potential negative consequences are invited: at worst, larger issues of cultural production, music distribution and creative independence, and the impact that advertising as a vessel of popular music has on each of these areas, will evade inspection. Corporate sponsors already have "a strong influence over currents of thought in our society" (Barnouw 1978: 74); popular music is employed in television commercials as yet another instrument of control.

Cola's Strategic Capture of Music Culture

Coke and Pepsi, with their advertising agencies, have utilized a number of strategies in attempting to avoid and alleviate tensions inherent to dealings between commercial and cultural entities. Both companies have partnered largely with artists for whom commercial affiliations are viewed by the public as less compromising, and both have drawn attention to the benefits of exposure through advertising, as well as the creativity of the advertising medium. Further, Coke and Pepsi have attempted to adopt qualities symbolic of rock 'n' roll, as a means of narrowing the gulf between the philosophies of corporations and of artists. Each of these strategies is examined more closely.

Commercialism Friendly Music

In popular music, artistic distinctions and positions with respect to commercialism are negotiated around variables involved in discourse of cultural difference, such as race, gender, and class. In the 1960s, the rock as art movement aligned rock music with other cultural products seemingly positioned in opposition to clear commercial ends, an example of Frith's claim, noted earlier, that, "The belief in a continuing struggle between music and commerce is the core of rock ideology" (1981: 41). Ultimately, it is a certain variation of music—largely white, male, and middle-class rock music—that is most philosophically at odds with commercial affiliation and most open to charges of "selling out." "While it's not surprising that people as historically crass as The Jacksons would sell their soul for a soft drink Michael wouldn't touch," wrote one journalist in 1987, "it's surprising that an artist of Bowie's calibre would join the corporate ranks" (Gross 1987: S18). In fact, David Bowie's involvement does stands out against the usual music selection of the colas, which tends towards more "commercial" artists, or those for whom commercial affiliation has less of a stigma attached to it.

While the "Things Go Better with Coke" campaign included a number of rock bands, by the 1980s Coke and Pepsi were using mostly pop and R&B songs and acts. For these artists, commercialism was not necessarily a bad word. As Madonna explained in 1989, "What I do is total commercialism, but it's also art ... I like the challenge of doing both, of somehow making art that is accessible and making commerce something artistic" (qtd. in Holden 1989: 1).

In 1990, with rap growing in popularity, Pepsi was one of the first advertisers to seek out the endorsement of a rap artist, featuring Young MC in its "Cool Cans" spot (Foltz 1990). While rap was not, at first, an easy sell to companies nervous about language and alienating part of their consumer base (Foltz 1990), it was an obvious choice for the colas. Much rap music was already littered with commercial product shout-outs (essentially free endorsements), and, focused as the cola corporations were on reaching both the youth and minority markets, rap presented a way to reach both simultaneously. According to the *New York Times*, "Middle America's growing acceptance of a variety of cultures has also fueled the boom in urban-inspired ads and promotions aimed at youth ages 12 to 24" (Day 2002: C2).

From the rap artist's perspective, an offer from Coke or Pepsi served as a kind of validation. As a New York brand consultant described, "The fact that Coca-Cola is using urban music says more about where urban music has moved than where Coke has moved" (qtd. in Howard 2003: 7B). In a country with a history of black artists not being treated the same as white artists, where black music trailed behind in radio, on MTV, and in sales for many years, despite being the obvious basis for much of the popular white music, marketers like the cola companies wasted little time taking advantage of black music's desire to be treated and used equally in the area of advertising. Yet whether these artists are truly treated equally by the corporations remains in question: in 2003, Pepsi withdrew its commercial featuring rapper Ludacris because of complaints about obscene lyrics on his album.

But Pepsi had featured artists before whose album material or behavior outside of the commercial campaign would have been inappropriate for a television spot. As rap impresario Russell Simmons pointed out, by featuring the historically outrageous Ozzy Osbourne in an ad, Pepsi appeared hypocritical (Carr 2003: C5). Finally, when less commercial or more socially conscious rappers, like Common, have appeared in cola ads, they have been subject to the same, if subdued, critiques of selling out as their rock counterparts.

Rap remains, alongside pop, the most common genre tapped by the cola companies in terms of featuring actual musicians and pre-existing music in their television spots. Rock-themed campaigns, like Coke's faux-documentary following the activities of an all girl rock band, tend to use composed music and fictional groups, partly because actual rock groups may be more hesitant to commit to a Coke campaign. The director of film and television for the Beggars Group reported receiving "Diet Coke and Coke pitches all the time; they're constantly looking for new artists," but the artists she represents have so far refused because they do not support the company (Lanchart, p.c., 2005). One of those groups, the Super Furry Animals, turned down an offer from Coke only to find the company respond by doubling the money to £1 million; the band maintained their stance, but this example reveals a disconnect between corporations and musicians, where the former can hardly imagine that an offer would be rejected for any reason other than financial. Singer and guitarist Gruff Rhys (p.c., 2006) explained, "Most of our peers think we are nuts," echoing the sentiments of other holdouts. "It's been a lonely road resisting the chants of the rising solicitations," expressed the Doors' John Densmore (2002: 35), whose refusal to consent has prevented his willing former bandmates from reaping a fortune in licensing fees. Lately even Densmore has tempered his position, telling *Rolling Stone* that the Doors would consider licensing to an advertisement for "something technology-oriented, or some hybrid car or something" (qtd. in Serpick 2006: 20).

As licensing to commercials has become more routine, there is a greater rock presence in advertising, including cola campaigns: the Rolling Stones' "You Can't Always Get What You Want" and Queen's "I Want to Break Free" were used to promote Coke's C2 in 2004, Green Day covered the Clash's "I Fought the Law" for Pepsi's iTunes promotion that same year, and Detroit garage-rocker Jack White of the White Stripes composed music for a 2006 Coke ad. White based his decision in some measure on his own status as a Coke drinker, echoing the abovementioned sentiments of Velocity Girl's Moore, the Spinto Band's Krill, and Joe Pernice. But White also insisted that he would have found it strange to license a song for the campaign, a sign, along with the fan critique that has followed each of these deals, that commercial involvement for rock musicians is still a complex negotiation.

Benefits to Artists

The partnerships between the cola companies and musicians have been framed by the corporations and sometimes in the press as beneficial to artists. For older artists, participating in commercial campaigns can spark a renewed interest in back catalogs; Ray Charles admitted being embarrassed by the Diet Pepsi ads he starred in (Bream 1992), but the campaign did bring attention to the artist during a relative lull in his career. Often commercial campaigns coincide with artist events, such as album releases or tours, acting as a cross-promotional tool. The 1989 Pepsi ad featuring Madonna's "Like A Prayer" was broadcast before the album was even released. The premiere of the ad, broadcast simultaneously in 40 countries, was described in the press release: "The ground-breaking deal is expected to change the way popular tunes from major artists are released in the future. Traditionally, new songs have been made public through heavy radio air-play. In an innovative twist, the Pepsi-Madonna deal uses television to provide unparalleled international exposure for her new single" (qtd. in Siegel 1989: 77). It is interesting that this case was framed in terms of bypassing commercial radio since, at the time, US commercial radio was nowhere near the disaster it is today for young artists, with ever-narrowing playlists, a plague of payola schemes, and practical if not technical oligopoly status.

The benefit to artists today is often explained as a salve against the hard times being experienced by artists, both in terms of commercial radio lock-outs and the perceived threat of the twin evils of dubious consequence, piracy and downloading. As the guitarist from the Counting Crows explained of the band's turn in a Coke commercial, "It's just such a tough world ... The economy and pirating and downloading. It's not a great thing" (qtd. in Laue 2003: 4go). Involvement in commercial campaigns has, for some artists, become not simply another way to gain exposure and make a living, but the only way.

As a further enticement to artists, in at least some cases of cola advertising, creative control is shared with the artist as a guarantee that the finished product will carry the artist's aesthetic and at times moral mark, occasionally in very bizarre ways. Michael Jackson, known for his belief in health food, agreed to do the Pepsi ad, but at his insistence refused to actually consume the beverage, or appear to be consuming the beverage, on camera (Gross 1987). Jackson also "demanded that the TV spots display his face no more than four seconds and feature one spin, not two, in his commercial's dance routine" (Engardio 1986: 16). Sometimes musicians are able to step outside the role of performer and into another creative position. George Michael agreed to do a Diet Coke ad on such premises: "In luring Michael as pitchman, Coca-Cola gave him the freedom to create his own pitch," plus producer and co-director duties (Collins 1989: 3D). As reported in *Creativity*, it has become more common for commercial campaigns featuring musicians to position "its hitmakers literally at the core of the creative team" (Lyon 1997: 16). By handing some creative control over to the artists, the typical advertising model is ostensibly turned on its head: "instead of asking the musician to celebrate the brand, each commercial, in effect, celebrates the musician" (Lyon 1997: 16). Or, at least, that is what artists are led to believe.

Advertising as Entertainment

The reason why creative control is a variable at all is because the cola corporations have consistently promoted their television advertising as entertainment, not just pitch, capitalizing on the changes in the advertising industry outlined in Chapter 3. It is not uncommon for musicians involved in the campaigns to talk about the ads as though they are any other creative project. For instance, in the PR report for Kanye West's Pepsi ad, the artist thanked the corporation as he might a music producer: "From concept, to execution, to post-production and effects, to revisions—a lot of work went into this creative process ... I want to thank Pepsi for working overtime to see this through" ("Kanye West and Pepsi" 2005). A writer for the *Boston Globe* considered the overlap between entertainment and advertising when he contended that viewers will be left wondering whether Madonna's Pepsi ad premiere will be "a) a great moment in music history; b) a great moment in broadcasting history; c) a great moment in advertising history or d) the end of Western civilization as we know it" (Siegel 1989: 77). His befuddlement sounds outdated now that television advertising as entertainment is an accepted part of everyday life.

The premieres of cola ads have sometimes been handled by the media and public as genuine cultural events, with families gathering eagerly around their television sets and an enormous number of viewers watching simultaneously. In 2001 Britney Spears appeared in a Pepsi commercial that, like Michael Jackson's 1984 ad and Madonna's 1989 ad, was anticipated as if it were a feature film. Millions of viewers tuned in to see the pop princess sing the praises of the sugary beverage. The framing of commercials as events assists in distancing these spots from their marketing origins. Further emphasizing its entertainment qualities, the Britney spot premiered on television during the Academy Awards, the highest cultural honor for filmic success in the US. And continuing the parallel between this spot and actual filmed entertainment, viewers could access, via Yahoo!, "behind-the-scenes footage of the commercial shoot, a 15-second 'teaser' preview, and Spears' diary documenting the making of the commercial" (Jeckell 2001). Through the hiring of well-known directors—Michel Gondry has directed for Coke, Spike Lee for Pepsi—and an emphasis on storytelling over product placement, Coke and Pepsi have asserted themselves as more similar to film than to traditional advertising.

Promotion of music-focused cola ads as entertainment has been facilitated by the popularity of the music video format following MTV's 1981 inception. According to a 1985 story in the *New York Times*, "At every turn, the imagery and sound of the music video, the first new form television has yielded in decades, is having a pronounced effect. Only three years old, the notion of melding highly stylized, rapidly cut video montages with rock music is echoing throughout the popular culture" (Smith 1985: 29). Because "music videos are fundamentally commercial, designed to sell rock musicians, songs and albums," in fact taking their inspiration from the European new wave commercials of the 1970s (Smith 1985: 29), it makes sense that the aesthetic was so readily adopted for television ads. If MTV is the ultimate postmodern vehicle (see Kaplan 1987), then by borrowing its aesthetic, advertising also adopts the postmodern position that collapses distinctions, including, self-servingly, the distinction between artistic and commercial intent. By the time Britney Spears was approached to appear in Pepsi ads, the association between cola advertising and entertainment was fully entrenched in (false) cultural consciousness, which explains how Britney Spears could say, "I'm a big fan of Pepsi products and Pepsi commercials" ("Britney Spears and Pepsi-Cola" 2001) as casually as one of her fans might say, "I'm a big fan of Britney Spears," and country star Faith Hill could unselfconsciously report, "It is an honor to be involved with Pepsi, who over the years has successfully blended a superior product with quality music, talent and creativity" ("Faith Hill to Star" 2000). Spears and Hill described their involvement with Pepsi in the same terms artists use to discuss working with music producers and film directors, and in so doing helped to move the discussion of cola advertising from the consumer market to the art world.

The Adoption of "Rock" Qualities

Frank described soda as "another product category that was quite thoroughly given over to hip advertising" and noted that "the best soda ads stressed the *values* of the counterculture rather than simple countercultural appearances" (1997: 163). As well as offering benefits and a degree of creative control to artists, cola advertising has adopted characteristics borrowed directly from the rock 'n' roll handbook: anti-authoritarianism, authenticity, and gravity, all in service of achieving the elusive but essential tag of "cool," are established through the choice of artist, and overall aesthetic and message of the spots. As Dawn Hudson, senior vice president for strategy and marketing for Pepsi, explained, "We try to choose celebrities not because they are hot and big but because their personalities or what they are known for reinforces our brand" (qtd. in Howard 2001: 3B). By adopting and then reinforcing "rock" qualities the cola corporations are able to make their advertising more attractive to musicians and less offensive to fans.

An anti-authoritarian stance is often expressed through the selection of notorious artists. Although Pepsi has conveyed surprise at the controversies sparked by their campaigns, the company's marketing department must be aware of the potential for controversy when divisive artists are selected to pitch for them. When Madonna's video for "Like a Prayer" was released, shortly after the Pepsi commercial that featured the song, conservative groups were up in arms over the images of cross-burning, stigmata, and, while not explicitly mentioned by the protestors, interracial love. Pepsi unsuccessfully requested that MTV withdraw the video and ultimately dropped the sponsorship of Madonna, removing the spot in the US. For a corporation to hire Madonna, who, as one journalist wrote, is known for "stirring up just enough controversy to advance her career without tipping the balance of public opinion against her" (Holden 1989: 1) and not anticipate potential controversy is either incredibly naïve or, more likely, a savvy business move.

Less predictable than the Madonna debacle, but just as headline making, was Michael Jackson's hospitalization after an on-set accident set his hair on fire. Again, by 1984 Jackson was already well-known for his strange habits; that this campaign might result in the establishment clucking disapprovingly was no mystery to Pepsi. In 1989, Mike Beindorff, Coca-Cola USA's vice president of advertising and associate director of marketing, described Pepsi's approach as "a high-risk, high-benefit strategy" (qtd. in Davis 1989), maintaining that Coke's method is less risky. Yet even in the absence of massive scandals and controversies, Coke's approach and use of music have since the 1960s carried an anti-authoritarian message. A jingle by the Troggs or the Left Banke sends a different message than one by Connie Francis, who had endorsed the cola only a few years earlier; surely these ads sounded to over-40s at the time much the same as the noise being played on the radio. Likewise, the gathering of youth on the hilltop was a conspicuous representation of the counterculture movement, aligning Coke and Coke drinkers in opposition to the authority who would have you cut your hair and drink a glass of milk. Both companies continue the tradition today, hiring musicians that, on the surface, teeter on the brink of controversy, through explicit sexuality, graphic lyrical content or attitude. Even Coke's fake girl band, featured in a mid-2000s campaign, adopted an anti-authoritarian stance through their outspoken, punky, devil-may-care attitudes.

For Coca-Cola, the most important and constant characteristic underscored by the ad campaigns is authenticity, epitomized by the slogan and "Hilltop" chorus "It's the real thing." Likewise, the concept of authenticity, even as it is revealed to be an ever-changing and indefinable construction, continues to be salient to the discourse surrounding rock 'n' roll. As the self-described "real thing" Coke sidesteps questions of unholy mergers between art and commerce; it cannot be a threat to authenticity because Coke itself is the authentic cola.

While other slogans have come and gone over the years, Coke has returned to the theme of "real" repeatedly, using the hilltop ad as a hallmark of that promise. In the 1980s Coke used nostalgia for *its own ad* as a campaign theme, allowing us to catch up with the wide-eyed idealists who populated the original ad, now with children of their own (and, one imagines, jobs working for The Man). In 2005 Coke revived the song again for its "Chilltop" spot, which featured corny blues-rocker G. Love and friends performing what one reporter called a "horrendously lame cover" (Lazare 2005) from a Philadelphia rooftop. A small group alone on a roof transforms the unity message of the original into a message of exclusivity, a subtle reminder of the malleability of brand and brand values. Though these later revivals of the ads could be generously labeled missteps, McCann Erickson's supposition that viewers had a nostalgic relationship to the original was probably correct: the spot, along with a disproportionately large number of other cola ads, regularly claims a position on lists of best ads or most memorable ads. Other uses of the "real" by Coke include the late 1980s and early 1990s campaigns proclaiming that you "Can't beat the real thing" and a more recent Coke campaign comprised of mini-documentaries featuring young people seeking to "make it real" through the joint consumption of cola and authentic music experiences, a thematic continuation of Coke's 2003 campaign featuring "real people and celebrities in 'real' situations" (Howard 2003: 7B).

The lure of the "real" and "authentic" has not escaped Pepsi either. Particularly the company's early adoption of the rap sound to convey its message signaled a reliance on authenticity to sell the Pepsi brand. In order to convey the brand as authentic, it was important to use music also perceived as authentic. Young MC dismissed imitations of rap music in commercials as "offensive," explaining, "If the point is to reach young people, an imitation isn't going to have the right effect … Rap fans will know right away when the music isn't the real thing, and the advertising is going to turn them off" (qtd. in Foltz 1990: D5). As noted earlier, one of the advantages of hiring non-white musicians is that, beyond appealing to consumers in minority markets, these artists often hold an appeal to mainstream, especially youth, consumers. The road to authenticity through minority marketing recalls Hebdige's claims about the role of the "other" in the formation of subcultures, where historically most subcultures have borrowed what are perceived as authentic aesthetic ideas, cultural products, and, by extension, outsider status from minority cultures (Hebdige 1979). Authenticity has been adopted by colas across the spectrum as a means of distinguishing their brand, through music, from presumably fake competition.

The use of music by the cola corporations also lends gravity to the spots. Music is a strong emotional connector and as Sarah Gavigan, founder of music house Ten Music, explained, "with every piece of music there is an emotion that went behind it and that's kind of what [advertisers are] borrowing, the emotion to go over the top of their visual" (p.c., 2005). Through their reliance on music, Coke and Pepsi have taken the message that music can change the world, which may actually be true, and transformed it into the suggestion that cola can change the world. Surely the success of Coke's "Hilltop" ad resulted from its overt similarities to the Beatles' *Our World* contribution of "All You Need Is Love"; both presented a throng of hippies singing to a global audience about making the world a better place.

Coke linked itself to peaceful protest again in 2004 in a spot that featured singer Sharlene Hector. As was written in the *Observer*:

> She softly, to the point of insipidly, sings the 1954 protest song "I Wish I Knew How It Would Feel To Be Free" that the fabulous Nina Simone would make her own. A song that was once a powerful, delicate cry for equality and freedom has its guts ripped out and is presented as if it is Coke that can be the ticket to a higher spiritual place. (Morley 2004: 53)

The campaign featuring the composition of White Stripe Jack White revolved around the theme of worldwide love too. Certainly the messages themselves are well-intentioned, and no doubt some Coke employees support them, but cola is hardly the most obvious tool to achieve the objectives of peace and freedom. Similarly, Pepsi's dependence on notions of generational difference, as per their "Pepsi Generation" slogan, and reliance on generation-defining artists like Madonna, implicates the beverage as somehow responsible for positive changes, as opposed to simply cashing in on them.

This combination of anti-authoritarianism, authenticity, and social significance recalls both the original rock 'n' roll ideological position and, more generally, the *modus operandi* of the 1960s countercultural movement, arguably a loose basis for subsequent notions of "cool" or "hip." The use of popular music and musicians in advertising provides a branding shortcut to achieving these qualities.

Inextricable Links?

Through their extensive histories with popular music, Coca-Cola and Pepsi-Cola have succeeded in the ultimate goal of branding, effecting an articulation between music culture and the colas. And although such articulation is by its nature "a linkage which is not necessary, determined, absolute, or essential for all time" (Hall qtd. in Grossberg 1986: 53), with companies like Coke and Pepsi, it becomes difficult to tease out which came first, the reputation of the colas or their association with popular music. In the end, the music-cola articulation acts as a self-perpetuating machine, where otherwise finicky bands may be willing to waive their no commercials policy for Coke or Pepsi. Through all of the strategies discussed here Coke and Pepsi have effectively become part of music culture, as well as part of the larger culture too; there are cola collectors, just as there are record collectors, and Coca-Cola has garnered free lyrical mentions by artists including the Beatles, the Kinks, and the Jam. If there is any doubt as to whether companies consider these references to be (usually) free and desirable advertising, consider brand strategy agency Agenda Inc.'s "American Brandstand" project, which tracks for its clients the presence of lyrical mentions of brands in the Billboard Top 20 singles chart (Coca-Cola was ranked 22nd with sixteen mentions in 2005; in 2004 Pepsi beat Coke eight mentions to one) ("American Brandstand").

But what does it mean for the colas to be so deeply insinuated into music culture? There are two concerns: what music is doing for the colas, and what the colas are doing to music. As this analysis of Coke and Pepsi advertising has shown, popular music allows the cola corporations to hide the physical content of their products, as well as the politics of their business, behind a veil of fabricated cool. We may be well-advised to listen to one reporter who suggested there should "be a law that the grosser, greasier corporate companies such as Coca Cola, McDonald's and KFC are closely monitored by official, independent watchdogs when it comes to the music they use in their commercials to disguise the fact that they are indeed morally, technically, emotionally and nutritionally gross and greasy" (Morley 2004: 53). For their part, the Super Furry Animals ultimately gave "Hello Sunshine," the song requested by Coca-Cola, to a video detailing human rights abuses produced by War on Want, a non-profit organization which campaigns against the causes of global poverty, and which has criticized the Coca-Cola company's impact on local communities.

As for what the colas are doing to music, while the totality of consequences is still becoming apparent, they are definitely playing a more prominent role in music culture and distribution. In response to the 1989 Madonna–Pepsi partnership, Leslie Savan commented on advertising as the new and future medium of music transmission, "But if that's the way to enter the pantheon, then what does that make Pepsi and Coke? They are the medium through which the word is passed. They are universal, speaking no languages and all languages. And each art/ad is like a prayer unto them" (1993: 90).

The universality to which Savan refers is evident in Coke and Pepsi's global campaigns: more than other American brands these products and their ad campaigns have spread worldwide, a process Pico Iyer has dubbed "Coca-Colonization" (see, for example, Iyer 1988). But the US is not only exporting cola and music through these advertisements, it is also exporting ideas about the relationship between cultural and commercial interests, which is why this case study is also a cautionary tale. At a time when musicians and record companies are increasingly desperate to explore non-traditional revenue streams, it is important to examine even seemingly benign partnerships and to recognize that, whatever the potential benefits to artists in the short term, when musicians and corporations enter into an agreement, the resulting partnership is not a symmetrical one. Bear in mind how many of the musicians who have been involved in cola campaigns are barely a blip on the popular culture radar today, while the names Coke and Pepsi remain in lights.

Over the years the colas have developed what amounts to a real relationship to the music industry. Coca-Cola's 1991 "Pop Music" program saw the company joining with Sony Music to provide free mini-CDs to buyers of multipacks and in 2004, through their partnership with the iTunes music store, Pepsi invited customers to download a free song with purchase of a soft drink. Such promotions call attention to the role of the cola corporations in the distribution of popular music. The system of music distribution imagined by Josh Rabinowitz, director of music for Grey Worldwide, where record labels become obsolete and singles are released directly through product advertisements, may offer solutions to some of the problems presented by major labels, but it also offers its own set of concerns. One advertising copywriter I spoke with worried that as corporations like Starbucks become more successful in music distribution they might, like major labels, "think they know better than the artist" (Kovey, p.c., 2005). He imagined a Starbucks executive commenting on the new Ron Sexsmith album, saying "the xylophone is too jarring, so if he could remove those then we'd be more willing to put it in the store" (Kovey, p.c., 2005).

The impact of advertiser interest on the cultural realm is already occurring, even without this sort of blatant wresting of control and power over the production of culture from the hands of artists. Writing of corporate sponsorship of the arts, McAllister asserted, "Art becomes less valued, less credible and less engaging. Art begins to equal other commercial entities. Art equals the sitcom; art equals the 15-second spot" (1996: 221). Likewise, the articulation between music culture and advertisers holds a similarly detrimental capacity; as the association becomes more conventional, and viewers more apathetic to it, the self-standing value of music culture may become threatened. No clearer is this threat than in cases where songs have been restructured or subverted by a commercial usage, sometimes in ways that are viewed by fans and critics as patently offensive. Chapter 6 considers advertisements that have been subject to this accusation.

Chapter 6
Taming Rebellion: Advertising's Control over Meaning

The previous chapters have implicitly and explicitly suggested that the use of popular music in advertising affects how we regard popular music. Interactions between different textual entities, the use of popular music in advertising representing one example, contribute to the hypercommercialistic media environment, and the relationships forged between artists and advertisers, as displayed through licensing to advertising, product placement, and sponsorship, tend to play to the commercial aspects of cultural texts. Yet the specific process through which advertising impacts popular music remains largely unexamined. This chapter seeks to analyze more closely the process that transpires when popular music and advertising are joined.

In many cases, the use of music in advertising has provoked discussions involving various conceptions of "meaning" and accusations that ads did not stay true to, or dishonorably changed, the meaning of the songs. The study of culture is, at its most fundamental, the study of how meaning is encouraged or discouraged and which kinds of meanings prevail. Yet, in understanding cultural forms and processes, few terms are more problematic and complicated than "meaning." "Meaning" is employed broadly and narrowly across cultural texts, and recognized as the currency by which culture circulates, even as users continue to designate different values to different meanings. Determining the source of meaning has proved as difficult as identifying meaning itself, which is not merely decoded, but fundamentally constructed by the readers, listeners, and consumers of cultural texts.

While it is common and traditional to treat the author as the origin of meaning, literary and cultural scholars have questioned the stability and structure of meaning presumed by privileging the author, instead declaring texts to be inherently meaningless except in the context of communities of readers in particular situations, rendering audiences to be active agents in the construction of meaning. Barthes offered a liberating challenge to author privilege, proclaiming a text to be "not a line of words releasing a single 'theological' meaning (the message of the Author-God) but a multidimensional space in which a variety of writings, none of them original, blend and clash" to be unified, made meaningful, by the reader (1977: 146).

Despite the popular discourse that continues to view the author as the source of meaning and despite the belief that popular music provides easy texts to read, popular music is never experienced as containing a single meaning. Messages expressed through popular music, like other media messages, are subject to audience work: "since there is no necessary correspondence between encoding and decoding, the former can attempt to 'pre-fer' but cannot prescribe or guarantee the latter" (Hall 1980: 135). Polysemy, argued Fiske, is a necessary component of the popular text: "A popular text, to be popular, must have points of relevance to a variety of readers in a variety of social contexts, and so must be polysemic in itself, and any one reading of it must be conditional, for it must be determined by the social conditions of its reading" (1989: 141). Fiske's insistence on the "polysemic openness of popular texts" (1989: 30) draws on de Certeau's (1984) notions of "making do" and "textual poaching" to assert that "the fact that the system provides only commodities, whether cultural or material, does not mean that the process of consuming those commodities can be adequately described as one that commodifies the people into a homogenized mass at the mercy of the barons of the industry" (Fiske 1989: 25–6). Song meaning is constantly being remolded by various music consumers to suit their purposes and experiences; polysemy, in this way, does not suggest merely a set of meanings from among which listeners select one. Texts are inherently meaningless but offer infinite possibilities of meaning to be constructed by the listeners who place the texts into a historical, situational, or interpersonal context.

Popular considerations of meaning still focus attention primarily on the author and adhere to the belief that there is a single "true" meaning to an artistic text. The idea that author-intended meanings determine audience meanings is perpetuated by music journalists who decode lyrics by trade, opponents who point the finger at musicians as responsible for moral decay, and programs such as VH1's short-lived *True Spin*, which revealed the so-called truth behind multiply-interpreted popular songs. Critiques of certain uses of music in advertising consistently quote lyrics, and often refer back to the artists' explanations of their songs as evidence that the commercial interpretation is both incorrect and immoral.

Although nobody would contest that popular music has meaning, and in very important ways, "What has been relatively neglected is the problem of just how popular musical texts produce meaning and how such meanings operate not only within the contexts of political economies but also within social history and lived experience" (Walser 1993: 34). The meaning of popular music is multifaceted, consisting of multiple dimensions that vary in valence. An understanding of popular musical meaning, and the restructuring of popular musical meaning, must take account of multiple layers through which meaning is created. I aim to understand the construction of meaning as interactive, involving exchanges between the text, often the object of study for popular musicology, and the uses of the text, long the charge of cultural studies. The meaning of popular music is, as Middleton expressed, "produced through dialogue at many levels: within the textures, voices, structures, and style-alliances of the individual musical event; between producers and addressees; between text, style, and genre and other texts, styles, genres; between discourses, musical and other; between interpretations, mediators, and other involved social actors" (2000: 13). To address advertising's role in directing audience meanings, multiple levels require consideration.

In the history of music in advertising described in Chapter 1, I referenced the work of various scholars who have made claims that musical meaning is influenced by the recontextualization of music into various settings, such as participating in concerts, listening to a CD, or hearing a song in a commercial. Tota explained that musical meaning "is modified when its use radically changes" (Tota 2001: 116) as it does when placed in an advertisement. Music pieces placed in advertising, described Frith, have "their emotional meaning defined by products and sales talk" (2002: 281). In fact, the use of popular music in advertising is motivated by particular purposes, not necessarily intended by the creators of this music; as Huron argued: "it is the overt knowledge of objectives and the consequent desire to control and handle the tools of musical meaning which make advertising such a compelling object of musical study" (1989: 572). Advertising's use of external media, such as pieces of music, or clips from films, or even recognizable entertainment and cultural figures, does not simply borrow with no effect: "when advertising engages in this social linkage process, it also changes the object to which it is linked. Advertising does not borrow meaning neutrally; it changes the meaning" (McAllister 1996: 125).

"Selling out," the charge that has traditionally been positioned at the crux of conversations about the use of music in advertising, is a distraction from how the use of music in advertising constrains, highlights, or suppresses meanings that audiences have the ability to create. Carrie McLaren, who has written about popular music's use in advertising for the *Village Voice*, as well as for her own magazine, *Stay Free!*, described her interest in the subject:

> The debates always focus on "Did so-and-so sell out?" "Should artists make these kinds of decisions to put their music in commercials?" But I was never really particularly interested in that personal decision that artists have to make because I understand people have to live in the world, and they have to survive and they have to pay their rents. I just feel that from the listener's perspective it fundamentally changes a song when that song appears in a commercial. (personal communication, 2005)

That placement into a moving-visual medium changes the meaning of music is by no means a new concept; a similar impact has been described with film and video, though not necessarily with the same disapproving undertones. Mundy wrote that film and television are "inextricably bound up with defining the meaning of popular music, that they are structurally and ideologically bound up with the popular music industry and those commercial enterprises through which we receive, interpret, delight in or reject our music" (1999: 214). Certainly as it has become standard to release a music video with a single, the relevance of visual layers to the meaning of popular music has increased. Fan discussions of popular songs often include "a reading of the song's interpretation in music video"; music video "provides preferred interpretations of lyrics" (Rose 1994: 8).

Yet if the use of music in advertising has its roots in film soundtracks and music video, there are qualities that necessarily distinguish the use of music in commercials from uses that are less explicitly tied to advertisers. As copywriter Fred Kovey put it, "just because advertising is generally insidious and annoying, it's kind of weird to associate something that's personal with it" (p.c., 2005). As discussed earlier, though commercials are sometimes treated as artistic works in and of themselves, it is impossible to entirely separate the spots from the aims of advertisers, whether they sell a product, promote a brand, or show the philanthropic nature of a corporation. Aesthetically, a commercial spot may do more justice to a song than a haphazard placement in a film, but the association with specific publicity changes or qualifies the original meaning. One dejected journalist identified this risk in describing "those moments when your soul is sort of raked across the coals as you hear a classic, epic song that actually sort of meant something sincere and cool and the tiniest bit profound to millions of fans, and represented everything that corporate profiteering did not, and it just makes you sad" (Morford 2004).

The association of popular music with the marketing objectives of advertising is the most commonly evoked explanation for how commercials change the meaning of music for audiences. It is therefore useful to consider the broader context of distribution as well as the specific details of critical cases in order to understand the entire process through which audience abilities to make sense of altered music are influenced. In considering the broader context, it is clear that even before a specific association is formed, the channel of distribution itself shapes musical perceptions. As Jones pointed out, though music "seems to be all around us … it rarely reaches us entirely accidentally" (2002: 216); the importance of understanding distribution is thus highlighted. When a song is heard in a concert, on a radio, on an iPod, or through a commercial, listeners are experiencing music quite differently: the distribution channel matters. Listeners may have choices among these channels but not what they hear. The attention paid to and investment in the music used in television commercials is made distinct from the listening habits attached to more traditional methods of distribution and, consequently, different meanings result. The detailed analysis of emblematic cases allows for an examination of the specific treatment of a song, and provides clues as to why some associations provoke stronger reactions from fans and critics than others.

Besides employing different distribution channels and using popular music with intentions outside listening experiences, new meanings are also encouraged by selecting parts of music out of context, reinstrumentalizing its score, altering the (words of the) lyrics, and mixing (remixing) one piece with another. These techniques of using popular music in advertising, and in fact all recycling of music, alter listeners' ability to construct meanings. Advertisers cannot control how a listener makes sense of music; however, by modifying the sensory qualities of music, advertisers take advantage of listener habits, predispositions, and potential responses.

The use of popular music in television commercials offers a locus through which the role of meaning in the relationships between popular musicians and advertisers can be examined. Some examples of popular music in television commercials have gained attention by pairing songs that take up presumably serious subjects with seemingly incompatible products or services. An examination of such cases, and the discourse surrounding them, highlights the changes in meaning anticipated by interactions between popular music and advertising. In organizing this study, I selected two cases that seemed to especially raise the ire of music fans: Wrangler's use of Creedence Clearwater Revival's "Fortunate Son" and Royal Caribbean Cruise Lines' use of Iggy Pop's "Lust for Life." My hunch that these cases define the issue of meaning transformation was validated when *Slate*'s Seth Stevenson announced the results of a 2005 poll, which asked readers to write in with what they considered to be the most egregious uses of music in advertising:

> The big winner, submitted by dozens and dozens of you, is Royal Caribbean Cruise Lines, which used Iggy Pop's Lust for Life in a series of spots. As my reader Andrei put it, Nothing says maritime comfort like a song about shooting up junk.
>
> A very close second was Wrangler's use of Creedence Clearwater Revival's Fortunate Son in an ad for jeans. Something about the patriotic vibe of the ads, mismatched with this fiercely defiant song, really got your hackles up. (Stevenson 2005)

Both cases upset fans and critics who were astounded by the advertisers' apparent ignorance and consequent rearranging of these songs. Individual consumers may be able to empower themselves by "making do" with the media available, as scholars from Hebdige and de Certeau to Fiske have argued, but this same strategy of bricolage can also be used against them, as is evidenced by an advertiser's capacity to pick out sections of song, rearrange them, write over them, and combine them with visuals. Through these cases, I explore the manipulation of audience meanings in the context of music's use in advertising, and the processes assumed to be at work when commercials use popular music; what is revealed are the ways in which various types of meaning—linguistic, instrumentational, personal, and socio-cultural—are used selectively by advertisers and critics, despite each being, for listeners, experientially intertwined with the others.

A Lust for Cruises and Fortunate Jeans

Royal Caribbean and "Lust for Life"

Known as the Godfather of Punk, Iggy Pop is notorious for his hard-living tendencies and shocking stage antics, from receiving oral sex from a fan to cutting himself with broken glass. His late 1960s/early 1970s group the Stooges was anti-establishment both in sound and in lifestyle, and, at the time, it would have been hard to imagine this singer's work going on to represent any product or service besides liquor or syringes.

Iggy Pop's "Lust for Life," a collaboration with producer and co-writer David Bowie, was released on the solo album of the same name in 1977. A documentation of the singer's own publicly acknowledged struggle with heroin, "Lust for Life" opens with a verse relating the lure of destructive behavior: "Here comes Johnny Yen again/ With the liquor and drugs/ And a flesh machine/ He's gonna do another strip tease." Amidst the references to drug abuse and the struggle of recovery, the chorus—"I got a lust for life/ Oh, a lust for life"—takes on an ironic tone, but does present, on the surface, an internal mismatch in message. In addition, the track's unrelentingly bouncy beat provides a strange home for the decidedly bleak lyrics.

Though less attentive listeners might not be expected to pick up on the dark theme of "Lust for Life," Iggy Pop fans widely understood the song to be about attempting to quit drugs. This presumed meaning of "Lust for Life" was reactivated in 1996, when it was featured on the soundtrack to *Trainspotting*, a film tracing the travails of a group of Scottish heroin addicts, suggesting that nearly twenty years after its release, the song's connotative connection to heroin persisted, at least for some listeners. The association was challenged in 2001, when the song was licensed for use in a Royal Caribbean Cruise Lines ad campaign (it continues to be used some seven years later as this book is prepared). Wrote one journalist of the Iggy Pop song, "His 1977 'Lust For Life' anthem is ubiquitous, a theme song for the dark film *Trainspotting*, as well as the upbeat jingle for the family-oriented Royal Caribbean cruise ships" (Moayeri 2003). Perhaps more impressive than the track's ubiquity is the span of contexts in which it has been placed; how many songs come to mind as a perfect fit for portrayals of both heroin junkies and wholesome cruise holidays?

The ads themselves are apparently intended to appeal to a younger demographic, who would be familiar, if not with the song, then with the punk spirit from which it hails: "'Lust for Life,' by the '70s proto-punk, is aimed squarely at younger, first-time cruisers and baby boomers who are moving into prime cruising age by the millions" (Hilton 2001: T12). When the spots were first set to air, *Adweek* reported, "A series of 30-second TV spots from the Boston-based agency utilizes the percussive pop song 'Lust for Life' as a soundtrack for colorful, quick-cut images of vacationers having fun aboard the client's cruise ships, splashing in the ocean with stingrays and enjoying the sites—including Tivoli and the famed 'Little Mermaid'—of Copenhagen, Denmark" (Gianatasio 2001). Subsequent spots offered variations on this theme: scenes of sparkling blue water and enthusiastic travelers engaging in various activities—shooting up not among them—are punctuated by the song, the lyrics of which are reduced to the "lust for life" chorus. If the advertising industry press largely failed to recognize the oddness of this song choice, the popular press immediately identified the disparity between song and service. Commenting on the use of anti-establishment music in advertising, a reporter for the *New York Times* noted, "Commercials for family friendly cruise ship vacations with Royal Caribbean are set to Iggy Pop's 'Lust for

Life,' a rousing ode to drug life from a punk firebrand who has acknowledged his own copious substance abuse" (Ives 2002: C3).

Due to the length and reach of the Royal Caribbean campaign, this placement of "Lust for Life" attracted a lot of attention, but as Iggy Pop explained, "the history with that song is actually very long" (qtd. in Lanham 2004: 53). "Lust for Life" had appeared in various movies and television programs at the time that Royal Caribbean sought to license it. Because covers of Iggy Pop's music, some sounding suspiciously close to the originals, had already been placed in ads without his consent, and because the song had been previously excluded from radio play, Iggy Pop, who controls the master rights to "Lust for Life," agreed to the use. As he put it, "I actually enjoyed Royal Caribbean's usage. And to me, it's just great that it's out there in any form for someone to hear. That track has just been all over the world" (qtd. in Lanham 2004: 53). Iggy Pop's perspective suggests that all placements should be considered equally as a means to exposure, but fans and critics disagreed, responding to the campaign with the type of indignation reserved for advertising. A writer for the *San Francisco Chronicle* asked readers, "Did you cringe at all when you heard Iggy Pop's fabulous 'Lust for Life' during that commercial for the utter dystopian nightmare that is Royal Caribbean cruises?" (Morford 2004). For many Iggy Pop fans and popular music experts, including some of the informants I interviewed, the answer was a definitive "Yes." Listeners without access to the history of this song had no reason to be upset or find anything odd with its commercial use.

Having licensed a song to Volkswagen, Archie Moore of Velocity Girl felt uncomfortable criticizing other musicians for licensing music to commercials, but acknowledged, "I'll see a classic tune that I like used on TV and I'll think it's pretty repulsive. Hearing 'Lust for Life' used on the cruise line thing. It's basically a song about all sorts of perversions and drugs and things like that that's been completely taken out of context because it has a bouncy beat and because it's called 'Lust for Life'" (p.c., 2005). Arnold creative director Chris Carl also found Royal Caribbean's use of the song nonsensical: "I think they just thought that was a piece of music that would make them seem cool and make it seem fun and so they used it. They could have created a piece of music that did that. I mean 'Lust for Life,' I guess it's saying you have a lust for life but … it doesn't really make any sense to me" (p.c., 2005).

For those who have experience with the original song and hold on to the popular privileging of author's intentions, the pairing of "Lust for Life" with Royal Caribbean is almost absurd enough to transcend the usual criticism of mismatched music in ads. Copywriter Fred Kovey called this example the "most egregious" use of music in advertising, and then declared it "ridiculous" (p.c., 2005). Royal Caribbean is viewed as having crossed the line to an extent that the use can be seen as humorous as well as offensive. The satirical newspaper the *Onion* responded to the Royal Caribbean campaign with an article headlined "Song About Heroin Used to Advertise Bank":

The soul-wrenching experience of recovery from heroin addiction was used to evoke the financial security of a major banking institution Monday, when Boston-based Metrobank launched a high-profile ad campaign featuring "Lust for Life" by seminal '70s proto-punk Iggy Pop.

"We needed something that conveyed Metrobank's global financial presence, high-powered transaction capabilities, and respected position throughout the business community," said Jared Morris, president of Ogilvy & Mather, the spot's creator. "So, we thought, what better way than to call to mind punk forefather Iggy Pop's long, terrifying struggle with a near-fatal heroin habit?" ("Song About" 2001)

In addition to its entertainment function, the *Onion* article illustrates the disconnect between the cultural understanding of "Lust for Life" among Iggy Pop fans and the way the song is implemented by Royal Caribbean in its ad campaigns. This tension hinges on the ability of listeners, be they fans or advertising creatives, to construct very different meanings from the same text, occasionally resulting in a struggle over the "true" meaning, itself a fluid social construction.

Royal Caribbean presumably considers the campaign and the use of "Lust for Life" successful, as suggested by its continued use. At the end of the day, reasoned Kovey, "It totally works for the purpose it's used for, but it's just bizarre more than anything else" (p.c., 2005). Josh Rabinowitz, director of music for Grey Worldwide, agreed that it "works really successfully" (p.c., 2005). That the song works for the ad, however, does not mean that the ad works for the song, which is why this case earned the top spot in *Slate*'s poll.

Wrangler and "Fortunate Son"

In the late 1960s, as Iggy Pop and the Stooges were stunning small audiences, Creedence Clearwater Revival was a mainstay on radio, combining the sounds of rock 'n' roll's roots with often compelling lyrics. The all-American aural packaging of CCR's material hid the sometimes challenging themes addressed by songwriter John Fogerty.

"Fortunate Son," released in 1969, was a powerful and rousing critique of the military draft during the Vietnam era. The song begins, "Some folks are born made to wave the flag/ Ooh, they're red, white and blue/ And when the band plays 'Hail to the Chief'/ Ooh, they point the cannon at you, Lord" before driving into the chorus: "It ain't me, it ain't me/ I ain't no senator's son, son/ It ain't me, it ain't me/ I ain't no fortunate one, no." By the third verse, there is no question as to what event is framing this discrepancy in privilege: "Some folks inherit star spangled eyes/ Ooh, they send you down to war, Lord." "Fortunate Son" was a defining song during the Vietnam era and was readily adopted by anti-war protestors. It would take a substantial amount of editing and reinterpretation to feature the song as a patriotic anthem.

In 2001, Wrangler did just that by using "Fortunate Son" in a television commercial for its jeans. The ad juxtaposed the song with images of people living in the American heartland, denim, hay bales, and the American flag. In terms of lyrics, only the first couplet of the song—"Some folks are born made to wave the flag/ Ooh, they're red, white and blue"—was included in the ad. According to one journalist, "In the context of the ad, the lines are an appeal to a sense of Americanism, just what a company would want viewers to associate with its product. There's only one problem: That opening couplet alone does not convey the theme of the song" (Baker 2002: C2). Cases like this one serve as reminders to music supervisors to handle music with sensitivity: Music supervisor Tricia Halloran reported experiencing situations

> … where I've tried a song with a spot and the part of the song that we would use for thirty seconds really works with the spot, but the deeper meaning of the song is completely inappropriate for the spot and I've nixed it. That's to me a bad use of licensing. For example, I think it was a Creedence song, "Fortunate Son" for Wrangler, and that's an inappropriate use because that's not what that song's about. Even though the chorus sounds like one thing and the song is about another, and that happens a lot and I just think it's wrong. (p.c., 2005)

The negative reaction that the Wrangler spot received was heightened by Fogerty's own disapproval of the use. Unlike Iggy Pop's relationship to "Lust for Life," Fogerty does not control the rights to Creedence Clearwater Revival's catalog and Fantasy Records did not consult with the songwriter when Wrangler sought to license the track (Baker 2002). Fogerty explained the origin of the song: "I was protesting the fact that it seemed like the privileged children of the wealthy didn't have to serve in the Army," adding "I don't get what the song has to do with pants" (qtd. in Ives 2002: C3). Where Iggy Pop was happy with Royal Caribbean's use of "Lust for Life," Fogerty admitted that the Wrangler ad "makes me angry. When you use a song for a TV commercial, it trivializes the meaning of the song. It almost turns it into nothing" (qtd. in Baker 2002: C2). Yet the Wrangler advertisers and presumably their target audiences saw no problems with the use of the song, largely because its history was unknown or did not matter to them.

The differences between the cases do not end with control of copyright. While some fans and critics found it possible to see the use of Iggy Pop by Royal Caribbean as humorous and maybe even a little subversive, nobody was smiling about Wrangler's use of "Fortunate Son," which was viewed by the critics as undermining the original meaning. The Wrangler spot even inspired a short documentary called *Fortunate Son*, in which director Greg Wilcox set out to explain the meaning of the lines excluded from the commercial. Shown at many film festivals, Wilcox's short illustrates the importance to CCR fans of understanding a song like "Fortunate Son" in its entirety and original context.

Manipulating Audience Meaning

If advertising's affair with popular music threatens to transform the meaning of music adopted for commercial ends, a nuanced understanding of how and why meaning is constructed is necessary to explore the process of converting popular songs into advertisements. Both of these cases illustrate how the use of music in advertising, and subsequent discussions of the practice, encourage various senses of meaning while suppressing the chance of other readings. Meaning may arise primarily from word choices in lyrics, instrumentalization produced by the combination of sounds, the personal backgrounds, knowledge, and preferences that fans invest in the music they consume, or the shared socio-cultural experiences that develop for certain songs salient to specific cultural contexts. The following sections explore each of these senses of meaning more closely, and insist that, try as advertisers may to separate one layer of meaning from another, each remains interwoven with the others and to change one is to challenge meaning at its most culturally powerful and significant.

Linguistic Meaning

The answer to "What does this song mean?" is often sought, by both fans and scholars, through looking to lyrics and, if uncertainty persists, the author's explanation of those lyrics. As Johnson commented, non-linguistic meanings are largely viewed as "either parasitic upon linguistic meaning, or else falling outside the study of semantics altogether" (1987: 2). By limiting "meaning" to lyrics, author's explanations and listener's verbal responses, non-linguistic, particularly bodily contingencies, such as the listener's personal experiences or the cultural context into which a message is distributed, are all but nullified. The implication of a linguistic approach to the discovery of meaning is that all of the information necessary for a message, in this case a popular song, to "mean" is included within the cultural object, and specifically in the lyrics.

This conception of meaning has its roots in Saussurean linguistics, where knowledge of the inherently arbitrary but culturally conditioned relationship between signifier and signified is essential to an understanding of a sign (Saussure 1966). Certainly the linguistic information conveyed by the two ads allows little room for varied interpretation: one proclaims, "I've got a lust for life," while the other declares, "Some folks are born made to wave the flag/ Ooh, they're red, white and blue." Abridging the lyrics of popular music is usually a necessary part of placing a song into a television commercial.

Advertisers are often drawn to choruses that represent the messages they are trying to convey; the chorus from a piece of popular music replaces the advertising jingle. HUM's Tricia Halloran explained, "Some clients really want the catchy, hooky chorus that just kind of reiterates their message. That's the most obvious form of licensing and probably that's done the most and then these other ways are kind of the more artistic ways that are slowly emerging, I think" (p.c., 2005).

In selecting just a portion of song to be featured advertisers are naïve, sometimes intentionally, to a phrase's ironic or metaphorical reading within the context of the entire song. "In advertising the clients are always incredibly literal" noted copywriter Kovey. "They have this idea that people are very literal about how they interpret everything. But with music they seem to be totally oblivious to that" (p.c., 2005). With clients so concerned about every nuance of a spot, it is expected that the generally accepted meaning of a song would be scrutinized before a track is licensed. Instead, advertisers seem to believe that by presenting only the words that support the ad's message, the baggage of previous interpretations is left behind. In this way, advertisers are still being "incredibly literal"; their understanding of musical meaning is privileging the literal, downplaying other possible layers of meaning, even as they use them. So it is that Johnny Cash's "Ring of Fire" seemed to one ad creative a reasonable choice for pitching hemorrhoid-relief products (the Cash family resolutely denied the use).

Placing linguistically mismatched songs into television commercials holds potential to be both funny and subversive. Arnold's Chris Carl described licensing the Magnetic Fields' "Kiss Me Like You Mean It" for use in an ad for Helzberg Diamonds, before a closer inspection of the liner notes forced a reassessment of the song's meaning. Said Carl,

> The company we did it for is like Bible Belt Kansas City, absolutely, totally conservative. They had no idea what that song was about. They thought it was a love song. And it's about B&D [bondage and domination] and all that shit. So it was pretty funny that they were televising this spot and it was all about this woman in love with this guy. It was totally pure and innocent, but at the same time that's not what the song was about at all. (p.c., 2005)

Royal Caribbean's use of "Lust for Life" has struck some fans as similarly subversive, as was suggested by the *Onion* article. But for others, the use of a song about one thing to sell something else entirely seems irrational. Of his work on a Starbucks campaign, Jeff Hale recalled, "It just never made any sense to me that someone would be using a pre-existing song presumably about something that isn't super-caffeinated coffee to sell it" (p.c., 2005).

By selecting and presenting a certain linguistic interpretation of a song, chosen to work in line with a marketing message, advertisers are participating in the production of musical meaning in much the same way as other listeners. Varied interpretations of lyrics result from the most seemingly transparent of popular musical texts (see, for example, Prinsky and Rosenbaum 1987). In the essay "Why Do Songs Have Words?," Frith suggested that "song words matter most, as words, when they are *not* part of an *auteur*ial unity, when they are still open to interpretation, not just by their singers, but by their listeners too" (1988: 123); it is through this openness that popular music provides its social use, giving listeners the terms through which they live experiences.

In terms of ambiguity, some popular music lyrics have more in common with the art of poetry than with other written forms. As with poetry, lyrics are constructed to fit into a fixed form, resulting in a text that is perceptibly less transparent than the text of, for instance, advertisements or instruction manuals, or other texts that have a vested interest in the audience decoding the message from Hall's dominant-hegemonic position. Artists ranging from folk legend Bob Dylan to rapper Tupac Shakur have been consistently referred to not as lyricists, but poets, suggesting that the artist-as-poet perception straddles genres and generations.

Poetic ambiguity makes it easy for advertisers to choose and rearrange lyrics to suit their preferred interpretation. Moreover, advertisers that take the entire song and the whole of its lyrics into account can nonetheless read the overall theme to fit with the campaign theme. Craig Errington, director of advertising for Wrangler, "said the company studied the lyrics and concluded that 'Fortunate Son' was not merely an anti-war song, but 'more an ode to the common man. The common man is who we have been directing Wrangler toward'" (Baker 2002: C2). Admirable though it may be that Wrangler's marketing executives "studied the lyrics" at all, their research only looked inward, neglecting to consider how the lyrics had been received when the song was popular, or how the lyrics are interpreted by current fans. Wrangler might have discovered that, while the theme of privileged few versus common majority is a salient one, fans who had experienced the whole song, and in the era it characterized, were uncomfortable with that aspect of the lyrics being excised from the context of war, whereas younger listeners without knowledge of that context fell more easily into the advertiser's reinterpretation.

For some music listeners and TV viewers, it is possible for the success of an individual ad to excuse the ad message's irreverence to the song's previous meanings. As Josh Rabinowitz, director of music for Grey Worldwide, offered, "Obviously 'Lust for Life': it's a great example of a commercial that has nothing to do with what they're talking about but works really successfully. The 'London Calling' thing that Jaguar did a few years ago is a great example of taking something that was completely antithetical to what Jaguar represents ... but it still resonated" (p.c., 2005). Yet even music fans who are generally unaffected by mismatched uses of music may still have a line that can be crossed; the changing, as opposed to rearranging, of lyrics often draws that line. Universal Music Publishing's Carianne Brown reported being generally unbothered by the use of music in commercials, even when the presumed meaning was turned on its head. But, she admitted, "I did have a weird reaction to, I don't know if you saw that Swiffer commercial that used [Devo's] 'Whip It' and changed the lyrics? That freaked me out a little bit" (p.c., 2006).

The manipulation of lyrics is a sensitive area, in part because it is through lyrics that listeners often choose to discuss popular music's meaning, and also because speech more generally is considered the most important right in democratic societies. Gruff Rhys of the Super Furry Animals, who have turned down multiple offers to license to commercials, explained that the use of music in advertising is "more problematic for lyrical music; your most personal means of expression may be used as sloganeering to endorse a suspect product" (p.c., 2006). In addition to being our "most personal means of expression," words remain the layer of meaning most readily accessed and articulated by listeners. Lyrics can thus be understood as the topmost layer of meaning for most people, most of the time and, as a consequence, the layer for which the restructuring by advertisers might provoke the greatest disapproval.

This was the concern expressed in Chapter 3 by Lost Planet's Tim Barnes over VW's use of "Pink Moon," about which he noted, "when you start getting into just slapping up a song, where you're hearing the singing and all this other kind of stuff, that's when I think you really get kind of locked in to the sort of torture of 'I can't listen to this song again'" (p.c., 2005). That feeling was experienced by some fans and critics who rejected Royal Caribbean's use of "Lust for Life" and Wrangler's use of "Fortunate Son." The dissonance between what fans had accepted as the linguistic meaning of the songs and what the advertisers offered in terms of interpretation was too powerful for many listeners to simply laugh at or shrug off.

The Meaning of Instrumentation

In some cases, accessing linguistic meaning is irrelevant: in the realm of popular music, there have been subgenres, such as surf and space-age music, that are almost entirely instrumental in nature. The role of the instrumentational component of popular song in how meanings are constructed, just as the role of typography in texts, is not to be overlooked; even in the absence of lyrics, songs still acquire meanings. One way in which meaning is created through sound is through the socially and culturally constructed connections that certain sounds have with certain emotions: "Just as communicative behavior tends to become conventionalized for the sake of more efficient communication, so the musical communication of moods and sentiments tends to become standardized" (Meyer 1956: 267). To use a very basic generalization as an example, in Western cultures major chord progressions often connote "happy," while minor chord progressions often connote "sad." When popular music has been taken up by traditional musicological approaches, the meaning of instrumentation has been appraised through analyses of sound structures.

Even for lyrics-based music, the inclusion of what appear to be highly evocative lyrics does not guarantee that listeners will rely on the linguistic structures. As Meyer described, "a potentially connotative passage may fail to evoke any concrete images whatsoever. Instead the listener may become aware of how the musical passage 'feels' in relation to his own designative emotional experiences … The music may, in short, be experienced as mood or sentiment" (1956: 266). So it is that a listener may be able to describe a song as "meaningful" without being able to explain its linguistic meaning.

Japanese fans have achieved legendary status in the rock world for their unbridled passion for songs the lyrics of which they may not understand.

When English-singing groups tour Japan, they are often struck by the crowd's ability and desire to sing along to all of the songs, despite not necessarily understanding the linguistic meaning of the lyrics. Clearly, popular music—including the sound of lyrics in a non-native tongue—can be very meaningful to fans, without that meaning being specifically tied to the linguistic aspect of the text. Tim Barnes' explanation that by using only instrumental parts of songs the product is being sold on "just the feeling of the music" illustrates the persistence of meaning in the absence of lyrics (p.c., 2005).

As an extension of the culturally encouraged meaning of instrumentation, specific sounds and genres of music are considered better fits for some products or services over others. Music that is experienced by listeners as soothing sends a different message for an advertiser than music that is experienced as aggressive. Tricia Halloran reported dealing with a "really aggressive, not quite metal, but pretty aggressive sounding band" (p.c., 2005) that was open to licensing to commercials, but was not interested in car commercials. To Halloran, the sound of the band narrowed their options: "What other kind of commercial is your music going to be used for? It's not like it's going to be used for tissue commercials—it had this really agro driving sound and that is used in car commercials" (p.c., 2005).

The fit of the sound of the music to the campaign's message is just as critical, if not more critical, to clients than the lyrics, which can be removed entirely. Justifications for why Royal Caribbean would use "Lust for Life" routinely return to the bouncy beat of the song and, likewise, Wrangler's director of advertising described how the company was attracted to "Fortunate Son" for "the energetic, uplifting sound and beat that makes you turn your head back to the TV" (qtd. in Baker 2002: C2).

As with lyrics, listeners play a crucial role in determining the meaning of instrumentation; Small described how "with a recording the relationships between sounds are stable, but the participants still change" (1998: 139). In other words, the position of the listener—physical, emotional, cultural—contributes to the individual interpretation of meaning, even when the sound remains internally the same. Sound relationships contribute to how meaning arises for listeners "but they do not constitute the whole of it" (Small 1998: 139). Advertisers change the sound of popular music by abridging it and rearranging it, but also by addressing the listener as occupying the particular position of consumer. At the same time, some listeners will experience the use of music in advertising with pre-existing and personal meanings already associated with the song, complicating the reductive and restrictive consumer subject position.

Personal Meaning

A model of meaning that focuses only on the lyrics and instrumentation refuses to engage with another very real sense of meaning in popular music: meaning as personal and emotional significance. The personal meaning of popular music may be derived partially from the lyrics and music, but is also inspired by external factors. Meaning can be influenced by any number of an infinite variety of personal connections that a listener has with a song—where a listener was physically and emotionally when introduced to the song, who introduced the song to the listener, how the listener has used the song, and so on. Where Adorno (1990/1941) feared the effect of standardized music on the passive consumers, the standard, universal themes in popular music also provide a site where listeners' personal experiences and beliefs can infuse different and deeper meanings.

Music is a significant part of our everyday lives, and its presence can be felt as near constant through the experiences of emotions and events. In an anecdotal account that addresses the role of experience in producing the meaning of popular musical texts, McDonald (1993) describes discovering the body of a friend who had committed suicide; after calling the police from a bar, he ordered a drink and listened to the Rolling Stones' "Gimme Shelter." Despite claiming to have "no idea" of the complete lyrics, he explained that "the traumatic memory of the event and the emotional intensity of that song have never been divorced" (1993: 1). McDonald's experience is an example of how texts "take on metatextual possibilities, each of which can change in nature given either the specific nature of the performance(s) under consideration, or given the manner of the subsequent audience response" (1993: 11). Listeners' expressions and explanations of the meaningfulness of music in their lives highlight the relationship between the practice of listening to music and the marking of memory:

> As one would expect from any practice so laden with emotional investment and so central to the invention of one's own identity, the use of music inevitably becomes conflated … with other important issues: how they make meaningful connections with others, how they monitor and remake themselves, how they remember the past, and how they dream of something better for the future. (Lipsitz 1993: xii–xiii)

Through evocative themes and sounds, popular songs can represent the past for future listeners to confront and reinterpret, emphasizing the openness and dialogic nature of popular musical texts: "while no cultural form has a fixed political meaning, rock and roll music has been and continues to be a dialogic space, an arena where memories of the past serve to critique and change the present" (Lipsitz 1990: 132).

The emotional meaning of music is created by contributions from both sides of the music experience; artists invest emotional meaning in the production of music and fans invest emotional meaning in the consumption of music, without necessarily sharing these emotions. Both origins of emotional meaning are taken advantage of by advertising's use of popular music. Ten Music's Sarah Gavigan described the process of licensing music, particularly unknown or lesser-known tracks, as "borrowing from the essence of their music" (p.c., 2005). Later, Gavigan acknowledged, "There are some artists that feel their music was created in so much emotion that they refuse ever to use it to promote a brand" (p.c., 2005). These two statements illustrate that it is the artist-invested emotion of popular music that advertisers seek to borrow, but they may encounter difficulties with the artist if the emotional investment is perceived as incompatible with the aim of the ad.

Ideally, advertisers would hope that listeners with a personal emotional connection to a song would also transfer that emotion to the product or service being marketed. But consumers do not necessarily want their emotions associated with a brand, and the use of popular music in advertising can alienate viewers previously acquainted with a piece of music. As Barnes put it, listeners become "fed up with hearing songs that they loved and have certain feelings for" used in commercials (p.c., 2005). Musicians who license to advertising are sensitive to fans' emotional connections to songs, even as they humbly deny that their music could be similarly meaningful to fans. Velocity Girl's Archie Moore was sympathetic to the destruction of emotional meaning that advertising may bring to popular music: "I remember reading recently where someone was talking about what disgusted him about it and again it's all personal ... The argument is 'I now have to watch the song that I' fill in the blank, you know, 'that I remember from my senior prom' or 'lost my virginity to' or whatever, is now selling French fries" (p.c., 2005). Yet, along with other musicians I talked to, Moore offered a songwriter's sense of perspective and was hesitant to grant his own music that same level of personal meaning. When I asked Joe Pernice why he did not view the meaning of his music as precious, like some of the more recognized songs that had been reinterpreted by advertisers, he responded simply, "Well, it isn't" (p.c., 2006).

Some informants suggested that the risk of offending fans was primarily a concern when ads use well-known pieces of music, where "people already have cherished memories of that song and a particular place and time" (Green, p.c., 2005). With new music, StarTime owner Isaac Green contended, "It's not taking people's memories or experiences with the record and then trashing them" (p.c., 2005). The use of lesser-known bands may still challenge memories among a smaller group of listeners familiar with the music. Perhaps more central, by introducing popular music to a larger audience through advertising, the commercial association may supersede the possibility of those songs holding an emotional resonance for future listeners.

Socio-cultural Meaning

Popular music also generates a collective experience for listeners, whose personal investments in a song are intertwined with their relationship to other members of groups. Though the goal of the music industry may be primarily commercial, this does not prevent groups from employing songs to mark identities, commemorate events, and observe relationships. Beatles fans can reflect on the commercial aspects of Beatlemania while maintaining that there was a genuine personal component to their fandom: "The Beatles seemed to be speaking directly to us and, in a funny way, *for us*" (Ehrenreich et al 1992: 99), as a generation with shared problems and concerns.

Groups make use of popular music to indicate shared identifications, and to celebrate and honor shared events. Audiences sing along with performers as groups, creating commonalities tied to music. Fans of sports teams use songs to distinguish themselves from fans of other teams, just as schools use songs to distinguish themselves from other schools. Groups drawn together through minority status or a lack of political power adopt songs to represent members' common concerns and interests. So it is that the 1960s girl-group style became associated with the gay community and the phrase 'the hip-hop generation' marks characteristics shared among American youths. The songs and genres shared by groups contain embedded memory, like the working-class memory in rock 'n' roll used by suburbanites detached from their working-class history (Lipsitz 1990), or the memory of the Holocaust available in Israeli music for use by post-war generations (Meyers and Zandberg 2002). As well as providing a space of embedded social memory, the interactive nature of popular music also offers the opportunity for embedding social memory. Whether in conjunction with the embedded memory or not, listeners are invited to forge social connections to popular music, to bring external social experiences to popular music encounters, and to construct social memories in relation to popular music. The important relationship between music and memory is underlined by Frith's description of music as "the most powerful of all *aide-memoires*" (1986: 76). As a space for producing and storing memory, popular music provides groups with an ideal marker; consider how even the smallest of groups, romantic couples, make use of the socio-cultural function of popular music through the cultural practice of establishing "our song."

The socio-cultural meaning of music, like personal emotional meaning, may not reflect the creator's intention. Rosenthal wrote that "the product as created by the producer is unlikely to be the product as received or used by the audience ... If we want to gauge music's powers to aid social movements, we must test that not by the intentions of the artists but by the effects on the audience" (2001). In the end, what the shared meaning is for listeners and whether it is reverent to the author's intention is less important than the fact that listeners perceive it as shared and meaningful to them.

Not all songs develop a socio-cultural significance for a large group of listeners, but both the Wrangler and Royal Caribbean spots used songs that, in addition to fulfilling each of the outlined categories of meaning, are also representative of specific moments in history that resonate widely. In these cases, the songs were licensed for commercial campaigns as a method of presenting information about a product or brand in part by capturing the pre-existing socio-cultural relevance of the selection. Music supervisor Tricia Halloran's consideration of "the deeper meaning of the song" (p.c., 2005) represents an acknowledgement of the socio-cultural layer of meaning; the "deeper meaning" in the case of "Fortunate Son" was adopted as the socio-cultural meaning shared by a large number of people for a social purpose. Jeff Hale reasoned that it was "sad to hear a song that was made for maybe other reasons ... being sort of colonized for marketing purposes" (p.c., 2005). One journalist wrote of Fogerty's objection to the use of "Fortunate Son":

> What hurts the most, he said, is the reaction he fears from men who were of draft age during the Vietnam War, men for whom Fortunate Son protested the unfairness of the loophole-filled Selective Service System. "It really ticks me off that they're thinking, 'Oh, they got to John. Musta given him a new boat or something.'" (Baker 2002: C2)

Ultimately, the advertiser cannot change the socio-cultural meaning of music for fans already familiar with the music. A spot can select and rearrange the lyrics and music, but if the song has a socio-cultural relevance for a listener, any amount of editing will encounter difficulties in expunging that meaning. Although it was reported that "Royal Caribbean International in Miami could do without Iggy Pop's outlaw image; its marketing executives just liked the pounding beat of 'Lust for Life'" (Ives 2002: C3), for listeners familiar with the song's provenance, its socio-cultural meaning was already formed. Arnold creative director Jay Williams insisted, "Iggy wasn't someone we were going to put out front" (qtd. in Ives 2002: C3), but while Iggy Pop is not visually put out front in Royal Caribbean's campaign, his presence and the ideologies represented by his presence exist in the use of "Lust for Life." The difference here between "Lust for Life" and "Fortunate Son" is one of numbers: fewer listeners were previously familiar with the Iggy Pop song, allowing Royal Caribbean to offer their interpretation to a new audience. When listeners are introduced to songs through the interpretation of an advertiser, the meaning of that music, while still subject to the agency of the consumer, is significantly transformed. Archie Moore wondered whether the risk of hearing a song out of context was worth reaching an audience that might otherwise never hear the song:

> There's going to be people that hate the idea that you're using a beloved song to sell a product. But there's also going to be other people who haven't heard that song and instead of hearing a jingle that was composed for a specific product they hear something that obviously a lot of people thought was a really cool song. They hear it completely out of context for the first time and it maybe makes an impression on them. (p.c., 2005)

Jack McFadden of March Records noted that the scenarios which have resulted in arguments about the meaning of the song affect classic artists much more than independent artists: "When they're selling these songs that are also quintessential, I mean the very staples of rock, and they're desecrating them by putting them in a shitty ad, then yeah that's going to be bad ... Like if Springsteen sold 'Born in the USA' to Walmart or something, all hell would break lose. It would be the most controversial thing of all time" (p.c., 2005). Because independent artists have a smaller fan base, and because independent artists have arguably more to gain by licensing to advertising, whatever disapproval might be voiced is muted and measured. At the same time, when independent or lesser-known bands are used in advertising, the socio-cultural meaning for a subset of listeners—the subcultural meaning—is threatened, which provokes another set of responses, revolving around the exclusivity typical of subcultures. The final chapter will consider more closely the tensions inherent to independent music being used in advertising.

The various layers of meaning discussed heretofore can be separated for the purpose of analysis but, in reality, are inextricably linked to one another. The meaning of popular music emerges in the multiple connections that listeners live in; whatever music comes to mean, audiences weave linguistic, instrumentational, personal, and socio-cultural layers. Moreover, with television advertising, as with music video, the combination of layers is also complemented by a visual experience. The meaning of popular music goes beyond its role as message-carrier; as DeNora wrote, "Music is not merely a 'meaningful' or 'communicative' medium. It does much more than convey signification through non-verbal means ... Music may influence how people compose their bodies, how they conduct themselves, how they experience the passage of time, how they feel—in terms of energy and emotion—about themselves, about others, and about situations" (2000: 16—17).

The polysemic possibilities offered by popular music exist both within and between categories. In using music, advertisers do what all listeners do: they poach and make do with the text, interpreting the meaning in the way that best suits them. Of course, the difference between an advertiser as a listener and most other listeners is that advertisers can disseminate the products of their interpretations to larger audiences than ordinary listeners can. Advertisers have the financial means and access to media that recontextualize music for a wide-reaching audience; the ability to create and distribute interpretations is not shared equally among all potential bricoleurs. In light of this power differential and the increased presence of licensed music in commercials, it becomes critical to examine advertising's perceived and real capacity to constrain the meanings of popular music.

Carrie McLaren described advertising's role in the production of meaning as analogous to seeing the filmic adaptation of a book:

> Listening to music is, I think, kind of comparable to reading a book, in the sense that when you read a book the characters and the way you picture things and the locale is very much an individual thing and those characters can become more alive to you for that reason. It's a cliché that people say they like reading more than seeing the movie. And I think that hearing a song first in a soundtrack or on a commercial is more like seeing the movie because it puts a specific image on a song. It puts it in a specific time and place. (p.c., 2005)

When they place popular music into a spot, advertisers are encouraging interpretations to listeners and with the specific goal of promoting something: a brand, a product, a candidate, a service, or an event.

Fogerty's discontent with the use of his music in advertising was informed by his response, as a Beatles fan, to Nike's use of "Revolution," another case in which copyright was out of the hands of the music's creators: "I happened to be on tour in a hotel room somewhere in America the first time I heard the Beatles' 'Revolution' used in a Nike commercial," he explained, "The trash can they provide in my room clanged against a wall. That was my reaction to that then—they're stealing something from me ... All my emotions welled up then at another nail in the coffin of the ideals of the '60s" (qtd. in Baker 2002: C2).

"How we relate [to music] is who we are" (Small 1998: 142), and when an advertiser becomes a part of that social relationship, we are relating to music through a brand. The insistence of Arnold's Williams that in placing "Lust for Life" the agency was "using a portion of the song that musically and lyrically fit with what we were doing ... The energy, enthusiasm and raw feel was right," (qtd. in Ives 2002: C3) fails to recognize the work that went into making the song fit: the linguistic and instrumentational layers were carefully selected, and the socio-cultural meaning was undermined.

This Music Was Brought to You by a Corporate Sponsor

When popular music is used in television commercials, it becomes attached to purposes extraneous to mere listening. Firstly, it becomes associated with the scene in the ad, encouraging rather specific interpretations, as McLaren suggested through her analogy with filmic adaptations of books. Secondly, music becomes associated with a brand. As agency producer Laura Pappanicholas commented, "With so much TV advertising, you start seeing it and then when you hear the song, it's like, 'Ugh, I'm thinking of [the brand]'" (p.c., 2005). Indeed, the ability of music to extend beyond the ad-viewing is one reason why advertisers use the strategy of licensing music: "Music has the possibility of reaching places that film does not. If you can connect a track of music to a brand and then that track goes on to a CD compilation that you play at your Christmas party and every time that song comes on somebody thinks of Target, you've done your job" (Gavigan, p.c., 2005). Finally, the meaning of music is attached to the objectives of commerce. Small described how the meaning of musical performance and listening comes from a "complex spiral of relationships" (1998: 48), comprising not only relationships between participants, but also "the participants' relationships to the world outside the performance space" (1998: 48). When music is used in advertising the relationship between performer and audience becomes mediated by the corporate sponsor. As a consequence, the relationships between listener and advertiser, and between artist and advertiser, are foregrounded.

The use of music in advertising campaigns has parallels in the use of music in political campaigns, though the latter is often acknowledged as having more clearly defined ideological ends. With advertising, instead of music being used to represent a liberal or conservative ideology, it is being used to advance a cause. Of the use of music in political campaigns, Street noted that it "serves to evoke particular images and associations" (2003: 114), functioning similarly to photo-ops with celebrities. He suggested that "songs and sounds are more powerful weapons in this armoury because of the way music works directly on our emotions. Just as the soundtrack to films or advertisements generates moods and feelings, so too do campaign songs" (Street 2003: 114). Some critics have also recognized and commented on the analogous nature of commercial and political campaigns. Of the Wrangler campaign, BBDO's senior creative director David Johnson concluded, "That's got to rank right up there in cluelessness with Ronald Reagan's brief, boneheaded embrace of 'Born in the USA' as a positive song about America, rather than an anguished wail from a Vietnam veteran chewed up and spat out by the country he fought for" (2002).

The response to such political gaffes has been strident and steady; artists have spoken out against their music being used by candidates with whom they do not share political perspectives, even issuing cease-and-desist orders, as Tom Petty did when George W. Bush used his song "Won't Back Down." It is worrisome that a similar response to music in commercials has become less frequent and is considered by many to be an old-fashioned viewpoint. Jason Fine, a senior editor at *Rolling Stone*, told one journalist, "It doesn't particularly bother me or steal the song's meaning from me. I know a lot of people do feel that way, but that's become an outdated way of thinking" (qtd. in Ives 2002: C3). Fine's statement suggests that we have, as a culture, become so inured to marketing practices that we no longer appreciate alternative ways of being, of questioning common cultural forms, which is the essence of art. What is hidden—intentionally or not—is that, in the end, all advertising has political and cultural consequences.

The Wrangler and Royal Caribbean ads topped the *Slate* list of most egregious uses of music in advertising because the feared influence of advertising on culture is its potential to control how people are encouraged to construct meaningful lives. Similarly, Small explained why he disliked music being pumped into malls and public transport:

> It is not so much the style of the sound relationships themselves that we may or may not like—in another context I might well find many of them pleasurable— but the relationships of the performance space themselves. Any performance, in fact, that the hearer has no choice but to hear affirms a relationship of unequal power that leaves the hearer diminished as a human being; for whatever else it might be, all musicking is ultimately a political act. (1998: 213)

Advertising is not a value-free filter; when it serves as the means to distribute culture, power shifts in favor of commercial interest. As DeNora described, "If music can affect the shape of social agency, then control over music in social settings is a source of social power; it is an opportunity to structure the parameters of action" (2000: 20). As the Wrangler and Royal Caribbean cases illustrate, advertisers control the dissemination of popular music and transform it by manipulation of content, rearranging the lyrics and instrumentation of the songs used, as well as through the very act of placing music into advertising.

SpinART co-founder Jeff Price reported his role as providing "every opportunity that exists to generate revenue for the artists or musicians through the—horrible word—exploitation of their music" (p.c., 2005). If "exploitation" is a horrible word, it is also a revealing one. "Exploitation," the word used within the music and advertising industries to describe the licensing of popular music, confirms the asymmetrical power relationship between musicians and advertisers. Even as some artists view their experiences with copyright exploitation as facilitation, the relationship between advertisers and musicians is not an equal one, but one between those in a position to exploit and those in a position to be exploited. In an interview on NPR, *Slate*'s Stevenson suggested that part of the reason why Royal Caribbean's use of "Lust for Life" took the top position was because the campaign had been running for such a long time. The longer a campaign runs, the more viewers will see it and the more the meaning of a piece of music will be informed by its commercial use rather than its original performance, both in terms of placing the song in other forms and in terms of restructuring its socio-cultural meaning. Dan Burt of JWT explained that most artists and labels "don't have things set in their mind about the media buy and how long they're going to use your damn song" (p.c., 2006).

The exploitation associated with licensing does not end with the artist; some critics believe that the viewer, too, is being exploited. The Super Furry Animals' Rhys remarked, "Exploitation is the key word and our guide in these matters, not some aesthetic principle of taste. One of our main reasons for not getting involved with adverts is that we may be exploiting people to buy a product that may be harmful to themselves or others through the companies' business practices" (p.c., 2006). The concern over how the audience is being exploited relates to the primary concern expressed by critics that commercials restructure the meaning of music. Accordingly, the cases that draw the most negative reactions are those that are understood to have strayed furthest from the perceived meaning or spirit of the song. Advertising's use of music in these cases can be a cause for alarm.

In a way, the Wrangler and Royal Caribbean ads are exceptions to the rule: usually television commercials do not use songs that have such a strong and shared meaning for the public. Creatives are usually more considerate in the way they use popular music in campaigns; for instance, Kovey (p.c., 2005) said that he and his co-workers joke about offensive pairings that they would not really pursue, an indication that they remain aware of the potential to offend. Besides, advertisers have reason to avoid distasteful pairings, if only because "these odd couplings of anti-establishment music and conspicuous consumption could end up alienating the very consumer the ads are meant to seduce" (Ives 2002: C3). As an example, Radioshack discovered through focus groups that their campaign featuring Marvin Gaye's "What's Going On" was provoking a negative response from consumers. The senior creative director for Radioshack explained,

> When you're going to use music that has history, you need to know what those songs meant to not even to certain people but to generations ... a lot of what we

heard in focus groups was "How dare you use this song that was so important to me, this anti-war song from the 70s for this cheap retail thing?" While we didn't get a lot of letters or anything like that, it was a point that we really hadn't taken into account. (Sabella 2004)

HUM's Tricia Halloran described being "surprised" by the Wrangler spot, noting, "most of the clients that I work with, like I said, they're totally artistic, they're music fans and they just wouldn't even want that kind of situation to occur" (p.c., 2005). At the same time, as Jeff Hale pointed out, there are music fans selecting the songs behind even the most atrocious pairings; creatives who "probably really cared about the band but were completely missing the message all those years" (p.c., 2005). Whether or not the ad is clearly at odds with the intended meaning of the song, the idealized goal of popular music and the goal of advertising are necessarily at odds.

The history of popular music, and popular culture, represents a struggle between meaning being imposed on consumers and meaning being produced by consumers. As Frith described, "the argument is either that the ideological meaning of music lies in the way it is commercially produced, in its commodity form, or that consumers create their own meanings out of the commodities offered" (1981: 56). While there may be no simple answer, it is undeniable that popular music has at moments and in places represented a powerful tool of resistance for people whose voices were not easily heard. Popular music's capacity to provide an emotional or social support for resistance against dominant lifestyles is limited when the forces being resisted control the selective reproduction and distribution of music. In a letter to the editor of *Adweek*, BBDO's David Johnson chided Wrangler for their disingenuous appeal:

Songwriter John Fogerty wasn't waving the flag, he was pointing the finger at those who do, falsely, in order to foist something on the gullible but well-meaning public, be it a war or just a pair of jeans.

Back then he was singing about Vietnam. Today, Wrangler, if you listen to the full lyrics and not your edited ones, he seems to be singing right at you. (Johnson 2002)

One reason why discussions of music in advertising are often reduced to accusations of "selling out" or claims that "selling out" no longer is relevant is because articulating the process by which listeners create meanings for what they hear is difficult. Yet meaning is essential to connecting the real tensions inherent to popular music's use in advertising with cultural policy formation. Monitoring advertising's relationship to popular music is particularly important when popular culture is in part determined by the interpretation formed by companies and imposed, through advertising, on the public.

Ultimately, popular culture relies on its independence from the forces it critiques, among these capitalism, commercialism, and government. If advertisers are able to tame the intentions of popular musicians, reimagining Creedence's scathing critique of privilege and the draft as a simple ode to the common man, or Iggy Pop's struggle with drugs and the trappings of modernity as a pithy self-affirmation, how can those songs continue to offer a place for both personal meaning-making and shared opposition? This worry extends to popular music and popular culture generally. The potential for popular culture to "mean" is necessarily constrained by advertising's appropriation of the channels of distribution and the right to rearticulate the very texts that provide the ground for constructing meaning. Gruff Rhys reported being galvanized by comedian and social critic Bill Hicks, who turned his refusal to do a commercial for Orange Drink into this stand-up routine: "When I'm done ranting about elite power that rules the planet under a totalitarian government that uses the media in order to keep people stupid, my throat gets parched! That's why I drink Orange Drink!" (Hicks 1997, ctd. by Rhys, p.c., 2006). By aligning with an advertiser, explained Rhys, "You sign away your right to speak out on any issue with any conviction … from then on anything you say may be suspect" (p.c., 2006). When it is used in the service of commerce, popular music risks losing its capacity to be taken seriously by fans and musicians as a bullhorn for free speech, both personal and political.

At the heart of tensions surrounding popular music's relationship to advertising are questions of the consequences of associating corporate intentions with the production of cultural objects. What does a fine art exhibit mean when it is sponsored by a corporation? Does a film mean something different when the commodities featured within it are a result of product placement rather than auteurial vision? How can a song address significant socio-cultural issues when it has been linked through a commercial to a brand? Cultural theory that has focused on the polysemy of texts has done so with the goal of empowering audiences, endowing consumers with the active agency that allows them to poach and make do as able bricoleurs. The polysemic text also enables advertisers, as potential bricoleurs, to produce interpretations with the limiting goal of encouraging commercial objectives. Television commercials may span a mere fifteen or thirty seconds, but advertising's restructuring of popular music threatens to exert an enduring influence on how members of the public can construct meaningful lives outside of commercial interests. It is no small price to pay for selling culture.

Chapter 7
Negotiating the Future of Popular Music in Advertising

The use of popular music in advertising is but one example of rising numbers of interactions between artists and advertisers in the United States and elsewhere. As advertising campaigns have turned to licensing music, advertisers have also explored opportunities across the range of arts and culture. From product placement in television and film to underwriting art exhibits, the role of commercial objectives in the creation, distribution, and consumption of culture, while always present within the music industry, has become more prominent than ever, and shows no signs of abatement.

This book has traced the reasons why the use of popular music in advertising has become more common and considered the reasons why this partnership is problematic. The consolidation in commercial radio that resulted from media deregulation has led to narrow playlists that exclude all but a small number of new artists, and the major record label system, which has begun to rely on licensing as a response to the perceived threats of piracy and downloading, functions with the expectation that most signed artists will be commercial failures. Video channels like MTV provide an outlet primarily for groups that are already topping or climbing the charts, and when MTV licenses the music of smaller groups as background music to original programming, the promise of exposure is used as an excuse to avoid adequate compensation. For all of these reasons, licensing to ad campaigns has become more attractive and, in rare cases, has proved an alternative avenue to financial gain and widespread exposure.

Yet, as the use of popular music in advertising has been championed as "the new radio," it also presents a number of concerns. The power of cultural authors is called into question by instances in which authors no longer control the rights to music. Even when creators do control the rights to their music, the helplessness expressed by musicians who have simply thrown their hands up and submitted to licensing to advertising as the only chance to make a living, reveals asymmetrical power dynamics that privilege the commercial entities over the cultural dimensions of popular music; musicians desperate to be heard and survive financially by any means possible make for easy marks to an advertising industry that will pay as little as possible to license music. Though some commercials have been deemed works of art themselves, on the surface providing a sensible match for the music placed within, ultimately the advertiser experiences the greater benefits from the partnership, using songs as tools for branding and exerting control over popular music texts.

Each of these issues is reproduced in some form across the range of interactions between artists and advertisers, allowing this analysis of the use of music in advertising to speak more generally to such partnerships and to reveal tensions deserving of critical, and possibly legislative, attention.

Independents at the Crux

Cultural producers who are struggling to survive, a category that includes new artists entering art worlds, are particularly susceptible to the lure of corporate sponsorship. As the opportunities to gain exposure and financial backing through commercial affiliation increase in number, we find ourselves ushering in a system of artistic production, distribution and consumption that differs from previous eras in its explicit and naturalized embrace of corporate sponsors, through underwriting and licensing. The experience of independent musicians who license to advertising illustrates the precarious position of less established artists caught within and implicated by this shift in the extent to which interactions between artists and advertisers are standard practice. A closer examination of the position of independent artists in this debate thus offers a point of entry through which the future of relationships with corporations can be envisaged, and precautionary measures proposed.

Although many of the cases that I have discussed involve bands that found mainstream success prior to licensing, the current debate about music in advertising is of particular importance for smaller, independent bands. For one thing, unknown and independent bands are being used more frequently in ad campaigns. Advertisers are drawn to independent music because the licensing fees for smaller bands can be substantially lower than those requested by more popular acts. Moreover, the use of indie music connotes a hipness that advertisers may want to use as an appeal, and that reflects the taste of many advertising creatives. Finally, as independent and credible bands have licensed to campaigns, musicians who might have formerly dismissed licensing to advertising as compromising are more willing to consider it as an opportunity. More than ever, independent bands are looking at licensing to advertising as a viable option for sustaining themselves as musicians. JWT's Dan Burt noted, "Even a year or two ago we'll try to license something and they'll be like, 'No, fuck off.' And then the next year they'll call me back, 'Um ... can you license our song? Is that commercial still available?'" (personal communication, 2006).

Lesser-known and independent musicians are forced to reconsider advertising campaigns as a potential vehicle for placement because they have the most to gain from it. While famous bands might benefit from the huge paydays presented by licensing hits to ad campaigns, most hardly need the exposure. On the other hand, the licensing fee received for a placement in an ad campaign, though substantially lower for unknown bands, is often enough to support musicians through a tour or the recording of a new album. Locked out from commercial radio, MTV, and the promotional support of a big-budgeted major label, placement in an advertisement also offers the possibility of exposure, even though, as I have suggested, the tangible results of this type of exposure are often minimal. Many music supervisors entered into the business because they recognized the lack of opportunities for most bands. Lost Planet's Tim Barnes explained why he became involved with licensing music for ad campaigns: "when you feel strongly about something, you want everyone else to feel the same way"; to Barnes, the fact that most bands would never be heard by most people "was a crime. I thought if more people heard this music, more people would like this music" (p.c., 2005).

If independent and less popular bands have the most to gain through licensing to advertisers, they also are arguably the most at odds philosophically and culturally with commercial objectives: appealing to the largest number of people by whatever means necessary. As a consequence, there was a time when licensing music to an advertiser could result in a hostile fan response. When the Del Fuegos and their music were featured in a 1985 Miller Beer commercial, the critical response, from music writers, musicians, and fans, was immediate. Former guitarist Warren Zanes described, "it did take us to another level of visibility but then there was the backlash. I think every guy in that band in hindsight, in that moment ... if we were to be back there again and the decision was in front of us, we wouldn't do it" (p.c., 2006). Over twenty years later, it is hard to imagine a reaction so severe to a practice that has become so commonplace. Instead, fan reactions to the use of songs in advertising tend to be mild, and almost apologetic in their critique. Fans, it seems, have come to understand the difficulty of being a working musician. In the music industry, getting somebody, anybody to listen to your work is no easy task; the interest of advertisers is comparatively flattering. Savan identified this view of advertiser interest as a form of validation: "While many boomers think the music's a sell-out, others have convinced themselves that it's a victory of their youth—multinationals are coming to *us*, our generation has something *they* want" (1994: 286).

That licensing to a commercial is unlikely to derail a band's career does not mean the tensions inherent to dealings between popular musicians and advertisers are now obsolete. When indie-rock group the Shins licensed to McDonald's in 2002, unwritten rules and boundaries present, but rarely articulated, in popular music subcultures bubbled to the surface. Wrote one journalist,

> Your band is the darling of the indie-rock world. How do you keep 'em loving you? Don't ask the Shins for career advice. After releasing 2001's "Oh, Inverted World," a mod-pop gem that made many critics' end-of-the-year lists, they let McDonald's use their melodically mesmerizing "New Slang" in a commercial. Then keyboardist Marty Crandall's girlfriend sported Shins wear on UPN's "America's Next Top Model." They're from Albuquerque, N.M., so maybe they never got that memo on cred maintenance. (Begun 2003: 16)

The McDonald's ad, aired primarily during the 2002 Olympics, placed an instrumental section of the song "New Slang" over a shot of a man holding a baby. A voiceover narrated, "There will be a first step, a first word, and, of course, a first French fry," followed by the appearance of the McDonald's logo. If Shins fans were surprised by McDonald's desire to use the Shins song, so, too, were the band and label. The creative director of film and television for Sub Pop, the Shins' record label, told one reporter that when the label was contacted, "initially, it kind of freaked everyone out … Why the hell have they heard of the Shins?" (qtd. in Scanlon 2002: E2). At the same time, he described the decision as an easy one to make: "They were like, well we don't really think this is compromising, someone wants to pay us to do what we do" (qtd. in Scanlon 2002: E2). Just as degrees of commercial affiliation are often collapsed by both defenders and critics as a way of excusing or condemning a particular type of interaction, the explanation that, by licensing to advertising, bands are simply being paid to do what they do refuses to acknowledge the specificities of the relationship. McDonald's is not simply paying the Shins to make music; if that was McDonald's interest, the corporation could anonymously fund the group's recording and touring. Rather, the company is paying the band to help sell and implicitly endorse its products.

McDonald's selection was surprising because the band was largely unknown, but also because the song seemed an odd choice. Thematically the song, which contains lyrics that may cause McDonald's PR department concern, is an unlikely fit for the company. The song includes the passages, "New slang when you notice the stripes, the dirt in your fries" and "God speed all the bakers at dawn, may they all cut their thumbs/ And bleed into their buns 'til they melt away." The *Washington Post* reported, "it was the featured music in a McDonald's commercial, a choice that suggests someone at Mickey D's has great musical taste, not to mention a sense of humor: There's a reference in the song to 'the dirt in your fries'" (Segal 2003: C05). Yet if the choice of "New Slang" was intended as an inside joke to be shared with Shins fans, the subversive or humorous possibilities of the placement stop with viewers already familiar with the track: in the act of poaching and the process of restructuring, the lyrics were entirely removed from the spot.

In the absence of lyrics, what set the use of "New Slang" apart from the company's typical musical leanings was to be found instead in the sound. The tone of "New Slang" is somber, in stark contrast to the bouncy R&B-influenced music usually used by McDonald's in ad campaigns, perhaps typified by Justin Timberlake's "I'm Lovin' It," which became both the theme song and tagline for the company. One Shins fan highlighted the contrast, posting to a message board "ba da ba ba baaaaah, I'm hatin' it," (Pot 2004) a parodic rephrasing of the Timberlake jingle in response to the ad featuring "New Slang." Against the backdrop of feel-good pop music normally employed to sell fast food, the serious and introspective Shins song stood out. A journalist remarked of the ad, "Doesn't exactly set the scene for the peppy, upbeat, fit kids-playing-in-the-sunshine ads that the burger chain is known for, does it?" (Bretherton 2005: 15).

This case draws attention to issues unique to underground and independent musicians, whose placement into commercials initiates debates about subcultural mores as well as commercial affiliation. Although the musicians I interviewed reported receiving very little negative feedback after their music appeared in ads, most confessed to entering the deals with some trepidation. Velocity Girl's Archie Moore described,

> You hear murmuring or you read about people complaining about losing their personal thing to the crass commercial world. Or having something that they felt was cool getting co-opted for kind of devious reasons. And we were worried a little bit about that … at the time there seemed to be this idea of a purity involved in certain types of music, underground types of music, and we were worried that it would sort of taint any perceived purity that we might have had. (p.c., 2005)

Although Hamilton Leithauser of the Walkmen explained that the potential reaction did not shape the process by which his band decided to license a song to an ad, he admitted, "I just figured people would sort of think it was lame and we'd probably lose a little respectability in the, whatever, rock world" (p.c., 2005). As was mentioned in Chapter 6, many musicians are aware of the stakes for other artists, but are hesitant to grant the same import to their own music. Hence, the assessment of the Ladybug Transistor's Gary Olson: "our little following that we have, they're not very precious about us" (p.c., 2005). At the same time, Olson offered that, with other independent bands, he could understand the potential response of fans as warranting worry.

The nature of such worry revolves around the subcultural meaning of music and the philosophies often adhered to among creators and consumers of independent music, where opposition to working with major labels assumes opposition to working with large corporations more generally. The meaning of music in independent and underground music scenes is attached to notions of exclusivity and intimacy, as opposed to the large crowds and distance from the performer that characterize mainstream popular music culture. Entering into the mainstream, whether through play on MTV, commercial radio, or advertising, is seen as a threat to the original fan base. Arnold considered the power of a new, mainstream audience to damage the intimate relationship between fan and band, describing the backlash that occurs "every time a band's fan base grows beyond the confines of those you could personally meet" (1993: 65) and the annoying "invasion of the ordinary people" (1993: 124). Jenn Lanchart, director of film and television for the Beggars Group, reasoned, "There's always going to be disgruntled fans. There's always going to be people—just recently we did a Stephen Malkmus song in a Sears campaign and so many people have been writing about it on the Matador website. They've been like, 'What the hell, Stephen's doing this, Stephen's selling out, and I can't believe this'" (p.c., 2005).

As the former frontman for celebrated indie-rock group Pavement, Malkmus is an icon in the independent music world, and his involvement in an advertising campaign, like the Shins' agreement with McDonald's, was viewed as speaking to a larger shift in the independent world, where fans witnessed music they considered "their own" not only entering into the mainstream, but led by corporate sponsors. Fans hold expectations that bands will "stay true" to them, as the fans perceive themselves to have stayed loyal to bands through the purchase of records and attendance at shows. Moore suggested that expectations of loyalty are unfair to bands: "Fans are often as or more unreliable than bands. I mean, fans don't stick with a band for a lifetime. People turn on bands quite frequently and feel that they're justified to do that. A band selling their record to an ad, they're probably not doing it to piss off any fans, but that might be an effect" (p.c., 2005).

As I have suggested, artists deserve the right to deny uses of their work that could be reasonably classified as having a potentially negative impact on their reputation. Likewise, it is ultimately the artists themselves who must weigh licensing opportunities and depend on their own decisions to survive as musicians. In defending the Who's choice to license songs to advertisements, Pete Townshend contended, "These songs are my property. They came out of my head. I have every right to do whatever I want with them. You own your personal reactions to them and whatever memories they evoke for you, but the songs are entirely mine and I will use them any way I like" (qtd. in Flanagan 2006). At the same time, insofar as fans represent in their objections some real and important concerns, to ignore dissent and disapproval is to ignore certain cultural discussions. As the Super Furry Animals' Gruff Rhys explained, "I think it's dangerous generally to take fans for granted. The fans of the band are above anything else, music fans, like me. It's very important that you can justify any artistic decision to yourself above anyone else. I imagine people can detect if you make an earnest decision or not" (p.c., 2006). Negative fan reaction can be used to gauge and monitor cultural practice, even when the target of criticism is not the most deserving.

Calvin Johnson, founder of K records, described how the "sell-out" debate often places blame on musicians as the easy target, ignoring the other parties involved in the exchange:

> There is an unfair onus people are putting on the musician. It's like when there's a baseball strike, or when people hear about a baseball player getting what they consider a huge salary out of proportion with what they deserve. And again there's this moral overtone put on that and no one ever says, "Well, if he's making that many millions, how much is the owner making? And he's not even playing." No one ever comes back and says, "Wait the owner must be making way more than that in order to be able to pay this guy." ... We look at the little guy but we never think about the bigger picture. (p.c., 2006)

Johnson is correct that the knee-jerk reaction to campaigns is a moral indictment of the artist. Yet, as the use of pre-existing and particularly independent music in advertising has become more frequent, fans and critics are beginning to look at the bigger picture, not least by pointing to the financial struggle of musicians and the state of commercial radio as important contextual factors.

Mediating Variables Matter

It is clear that in all cases, whether the song and band are very well known or not, mediating variables matter. Who controls the rights, what the product is, how aesthetically successful and reverent to the song's perceived original meaning the ad is, and whether the band is in need of exposure and money, are all variables that may shape the fan response. That the musicians I talked to experienced, for the most part, neutral or positive responses to their licensing music to television commercials can be attributed to the combination of circumstances surrounding the spots: the artists maintained at least some control over the rights (publishing, if not master use), stood to gain potentially from both the fee and exposure, the products and companies were relatively uncontroversial, and the ads themselves were visually interesting. These are conditions that tend to result in more positive appraisals of licensing to advertising.

In the case of the Saturn ad that featured the Walkmen's "We've Been Had," for instance, the product is one that has more of a natural connection to music, since the car is where many people do much of their music listening. The theme of the ad, cautiously approaching adulthood, matched the theme of the song, and the ad, which included scenes of young adults driving by nostalgic childhood activities, such as swinging on swingsets, on their way to a roadside sign marking adulthood, received accolades in and outside of the advertising industry. Lastly, the Walkmen benefited from the song, both in terms of the fee, and through record sales that resulted from the placement. Whatever fears singer Hamilton Leithauser had going into the contract remained unrealized. Had any one of these variables been different, so too might have been the response. Such was the situation with the McDonald's ad featuring the Shins' "New Slang." Although an extreme reaction, the sort of which some artists experienced in the 1980s, may not occur in the current media environment, this example displays the existence of ongoing tensions and the weight of the factors outlined in earlier chapters.

The reaction in the press and on internet message boards was a mix of astonishment that the Shins would license to McDonald's, honest attempts to understand why the band agreed to, and insistence that complaining about the use of music in ads or selling out is outdated. Wrote one journalist, "The song 'New Slang' ending up appearing in a widely aired McDonald's commercial and the ensuing debate of whether the band had sold out further heightened their profile in indie rock circles" (Kielty 2003: D16). In actuality, the group already enjoyed a relatively high profile in the indie rock world; it was the potential that the ad might heighten the group's profile in the mainstream, and through the channel of a corporate sponsor, that drew a negative reaction from some fans. "There's nothing more annoying to a music geek than an ad exec who's ahead of the curve," reasoned an *SF Weekly* writer. "How many indie rockers cringe whenever they see that McDonald's commercial that financed the Shins' last tour, or hear Isaac Brock's tortured bark in the background of an ad for minivans?" (Kroth 2004).

The coverage surrounding the case concentrated on the perceived benefits to the band, recalling the documentation of Moby's success with licensing. As one writer put it, "Instead of radio, the Shins have relied on the pop-culture market to push their music" (Baumgarten 2005). The Shins' music has appeared in visual media outside of advertising, including television shows like *The O.C.* and films like *Garden State*, supporting the presumption that placement in advertising may lead to other, less fraught, licensing opportunities. Another reasoned, "While purists cried 'sellout,' the Shins used the money to relocate to Portland and build a basement studio, which is where they recorded their second album, 'Chutes Too Narrow'" (Segal 2003: C05). Sub Pop's creative director of film and television also stated this point: "It's a way for a band that doesn't get signed for huge advances to be able to quit their day jobs for a while and concentrate on making music" (qtd. in Scanlon 2002: E2).

Although control of rights was not an issue in this scenario (the Shins own their own publishing), some fans, hoping to contain their disappointment, suggested that it was not the Shins' decision. Wrote one, "Some bands sell their music to a licensing agency not knowing where it will go. My guess is that the Shins didn't intend for 'new slang' ending up as a McDonalds [*sic*] promotion" (Garcia 2002). In a sense, fans with this perspective were correct; the Shins did not intend the usage. As noted earlier, in an environment that offers very few opportunities for financial gain and widespread exposure, licensing to advertising seems the only choice and, thus, not a choice at all.

In addition, the juxtaposition of the spot with the presumed meaning of the song was considered by fans, who wondered if the lyrical content of "New Slang" introduced an element of subversion to the spot. But, as with Royal Caribbean's use of "Lust for Life," the omission of the lyrics in question renders the ad subversive only for fans already familiar with the song. Velocity Girl's Archie Moore commented on McDonald's use of "New Slang," "Especially in their hometown of Albuquerque, there was almost outrage about it, and then people would say 'Well, that's kind of a subversive thing because the song says something about the dirt in your fries and the bakers may they all cut their thumbs.' But at the same time I don't think there were any words in the ad" (p.c., 2005).

The aesthetics of the ad were also scrutinized, both for straying from McDonald's usually upbeat themes, presumably an attempt to correspond with the tone of the song, and for essentially conveying a story about French fry consumption. StarTime International's Isaac Green considered the role that the visuals of the ad played in mediating the reaction; comparing the McDonald's ad with the Saturn ad featuring the Walkmen song, he explained, "I don't think [the ad] helped sell any Saturns because it was a beautiful ad, but if the McDonald's ad had some sort of beauty to it, maybe that would've helped. It was a standard ad of people eating French fries. It just reminded you that people all over the country are eating greasy food and getting fat instead of, like, reliving your fantastic childhood memories" (p.c., 2005).

The language employed by the press suggested that the use of "New Slang" was not embraced as another uncontroversial point in advertising's history of adopting popular music. Newspapers described the situation as McDonald's "swiping the tune" (Pruett 2003); though the deal itself was legal, such description implies that the company is still guilty of theft, if not of copyright, then of the text's use by fans. In another account, the success of the band is attributed to TV placements, but the writer offers further rationalizations regarding the ad: "Due to difficult financial circumstances, at one stage the band even agreed to sell the song for a television commercial when McDonald's came knocking on the poorhouse door" (Bretherton 2005: 15). It seems not enough to make a case for the use by identifying the positive consequences of the placement: emphasis on "difficult financial circumstances" and metaphors like "the poorhouse door" characterize the scenario as a desperate one and the relationship as a necessary evil.

Even proponents of the use of music in advertising found this ad a tough pill to swallow, as music fans. Lanchart described the placement as "scary," but noted, "It didn't prevent me from buying the Shins record. At this point in time, I understand what it's like when you get one placement and you're on the road for a year straight and you need to pay your rent and there you go. It's done" (p.c., 2005). For many people, the use of "New Slang" by McDonald's crossed a line into excessive commercialism that is barely recognized as existing anymore. A writer for *Pitchfork*, an online publication covering independent music and one of the only venues in which vociferous disapproval of licensing to advertising is still frequently heard, could barely control his condemnation, declaring, "I don't even want to get into that McDonald's spot during the Olympics that used the Shins' 'New Slang'" (Bryant 2002).

It was not simply appearing in a commercial that prompted disapproval. Arguably the most significant variable in this case was the name and reputation of the advertiser. Had "New Slang" been placed in a commercial for another product or company, it is likely that the reaction would not have carried the same strength. As a company and advertiser, McDonald's is representative of cultural concerns beyond that of advertising's relationship to music. McDonald's is an exemplar for corporatization and the resultant homogenization that occurs when ubiquitous franchises spread out and displace local businesses. Intersections where McDonald's, Gap, and Starbucks meet, a scene easily imagined in most American cities, present modern onlookers with a view of localism lost, where determining local specificity based on the appearance of businesses becomes near impossible. As the golden arches of McDonald's have extended globally, the company has also been implicated as a major perpetrator of cultural imperialism, imposing its homogenizing presence, with Coca-Cola and Disney, in a wide variety of regions and over myriad cultures. Finally, critics of the growing epidemic of obesity in the United States have pointed to McDonald's, America's most popular fast food chain, as one of the foremost culprits.

Critiques of fast food content and the circumstances surrounding its production invariably use McDonald's and its instantly recognizable icons as the example through which negative effects are measured. Evaluations of the effects of McDonald's on our bodies and our body politic have become part of the fabric of academic and popular culture. Ritzer's *The McDonaldization of Society* identified "the process by which the principles of the fast-food restaurant are coming to dominate more and more sectors of American society as well as of the rest of the world" (Ritzer 1993: 1); McDonald's, suggested Ritzer, adheres to an ideology of efficiency that is sold as benefiting consumers but ultimately serves the financial interests of industry, suppresses difference, and threatens social traditions, such as communal eating. In 2004 the documentary *Super Size Me* tested out the hypothesis that McDonald's is literally killing us. Filmmaker Morgan Spurlock ate only McDonald's for a month, against the advice of his alarmed doctors.

When the Shins licensed "New Slang" to the McDonald's campaign, the song became bound with the thirty-second spot, as well as with the larger issues attached to the fast-food chain. The use of popular music in advertising is now so commonplace that it requires relatively extreme cases—a particularly offensive mismatch, or a controversial company—to provoke a vocal reaction. Rather than view these cases as extreme outliers, or exceptions to a generally innocuous rule, we can understand critical instances as playing an important role in highlighting issues that have been obscured by America's capitulation to hypercommercialism.

Even if the negative critique may seem undeserved or misplaced, fan feedback can remind musicians of their own fandom; however humbly musicians sometimes approach their own music says nothing about how fans understand and use their songs. Responding to the fan reaction to the McDonald's ad, the Shins' James Mercer reevaluated his own perspective regarding the import of his work:

> It's funny because you write these songs and you perform these songs and stuff. And we don't take them that seriously at all. At all. Not even nearly. I think that when you realize that somebody else does, and I know that I have songs that I personally connect to, just fucking pop songs that fucking make you feel like you maybe shouldn't jump off a fucking cliff. It makes me feel like I should maybe have a little more respect for my own stuff ... I think also over the last year I've really come to understand that people don't just feel like our songs are silly, stupid, boring or whatever. I would have hated it if, oh God, if any fucking beautiful Smiths song that I loved would have been in a fucking McDonald's commercial. (qtd. in Draizin 2003)

In the end, the Shins' involvement in the McDonald's campaign was rife with conflict. Like other independent bands that have been offered money to license to television commercials, the Shins weighed the benefits and detriments before making a decision that, if hard to approve for some fans, is also easy to understand. Mercer discussed the spot as providing necessary aid to the band, describing the placement as "a hook" and asking, "And what else is there? What else do we have? We're pretty much just a rock 'n' roll band, and any extra bit helps" (qtd. in Zaleski 2003: 10). But he also recognized the detrimental capacity of linking music with advertising:

> It's not something that we really want to be associated with … It would have been totally lame if it had become one of those things where the commercial was always on the TV. You know, people walking around going, "That fucking song is drilled into my head." Imagine us playing "New Slang", and everyone in the audience going, "That's the song from the McDonald's commercial — I'm loving it". (qtd. in Usinger 2004)

As an interesting footnote to the story of the McDonald's ad that used "New Slang," Mercer later sold a piece of music to Gap. He explained, "They came to me; just to me and I had a bunch of stuff that I didn't really want to use for the band. I picked a couple things and sent it to them and they told me, 'We don't like any of this,' and then a month later they were like, 'Actually we like one of them.' So they used it" (qtd. in Draizin 2003). Mercer's decision to license music that was not attached to the Shins' pre-existing catalog suggests one possible route through which relationships between popular music and advertising may be experienced as more mutually beneficial and less destructive. It is one among many changes and trends that offers alternatives to the current arrangement by which advertisers use popular music.

Reaching Compromises

Many artists continue to refuse to license to advertising, citing various explanations. In earlier chapters, I referenced bands that have turned down offers both because the specific product or company was opposed, and because the idea of linking up with a corporation, regardless of the specifics, was considered inappropriate. Like the Thermals, Trans Am and LiLiPUT, all indie bands that have turned down offers of between $50,000 and $180,000 from Hummer, many bands are selective about the type of product or company with which they are willing to pair their music.

There are also artists, such as Neil Young, Bruce Springsteen, Elvis Costello, and Tom Waits, who have refused to license to any advertising, occasionally lending their oppositional voices to debates about the use of music in advertising. While these artists are all successful enough not to feel compelled to seriously consider licensing to advertising, some non-mainstream acts have also taken a firm position. Like the Super Furry Animals, several independent or lesser-known musicians have expressed that advertising is not a vehicle into which they are interested in placing their music, though most are careful to add that a particularly fitting alliance would be cause for deliberation; Rhys half-jokingly reported that the band is "holding out for the 'Red Stripe' advert in Jamaica. We live in hope that a great product will, one day, rescue us from the clubs" (p.c., 2006).

Some musicians, including those that refuse to license pre-existing music, have, like the Shins' Mercer, composed music for television commercials. Jeff Hale, a former art director at Fallon, arranged for the band Yo La Tengo to compose music for a Starbucks campaign. "I think they had said up front if they were going to get involved they wouldn't license a song," he recalled. "And we weren't really interested in doing that anyway because I don't think we thought we'd get to work with someone that we were as interested in if we were going to license music" (p.c., 2005). Yo La Tengo has turned down multiple offers to license their music for ad campaigns, each time offering to compose music for the spot instead. In addition to Starbucks, the group has composed music for Coca-Cola, and two anti-smoking public service announcements. Not all ad creatives or clients are willing to compromise, however; their offer to compose has not always been accepted, and one company instead apparently commissioned other musicians to write a song based on the Yo La Tengo track originally requested.

Composing music for advertising, as opposed to selling pre-existing music for commercial spots, can be easily situated as a practice in a long history in the art world, whereby artists received commissions for works-for-hire as a means of supporting the creation of their non-commissioned art. While this type of work has also come under fire at times, the relationship to advertisers can be clearly distinguished from scenarios that place pre-existing art into a new, commercialistic context. Most pointedly, by keeping separate the category of works-for-hire, an artist preserves the independence of his or her non-commissioned art.

Popular musicians composed music for ads long before licensing became popular. In his early career, Barry Manilow penned some of the most memorable jingles of all time, including the themes for Band-Aid ("I am stuck on Band-Aid, 'cause Band-Aid's stuck on me"), and State Farm Insurance ("Like a good neighbor, State Farm is there"). Contemporary musicians join the tradition; recently, Joey Santiago of the Pixies joined EliasArts as a composer and creative director for television commercials. Like the many ad creatives and music supervisors who use their full-time jobs in part to support the artistic endeavors they enjoy in their off time, musicians continue to experiment with advertising as a lucrative outlet for their talents, and method of supporting their artistic work.

Walrus copywriter Fred Kovey explained why musicians might prefer to compose music over licensing: "I think part of it is that scoring films sort of has an honorable past. It probably feels a lot more like that to people. It's kind of like, 'I'm doing a film score. That's what I'm doing'" (p.c., 2005). Sarah Gavigan of Ten Music agreed, noting, "I think some artists feel that it's a way that they can partake and make money but not alienate possible people that would think they were selling out or whatever" (p.c., 2005). Many of the ad creatives and music supervisors I interviewed were enthusiastic about the prospect of musicians composing for television commercials. HUM's Tricia Halloran described the increasing use of popular musicians as composers:

One thing I've been doing more and more, I've been bringing in artists instead of licensing from them, having them create a new piece of music for a specific commercial. And they seem to really like that because it gets around the whole idea of 'Oh, I licensed my song to a commercial' and it can still give the client the feel of that artist that they love. So that's a new trend that we're trending towards that may balance out to be equivalent with licensing in the future. (p.c., 2005)

The ability to compose music does not necessarily or easily translate into the ability to compose music for advertising. Tim Barnes supported the development of opportunities for musicians to compose, citing "home digital recording" as helping to realize the possibility, but he also wondered whether musicians could adapt to the parameters set by advertising: "When it comes down to it, bands write songs. They don't write 30 second jingles, they don't write 30 second pieces of music … I don't think many bands could wrap their head around that kind of idea and be successful at it, just because it's not in the way they think in terms of constructing music" (p.c., 2005). Still, composition potentially offers an alternative to musicians who are uncomfortable with licensing pre-existing work. Composed music for ads has drifted away from its roots in corny jingles and towards an aesthetic that shares more in common with popular music; Deborah Fisher, a key account director for Associated Production Music, which controls a large catalog of music composed specifically to be placed in moving-visual media, asserted, "It sounds as good as the music you hear on the radio. People have called us wanting to buy our music. They want to know why it's not in Tower Records or in Virgin Megastore. They want to know where they can purchase it because they love it so much they want to use it for personal reasons" (p.c., 2005).

As long as licensing remains a popular choice for advertisers, it is important that the contracts retain a sensitivity and respect for the cultural producers involved in the exchange. In Chapter 2, I proposed that a version of *droit moral*, or moral rights, should be applied to the system of music copyright, if only to protect the integrity and work of artists who have no legal control over copyright. A broader arrangement for artists' rights would also serve to protect those musicians who may control their rights, but enter into licensing deals with little sense of the financial and logistical compensation they deserve. A right to refusal should be a standard term of licensing deals, particularly for placements that imply an artist endorses a product or company. When artists do license, fair standards for compensation should be employed; the synchronization fees paid to famous musicians may continue to rise, but independent artists are increasingly being offered the possibility of widespread exposure in lieu of fair monetary compensation. "You're dealing with the ad world," explained Tim Barnes, "They're always going to try to get something for less than what it's worth" (p.c., 2005). As Barnes advised, "The people at the labels have to be aware of that and come back at them and not be afraid that this one might get away from us. 'If we don't say yes we're not going to make ten thousand dollars without having to lift a finger.' That's totally true, but are you really willing to sell a track for ten thousand dollars?"

(p.c., 2005). Allowing advertisers to license music for relatively miniscule fees affects not only the immediate financial circumstances of the band, but also the value of that copyright, and the value of music copyright more generally. Universal Music Publishing's Carianne Brown remarked, "There is a fine line right now between the marketing value thing that people are claiming and devaluing that property" (p.c., 2006).

There are small concessions that can be made on the part of the advertiser to encourage the likelihood that bands will benefit from the exposure. At the very least, companies can credit the group on websites, linking either to the band's site or to a point-of-online purchase. Gavigan suggested, "If the client truly wants to help the artist and the label sell records then they have to be responsible for linking the consumer to the music" (p.c., 2005). When bands license to television commercials, they potentially reach a larger audience than they would through any other visual form, but if listeners cannot identify the band, the exposure is for naught. As Brown put it, "The exposure is greater but it's not as easy to find out what that is … You see a film, wait until the end, and then there are the credits and you can see which songs were used. Or a TV show, you go on the website. Yeah, you can probably dig and find out what the songs are in commercials but that's not the purpose. The purpose is to sell the product" (p.c., 2006). Although there are a number of sites devoted to tracking the use of music in advertising, they tend to be incomplete and there is a lag time between when the ads air and when the music is identified. Advertisers can facilitate the consumer search by identifying the music they use.

With "no comprehensive way to figure out who the hell the artist is," Jenn Lanchart wondered, "What's the point? … I would like to see more of a comprehensive correlation between these advertising spots and the credit which is due" (p.c., 2005). Identifying the song in the spot itself, as in music videos, would provide consumers with the most direct path to supporting bands that have licensed their music. Unfortunately, just as mainstream bands have more leverage to demand higher fees, mainstream bands are also more successful at negotiating the inclusion of in-spot credit. Usually when the music in a commercial is identified, the artist is already popular and, to well-versed ears at least, easily recognizable. Phil Collins and Sting, for example, are among the artists who have been identified in spots.

Some bands might not want their name in the ad, because this type of inclusion further implicates them as endorsing the product or company; Jeff Hale noted that Yo La Tengo refused to be credited on the Starbucks website for the campaign that featured their compositions (p.c., 2005). But if advertisers and agencies are genuinely committed to providing the artists with exposure, the decision should be the band's to make.

Finally, even as licensing continues to grow as a channel through which music is distributed and musicians are paid, the systems whose failure has led to the increase in licensing still require attention. Rather than writing off commercial radio as an irredeemable failure, measures should be enacted to restructure it.

McChesney noted that "the real issue is not regulation versus free markets"—even deregulated media relies heavily on government policy—"but, to the contrary, regulation in the public interest versus regulation to serve purely private interests" (2003: 126). In a democratic system, media policies should entail public debates. However, as McChesney explained, deregulation has served to lessen the public's already limited knowledge about and involvement in media policy-making (2003: 127). The survey work conducted by the Future of Music Coalition suggested that, when provided with information and asked for opinions, radio listeners know what they want, and know that the current structure of commercial radio is not it. The industrial structures and changes described in Chapter 4 are not irreversible, but consumers—as citizens and as taxpayers—require education and deserve involvement in the process of media regulation and legislation.

Similar to fine artists, whose options for funding have been limited by the withdrawal of support by organizations like the National Endowment for the Arts, popular musicians would also benefit from greater state support of cultural pursuits. In the fine art world, the dearth of grants has led to an increased role for commercial sponsors. The "Sponsorship" exhibition presented in 2003 at BLK/ MRKT in Los Angeles parodied this trend, displaying as its sole installation a wall of corporate sponsor names and logos arranged according to level of contribution. As the organizer/artist described, "My hope was that an empty exhibition would create enough pause for us to consider both the fine art of corporate sponsorship and the corporate sponsorship of fine art" (McGinness 2005: 13). For popular music, too, the degree to which corporate sponsors are present in its distribution is reaching farcical levels. But the underlying message is a serious one. Tim Barnes suggested, "Maybe if there were more comfortable opportunities, maybe they wouldn't feel the need to take on these offers or even solicit these kind of things, saying 'Send out our CD to all these music supervisors'" (p.c., 2005). In other Western countries, including the United Kingdom and Australia, it is not uncommon for popular musicians to apply for and receive state grants to support their work. That corporate sponsors can replace state funding of art does not mean they should, or that there are no cultural consequences to such a shift.

Culture versus Commerce: A Dated Debate?

Of twentieth century movements that used tools of commerce to combat cultural degeneration, Allen explained that the history can be read in two ways: it can be read as alliances beneficial to both sides, or as a story of "how capitalism gained hegemony over high culture by turning artists and intellectuals into its agents, thereby robbing them of their ability to criticize or pose alternatives to the kingdom of consumer commerce" (Allen 1983: xiv). The history of popular music in advertising has similarly been read in both ways, as a story of mutually beneficial alliance or of hegemonic control. This book offers a more nuanced reading of the blending of commercial and cultural concerns. It suggests various blends of the culture-commerce intersection that can be mutually advantageous or disadvantageous in different ways.

My intention has been to present the use of music in advertising as a complex interaction between two entities, both of which possess cultural and commercial aspects, with conclusions that are similarly complicated. In the end, it remains the right of artists to license their work where they feel comfortable. And it is hard to disagree with Jack McFadden of March Records, who suggested that it is preferable to have good music used in commercials, if only because it makes the world a prettier place. Likewise, it is clear that advertisements can be art, even as they are inextricably tied to commercial intent. In sum, advertising provides an opportunity for music, which might otherwise not be heard by many people, to be heard by millions; it is a way to have music heard, but hardly the ideal way, giving to advertisers a tool for branding through the reinterpretation of songs.

In *Owning Culture*, McLeod referenced Williams' claim that "the logic of capitalism necessarily requires previously untouched areas of cultural activity to be brought into this web of commodity relations" (2001: 5). By treating culture as any other commodity, the market narrows the range of culture that is promoted. McChesney wrote, "It is said that competition in the market forces media firms to 'give the people what they want'. In truth, competition in the market forces firms to 'give the people what they want within the range where they can make the most profits'" (McChesney 2003: 130). The incorporation of culture into a system driven primarily by economic concerns is an attempt to place a value on an invaluable form. While an arbitrary value can be placed on the tangible artifacts associated with popular music, such as compact discs or concert tickets, the *cultural* value of popular music, what popular music means to individuals and societies, denies easy pricing. Yet this is exactly what advertisers (and musicians) do when they negotiate the fees for synchronization licenses: put a price on the cultural value of popular music.

Muted reactions to the use of popular music in advertising indicate submission to commercial aims. Calvin Johnson, founder of K Records, observed,

> I think it's that people are more and more raised in a world that is so media-saturated that they no longer draw this distinction between the commercial world and the artistic world—and might say there is none. It's like Andy Warhol played with commercial art as fine art and that's what a lot of pop art was, it was taking commercial art and presenting it as fine art. And I think that there's great value in viewing commercial art in that light, but I think there still can be a line drawn between making your art for commercial purposes and making your art for your own purposes. (p.c., 2006)

Advertising is ubiquitous, and the desperation of advertisers to cut through the clutter calls into question how effective any individual ad is, as an atom in a sea of white marketing noise. The Shins' James Mercer commented, "It's a fucking commercial, you know? That's the thing too. I have a hard time feeling that commercials are so affective [*sic*], and then caring about the people they are affective [*sic*] on, if they are affective [*sic*]" (qtd. in Draizin 2003). Perhaps Mercer is correct, and using the Shins' "New Slang" did not sell any French fries for McDonald's. However, that is only part of the potential result of pairing music and advertising: another part is what McDonald's did for, or to, the Shins. Carrie McLaren, journalist and editor of *Stay Free!*, bemoaned the extent to which "commerce really shapes so much of our world aesthetically and kind of sucks all the life out of it" (p.c., 2005). The ability of advertisers to shape our aesthetic world was the concern of upset Shins fans, not that the placement might propel them to the drive-thru.

On the infrequency of backlashes towards the use of popular music in modern advertising, Joe Pernice wondered whether we have reached the point where the "outrage is as hip" as the placement was meant to be: when the Backstreet Boys "can be singing a love song to a freakin' cheeseburger and you know, all over the world, that says something about what's going on" (p.c., 2006). Boy bands, already subject to charges of manufacture and commercialism, may not represent the direction that all popular music is heading, but the point remains relevant. In fact, a recurring trope in stories about boy bands was the insistence of members that they were genuine artists, not puppets; that the Backstreet Boys did not think twice about singing, "Hold the pickles, hold the lettuce, special orders don't upset us," suggests that, for some artists at least, the construction and maintenance of a credible image is disconnected from affiliation with advertisers. Interestingly, the Burger King commercial's plot involved the Backstreet Boys altering their "We don't do commercials" stance in response to the offer of a lifetime supply of Whoppers. Licensing music to advertising has become an additional method of promotion and revenue generation, with no negative valuation necessarily attached, even as the tensions for some artists are recognized.

The shift in attitudes towards the use of popular music in advertising is an admission that hypercommercialism is inevitable. In response to the claim that through his association with the beer, "every time you hear a Phil Collins song you think of Michelob," Savan sarcastically noted, "How great for Phil. Maybe one day every hit will jam a product into the listener's mind" (Savan 1994: 286). That day, if it has not already arrived, is drawing closer. As mentioned earlier, a growing trend in non-traditional marketing involves companies paying artists for approved mentions of their products in songs. McDonald's, for instance, offered rappers $1 per radio play of songs that mentioned the Big Mac. If the control of advertisers over the distribution of popular music is irritating, the insinuation of advertisers into the *production* of culture is more troublesome.

Many individuals, and perhaps especially those who have direct involvement in the deals forged between popular music and advertising, express uneasiness with the notion of bringing morality into discussions of the market. Deborah Fisher, whose company sells production music to advertisers, explained, "That's the advantage of not being directly involved with working with commercial artists because I don't have to come home at night and have a conflict about it" (p.c., 2005). Jenn Lanchart determined that her own moral judgments of commercialism, "music in commercials and stuff, doesn't really have any relevance in what I do. It doesn't" (p.c., 2005). But the moral stance of individuals directly involved with the licensing of popular music to advertising is germane insofar as it is reflective of a loosely shared cultural morality. The presence of tension and conflict, however suppressed, around the use of popular music in advertising, necessarily demands the inclusion of morality as a component of the debate. Concerns over the rightness or wrongness of popular music's use in advertising are only as outdated as the concept of morality itself.

There is a belief sometimes conveyed in conversations about interactions between popular music and advertising that, because we are all consumers of the products sold by advertisers, we have surrendered our right to critique advertisers and advertising. Mercer's explanation of his position with respect to licensing "New Slang" illustrates the perceived connection of practices that forge relationships between cultural and commercials objectives to broader political concerns:

> Yeah we got a lot of shit. But then again not a lot of people who were actually in bands though. Unless they have really strong political beliefs about that sort of thing, which I don't – Have any strong political beliefs – about anything. Because I feel that these issues are extremely complex. Actually the issues are not what's complex, it's whether or not you should give a flying fuck about the human race that is a complex issue. So if you start arguing about what a company like McDonalds [*sic*] has done, and coming from a nihilist background you'd have a hard time really being able to commit to certain things. (qtd. in Draizin 2003)

The expression of concern over the reach of commercialism does not need to represent an indictment of capitalism. It is not only our right to monitor the role of advertisers in the production and distribution of culture: it is our duty as wardens of culture. Even advertising creatives, whose livelihoods depend on the dissemination of advertising, recognize the need for boundaries. Arnold's Chris Carl described, "I'll be in meetings where like, 'We could tattoo this shit on people's foreheads.' Like people say that shit and you're just like 'Oh my God.' I think there's definitely places it should be and places it shouldn't but it's really out of control in that way. It's gotten completely out of control because everything has a price now" (p.c., 2005). The use of popular music in advertising is an unsettled issue because, as video director Julien Temple suggested, corporate sponsorship is "like having an invisible Pepsi sign engraved on your forehead" (qtd. in Reed 1988).

That critics, music fans, and musicians express discomfort with and disapproval of the increasingly comfortable relationships between artists and corporations indicates a genuine cultural dilemma. Perhaps an even more pressing dilemma is the quieting of such discourse over time, suggesting a powerless resignation to the contemporary media environment and its associated objectionable trends and practices. Both popular music and advertising exist as cultural-commercial hybrids, making claims of art as well as charges of commercialism subject to deliberation. Dismissing the art versus commerce divide as constructed and the "sell-out" debates as antiquated conceals the importance of acknowledging and investigating these tensions within and between the popular music and advertising worlds. When fans and critics perceive a line to be crossed, it is not necessary to redraw or reject the line, but to assess who is in control and to what end. It is through such scrutiny that the balance between cultural and commercial objectives, and its role in hypercommercialism, can be monitored.

Appendix

Informants

Barnes, Tim. Sound designer, Lost Planet, New York. Phone interview, November 3, 2005.

Brown, Carianne. Director of film and television music, Universal Music Publishing Group, New York. Phone interview, February 28, 2006.

Burt, Dan. Music coordinator, JWT, New York. Phone interview, January 25, 2006.

Carl, Chris. Creative director, Arnold Worldwide, Boston, MA. In-person interview, October 8, 2005; email, April 6, 2006.

Eaton, Jon. Guitarist, The Spinto Band, Wilmington, DE. In-person interview, November 18, 2005.

Fisher, Deborah. Key account director, Associated Production Music, New York. Phone interview, October 30, 2005.

Gavigan, Sarah. Owner/Creative director, Ten Music, Venice, CA. Phone interview, November 14, 2005.

Green, Isaac. Owner, StarTime International Records, New York. Phone interview, October 26, 2005.

Hale, Jeff. Former art director, Fallon, New York. Phone interview, September 29, 2005.

Halloran, Tricia. Music supervisor, HUM Music + Sound Design, Santa Monica, CA; DJ, KCRW, Los Angeles, CA. Phone interview, October 27, 2005.

Heasley, Kurt. Singer/Guitarist, Lilys, Philadelphia, PA. In-person interview, September 15, 2005.

Johnson, Calvin. Founder, K Records, Olympia, WA. Phone interview, March 29, 2006.

Kovey, Fred. Copywriter, Walrus, New York. Phone interview, September 18, 2005.

Krill, Nick. Guitarist, The Spinto Band, Wilmington, DE. In-person interview, November 18, 2005.

Lanchart, Jenn. Director of film and television, Beggars Group and Matador Records, New York. Phone interview, October 20, 2005.

Leithauser, Hamilton. Singer/Guitarist, The Walkmen, New York. Phone interview, November 15, 2005.

McFadden, Jack. Owner/A+R representative, March Records and We Are Records, New York. Phone interview, September 19, 2005.

McLaren, Carrie. Editor/Designer, *Stay Free!*, New York; Writer, *Village Voice*, New York. Phone interview, September 29, 2005.

Moore, Archie. Former Guitarist/Bassist/Vocalist, Velocity Girl, Washington, D.C. Phone interview, September 17, 2005.

Neri, Dan. Associate creative director, Tierney Communications, Philadelphia, PA. Phone interview, November 11, 2005.

Nieves, Michael. Founder/Managing director, Sugaroo!, Culver City, CA. Phone interview, December 6, 2005.

Olson, Gary. Singer/Trumpeter, The Ladybug Transistor, New York. Phone interview, November 11, 2005.

Pappanicholas, Laura. Agency producer, Red Tettemer, Philadelphia, PA. In-person interview, October 28, 2005.

Pernice, Joe. Singer/Guitarist, Pernice Brothers; Owner, Ashmont Records, Dorchester, MA. Phone interview, April 21, 2006.

Price, Jeff. Co-founder/General manager, spinART Records, New York. Phone interview, October 17, 2005.

Rabinowitz, Josh. Senior vice president/Director of music, Grey Worldwide, New York. Phone interview, December 5, 2005.

Rhys, Gruff. Singer/Guitarist, Super Furry Animals, Cardiff, Wales. In-person interview, November 9, 2005; email, March 28, 2006.

Scully, Dryw. Music promotions director, Urban Outfitters, Philadelphia, PA. In-person interview, September 1, 2005.

Zanes, Warren. Former Guitarist, The Del Fuegos, Cleveland, OH. Phone interview, June 15, 2006.

About the Informants

By interviewing musicians, ad creatives, music supervisors, and licensing managers, my intention was to approach the use of music in advertising from multiple perspectives and through the work of the various parties involved in music placement. While the press coverage of the subject represents a range of positions and interests—particularly between the popular and trade coverage, but also within each—the amount of space devoted to the subject is limited. Long interviews allowed the involved parties to consider the nuances of the practice, as well as the contradictions that arise in discussing the use of music in advertising, without concern of being reduced to a soundbite or forced to fit a certain perspective. Although I occasionally use a shorthand to express main ideas ("Music supervisors think" or "Ad creatives feel"), I hope that my treatment of the informants portrays them as the individuals they are, united as music fans but each with a unique sense of the meaning of music licensing.

While not ethnography in the classic sense, whereby the researcher takes part "overtly or covertly, in people's daily lives for an extended period of time, watching what happens, listening to what is said, asking questions" (Hammersley and Atkinson 1995: 1), I endeavored to invoke the spirit of ethnography, collecting the richest detail available to me through the long interviews. I used in-depth interviews over a traditional ethnographic approach primarily because there are very few informants whose jobs are devoted solely to the use of music in advertising, nor are there many environments in which the use of music in advertising is a constant activity. Rather, for nearly all informants, situations involving placing the use of pre-existing music into a television commercial appear unpredictably and in fits and starts. That is, ad creatives do not always use pre-existing music in their campaigns, licensing managers only sometimes deal with licensing to television commercials, labels may receive multiple requests for songs in a week or none for months, and musicians cannot predict when one of their songs may be requested. Thus, a researcher thrust as a participant observer into the office of an ad agency, music supervision agency, or record label could wait weeks or months before anything relevant to the use of popular music occurs. On the other hand, in-depth interviews allow for a complex understanding of both the details involved in placing music in commercials, and the perspectives and experiences that inform those involved.

Interviews were conducted between September 2005 and June 2006. The length of interview ranged from 20 minutes to two hours, with the average length at around one hour. Informants were contacted via email or telephone; most interviews were conducted by phone, though some Philadelphia-based informants were interviewed in-person. In my initial request, I explained my position (PhD candidate at the University of Pennsylvania), the focus of my research, and the types of individuals with whom I was conducting interviews. I offered to talk whenever it was convenient and by whatever method was preferred. When asked for further information I explained that it was my intention to discuss the use of popular music in advertising as a complicated cultural practice, by examining both how it presented opportunities and created tensions. I offered the names and job titles of other informants upon request. Four interview requests were denied by the individuals, or in the case of musicians, their publicists, through the failure to return phone calls and emails. In one case, the publicist twice responded that the individual was too busy to schedule an interview. Twenty-nine informants agreed to be interviewed.

I had met seven informants prior to interviewing them, through my experiences as a music journalist, amateur musician, and regular attendee of music events since the 1990s. Names and contact information for all other informants were obtained through early contacts and local musicians, as well as through popular press coverage of the use of music in advertising (several informants were quoted in newspaper or magazine articles). The use of snowball sampling for this research presented several advantages. Firstly, by following contacts provided by informants, I was able to track specific cases in order to obtain the perspectives of multiple parties. For example, I was able to talk to both the musician and the label owner, or the musician and the music supervisor, involved in a placement. Secondly, because the use of music in advertising can be a touchy subject, as wrapped up as it is with notions of selling out and commercialism, contacting an individual through another informant created somewhat of an instant rapport or social connection, which helped to alleviate any suspicion of my motives.

Although I kept a list of general questions, interviews were allowed to go in whatever direction they headed, permitting the discussion of topics unforeseen. At the start of the interviews I let the informants know that if there was any topic they would rather not discuss, or anything they would rather leave off the record, I would oblige. I asked if it was okay to tape-record the conversation, and confirmed that using real names would not be a problem. While preserving the anonymity of informants in some research situations can broaden the sources and type of information gathered, in this case I felt it important to use identifying information in order to present the fullest portrayal of experiences. None of the informants requested that their identities be disguised.

Interviews began with a discussion of an informant's job and experiences with music placement in television commercials. Conversations often turned to high profile cases of popular music in advertising, including those analyzed throughout this book. While I sometimes brought up examples as a starting point, Nike's use of "Revolution," VW's use of "Pink Moon," Wrangler's use of "Fortunate Son," Royal Caribbean's use of "Lust for Life," and McDonald's use of "New Slang" were all referenced often by informants too. Some subjects were less easily discussed: informants who were not musicians were hesitant to speculate about why specific musicians might have chosen to or refused to license to an advertising campaign. A few informants also preferred not to disclose what they viewed as more sensitive information, including revealing the names of musicians involved in campaigns that did not work out, or the dollar amounts of licensing fees. All informants agreed to future contact if needed.

Each of the informants I interviewed engaged in work related to the use of popular music in advertising, either through direct involvement in placements, refusal to be involved in placements, or involvement with an activity closely connected to the licensing of popular music. Their roles fall under the categories of music supervisor, ad creative, licensing manager, musician, or other, though, as I noted earlier, many enjoy multiple roles (music supervisors and ad creatives often have at least part-time experience as musicians, for example). Here, I group the informants under the categories that best describe their roles with regard to the use of popular music in advertising.

Music Supervisors

Music supervisors are individuals who either work full-time for companies that are dedicated to providing sound and music to advertising agencies, or are employed by agencies in positions that are solely devoted to the placement of music into commercials. The types of services they provide are dependent on the needs of the clients and the requirements of the hiring agency. Music supervisors may be marginally involved in the production of a commercial, by suggesting a number of possible songs to fit an ad, or may be very closely involved in the process, offering input from beginning to end. I spoke with five music supervisors, three who work for music and sound design houses, and two who are employed by advertising agencies.

Tim Barnes is a sound designer at Lost Planet in New York. His experience with music supervision began in the mid-1990s and he has since helped to place numerous songs by lesser-known and independent bands in commercials. I made contact with him at the suggestion of a couple of other informants, and after seeing him quoted in a 2001 *New York Times* article on the use of popular music in advertising. Sarah Gavigan is the owner and creative director at California-based Ten Music, a music house that provides licensing and scoring services to advertisers. Like Barnes, Gavigan had been quoted in newspaper articles addressing the use of popular music by advertisers. Tricia Halloran is a music supervisor for HUM Music + Sound Design in Santa Monica, CA, and a DJ on the Los Angeles radio station KCRW. I contacted Halloran after seeing the 2005 series of Honda ads for which HUM supervised the music selection.

Dan Burt is the music coordinator for advertising agency JWT in New York, where he supervises music selections and hires composers. One of the composers he has hired is Gary Olson from the Ladybug Transistor. Josh Rabinowitz worked at various music houses and ad agencies before taking his current position as the director of music at Grey Worldwide. He has extensive experience in both music supervision and arranging for musicians to appear in commercials. I contacted him after seeing his name in credits for ad campaigns involving the use of popular music and musicians.

Advertising Creatives

When advertising agencies do not hire outside music supervisors to assist in selecting songs and securing the rights to their use and do not have full-time in-house employees dealing with music, other individuals within the agencies fulfill this duty. Advertising creatives, as the title suggests, are involved in various aspects of the creation of advertisements. The five advertising creatives I spoke with had worked on spots that either licensed popular songs, or commissioned popular musicians to compose for ads.

Chris Carl is a creative director at Arnold Worldwide in Boston who has worked on multiple campaigns that have licensed popular music. We were previously acquainted through a mutual friend, which is how I was aware of the work he had done. Carl put me in touch with Dan Neri, who made the award-winning anti-Nike ad that featured the Beatles' "Revolution" as its score. The two had worked together on projects for PETA and Carl was familiar with the anti-Nike ad that Neri had produced.

Fred Kovey is a copywriter at the small creative agency Walrus in New York, where he has been involved in campaigns that have licensed and commissioned music. We first met through my brother Josh Klein, who had been in a band with Kovey, and later a mutual friend suggested I contact Kovey for this research. Kovey recommended that I talk to Jeff Hale, a former art director for Fallon in

New York, who had worked on a Starbucks campaign for which Yo La Tengo composed music. A friend and former advertising creative put me in touch with the creatives at Red Tettemer in Philadelphia. I spoke to agency line producer Laura Pappanicholas, who was less involved in the selection of music, but who described to me the complete process by which popular music is licensed and placed in commercials.

Licensing Managers

In order for popular music to be placed in an advertisement, master use and publishing rights must be secured through the individuals who manage the copyrights of musicians. I include under the category of 'Licensing Managers' both informants whose jobs are specifically to manage the licensing rights of artist catalogs, and record label owners, who, if they have not hired an outside agency to manage the licensing of their bands, will deal directly with offers.

Carianne Brown is the director of film and television music for the Universal Music Publishing Group in New York, where she pitches the Universal Publishing catalog for use in all moving-visual media. JWT's Dan Burt recommended that I talk to her. Jenn Lanchart is the director of film and television for the Beggars Group and Matador Records in New York. I was familiar with ad campaigns that featured musicians from the Beggars Group, and I retrieved her contact information through their website. Michael Nieves is the founder and managing director of California-based Sugaroo!, a company that manages the licensing rights for a large number of independent labels and groups. A musician whose work is represented by Sugaroo! (my brother again) suggested I get in touch with Nieves.

Four of my informants run (or ran) independent record labels representing bands that have licensed music to advertising campaigns. I contacted Isaac Green, owner of StarTime International Records in New York, to talk about the Saturn commercial that used a Walkmen song, as well as other experiences with licensing. Calvin Johnson is the founder of Olympia, WA-based independent label K records. I was previously acquainted with Johnson through mutual friends, one of whom recommended I contact him. I have known Jack McFadden, owner of (no longer operating) March Records and We Are Records in New York, for years through involvement in the independent music scene. I contacted him for this research because I was aware of a couple of ad campaigns that featured March bands. Jeff Price is the co-founder and was the general manager of now defunct spinART Records in New York. Many spinART bands have been featured in ad campaigns and the group the Apples in Stereo was the focus of the same *New York Times* article that quoted Barnes.

Musicians

I interviewed nine musicians who were members of bands that either licensed to advertising campaigns or refused offers to license to advertising campaigns. Some had experiences with licensing to advertising going back more than a decade, while others had licensed for the first time only recently. Four had licensed to multiple ad campaigns and one was a member of a band that has turned down multiple offers to license their music.

Kurt Heasley is the singer and guitarist for Lilys, a group based in Philadelphia at the time of this research that has licensed to ad campaigns for Nike, Calvin Klein, and Levi's. We originally met when Heasley moved to Philadelphia in the late-1990s. Jon Eaton and Nick Krill are both members of the Spinto Band, a Wilmington, DE group whose debut album garnered a lot of press attention in 2005. I contacted the group after reading that their song "Oh Mandy" was being featured in a Sears spot. Hamilton Leithauser is the singer and guitarist for the New York group the Walkmen. I was put in touch with Leithauser by an acquaintance to talk about the Saturn commercial that used "We've Been Had"; the ad was nominated for multiple advertising industry awards.

Archie Moore is a music producer and former member of Washington, DC-area band Velocity Girl. I had met Moore at an indie-rock show in the late-1990s and was familiar with the VW ad that featured "Sorry Again" by his former band. Gary Olson is the singer and trumpeter for New York's Ladybug Transistor. He first told me about his experiences with licensing and composing for ads when we met though members of another band in 2005. Joe Pernice is the singer and guitarist for the Pernice Brothers and the owner of independent label Ashmont Records. I contacted Pernice after Chris Carl and I discussed a Sears ad that featured the song "There Goes The Sun" by the Pernice Brothers. Joe Pernice put me in touch with Warren Zanes, former member of the Del Fuegos, who were featured in a Miller Beer commercial in 1985. I contacted Gruff Rhys, the singer and guitarist for Welsh band Super Furry Animals because Jenn Lanchart, director of film and television for the Beggars Group, mentioned that the band had turned down multiple offers to license their music to advertising campaigns, including offers from cola companies.

Other

Three of my informants had jobs that did not fall under the aforementioned categories, but nonetheless involved them in the conversation about popular music's use in advertising. One was a journalist, another worked for a production music house, and the last worked as a music supervisor for a chain of retail stores.

Carrie McLaren is the editor and designer of the magazine *Stay Free!* and a contributing writer for the *Village Voice* in New York. Before I began this research I was familiar with her work for both publications on the use of popular music in advertising. Deborah Fisher is a key account director for Associated Production Music in New York, where she oversees an extensive library of production music. A friend of mine met Fisher at a wedding and dutifully collected her contact information for me. I contacted Fisher to discuss the similarities and differences between licensing production music and licensing popular music. Dryw Scully is the music promotions director for the retail chain Urban Outfitters in Philadelphia. We have known each other through involvement in music events in Philadelphia and I contacted Scully to talk about the use of popular music in marketing.

About the Articles

Although I focused primarily on the press coverage involving the specific cases I have chosen as examples, I also examined selective coverage of the practice more generally and other relevant articles from major newspapers, consumer music magazines, and trade music and advertising magazines. The search for general articles was conducted through Lexis-Nexis Academic, EBSCO MegaFile, and IIMP (International Index to Music Periodicals) using the keywords "music," "song," "commercial," and "advertising"; more precise keywords were employed to track the specific cases selected for closer examination. For instance, in researching Nike's use of the Beatles' "Revolution," I searched databases for combinations of the terms "Nike," "Beatles," and "Revolution." Other articles were obtained through Google searches (particularly for online magazines), and the thoughtfulness of friends and colleagues, whose forwards kept me from missing the latest developments. In the end, I analyzed over 300 discrete popular and trade press articles that concerned the use of music in advertising. Articles came from major and minor newspapers, popular music magazines, general magazines, online publications, news wires, music trade magazines, and advertising trade magazines. The time span covered was established by the selected cases, from the use of music by the cola companies, which began to receive coverage in the mid-1980s, and Nike's 1987 use of "Revolution," which I suggest was the first use of music in advertising that attracted a significant amount of coverage and reaction, to cases from the 2000s. Since the cases were selected partly because they received a great deal of attention in the press and from the public, early cases continue to be discussed as landmarks of the use of popular music in advertising. By giving attention to the earliest mentions of the practice, as well as the most recent, historical shifts in attitude towards the commercial placement of popular music were identified.

Bibliography

Abelson, J. (2005). Brand on the Run: Struggling Fidelity Turns to Ex-Beatle to Lure Boomers. *Boston Globe*, September 8, p. F1.

Adorno, T. (1990). On Popular Music. In S. Frith and A. Goodwin (eds), *On Record: Rock, Pop, and the Written Word*. London: Routledge, pp. 301–14. (Original work published 1941.)

Allen, J.S. (1983). *The Romance of Commerce and Culture: Capitalism, Modernism, and the Chicago-Aspen Crusade for Cultural Reform*. Chicago, IL: University of Chicago Press.

American Brandstand. (2006). *Agendainc.com*, April 18. Retrieved from http://www.agendainc.com/brand.html.

Arnold, G. (1993). *Route 666: On the Road to Nirvana*. New York: St. Martin's Press.

Baker, B. (2002). Fogerty Furious That His Song Sells Jeans: Fortunate Son Was a War Protest. *Ottawa Citizen*, October 28, p. C2.

Barnouw, E. (1978). *The Sponsor: Notes on a Modern Potentate*. New York: Oxford University Press.

Barthes, R. (1977). *Image, Music, Text* (S. Heath, trans.). New York: Hill and Wang.

Battaglio, S. (1987a). Beatles Sue Nike, Agency Over Use of "Revolution." *Ad Day*, June 29, p. 1.

Battaglio, S. (1987b). Beatles' Lawsuit against Nike Raises Questions on Use of Original Tracks. *Adweek*, August 3.

Baumann, S. (2001). Intellectualization and Art World Development: Film in the United States. *American Sociological Review* 66(3): 404–26.

Baumgarten, M. (2005). Killing It Softly: The Shins Bring Out the Dead at the Crystal Ballroom Last Thursday. *Willamette Week*, April 13.

Baxandall, M. (1972). *Painting and Experience in Fifteenth-Century Italy*. Oxford: Oxford University Press.

Beatles Still Mean Business. (1987). *Advertising Age*, May 18, p. 16.

Becker, H. (1982). *Art Worlds*. Berkeley, CA: University of California Press.

Begun, B. (2003). Music: Hymns for Hipsters. *Newsweek*, October 27, p. 16.

Bellafante, G. (2001). Talking Revolution and Showing Suits. *New York Times*, February 12, Fashion p. 8.

Benjamin, W. (1968). *Illuminations*. New York: Schocken Books.

Berger, P.L. and Luckmann, T. (1966). *The Social Construction of Reality: A Treatise in the Sociology of Knowledge*. New York: Anchor Books.

Bogart, M.H. (1995). *Artists, Advertising, and the Borders of Art*. Chicago, IL: The University of Chicago Press.

Boucher, G. (2000). Why You Know This Guy. *Toronto Star*, June 10, Entertainment.

Bowley, G. and Rawsthorn, A. (1998). Beetles Want Beatles, if VW Can Afford It. *Financial Times*, February 5, p. 25.

Bream, J. (1992). Ray Charles' Genius Leaves State Crowd Saying, "Uh-huh." *Minneapolis Star Tribune*, June 5, p. 4B.

Breen, M. and Forde, E. (2004). The Music Industry, Technology and Utopia—an Exchange between Marcus Breen and Eamonn Forde. *Popular Music* 23(1): 79–87.

Bretherton, M. (2005). Film Break Kicks the Shins Along. *Courier Mail* (Queensland, Australia), February 1, p. 15.

Britney Spears and Pepsi-Cola Ink Global Sponsorship and Advertising Pact. (2001). *PR Newswire*, February 6.

Brown, M. (1984). Just in Grammy Time: The Jackson Soda Sell. *Washington Post*, December 5, p. C3.

Bryant, W. (2002). Modest Mouse, Smog Sell Miller Beer: The MGD Blind Date with Cat Power and Silver Jews is Gonna Rawk! *Pitchfork Media*, April 10. Retrieved from http://www.pitchforkmedia.com/news/02-04/10.shtml.

Carr, D. (2003). Hip-Hop Impresario Urges Pepsi Boycott. *New York Times*, February 6, Section C, p. 5.

Caves, R.E. (2000). *Creative Industries: Contracts between Art and Commerce*. Cambridge, MA: Harvard University Press.

Certeau, M. de. (1984). *The Practice of Everyday Life* (S. Rendall, trans.). Berkeley, CA: University of California Press.

Clio Awards Press Releases. (2006). Retrieved March 2006, from http://www.clioawards.com/press/index.cfm.

Collins, M. (1989). George Michael Creates an Ad. *USA Today*, January 30, p. 3D.

Crane, D. (1992). *The Production of Culture: Media and the Urban Arts*. Newbury Park, CA: Sage.

Creativity. (2003). *The Music Issue*. July.

Daniel, J. (2000). Death is the Mother of Success: (Sometimes). *St. Louis Post-Dispatch*, April 9, p. F1.

Davis, T. (1989). What Ever Happened to "Be a Pepper"? *Beverage World*, April, p. 26.

Day, S. (2002). Pepsi Says Its Pop Music Stars Can Reach Minorities and the Mainstream at the Same Time. *New York Times*, August 27, Section C, p. 2.

Debut Set for Pepsi's "Glasnost" Commercial. (1989). *Journal of Commerce*, January 20, p. 5A.

Dee, J. (1999). The Naked Pitchman. *Ottawa Citizen*, February 10, p. A15.

DeNora, T. (2000). *Music in Everyday Life*. Cambridge: Cambridge University Press.

Densmore, J. (2002). Riders on the Storm: Why the Doors Don't Open When Corporate Ads Come Calling. *The Nation*, July 8, pp. 33–6.

Dickie, M. (2005). Inside the Mind of Moby: Finding a Balance in a Commercial World. *Toronto Sun*, February 17, p. 46.

DiCola, P. and Thomson, K. (2002). Radio Deregulation: Has It Served Citizens and Musicians? A Report on the Effects of Radio Ownership Consolidation

Following the 1996 Telecommunications Act. Future of Music Coalition. Retrieved from http://www.futureofmusic.org.

DIG! (2004). Ondi Timoner (dir.). New York: Palm Pictures.

Draizin, C. (2003). Shins, Not Assholes: Fans, Fame and French Fries. The Shins Struggle with Becoming a Serious Band. *Music Liberation Project: A Journal of Portland Music*, October. Retrieved from http://www.musicliberationproject. com/3/10/shins.html.

Dylan, B. (1985). *Biograph*. Columbia Records.

Eagleton, T. (1983). *Literary Theory*. Minneapolis, MN: University of Minnesota Press.

Ehrenreich, B., Hess, E. and Jacobs, G. (1992). Beatlemania: Girls Just Want to Have Fun. In L.A. Lewis (ed.), *The Adoring Audience: Fan Culture and Popular Media*, London: Routledge, pp. 84–106.

EMI Calls Beatles Suit "Absurd." (1987). *Washington Post*, July 30, p. E1.

Engardio, P. (1986). Cola Wars II: The Battle of the Books. *Business Week*, December 1, Books, p. 16.

Ewen, S. (1988). *All Consuming Images: The Politics of Style in Contemporary Culture*. New York: Basic Books.

Fahey, A. (1991). Coke's $100M blast: Mini-CDs Star in Huge Summer Promotion. *Advertising Age*, March 11, p. 1.

Faith Hill to Star in New Pepsi Commercial: "Joy of Cola" Spot to Debut on Academy Awards Telecast. (2000). *PR Newswire*, March 13, financial news.

Farber, J. (2001). Exposure at All Costs: "Edgy" Musicians Reap the Rewards of TV as Tie-ins. *New York Daily News*, January 7, p. 12.

Farber, J. (2002). Ad-vantage to Dirty Vegas. *New York Daily News*, June 11, p. 46.

Farhi, P. (1992). Well, We All Shine … Shoes? Is There Any Song Madison Avenue Won't Steal? *Washington Post*, March 22, p. G1.

Fiske, J. (1989). *Understanding Popular Culture*. Boston, MA: Unwin Hyman.

Flanagan, B. (2006). Selling Records or Selling Out? Bill Flanagan Debates Whether Musicians Should Use Their Music in Ads. *CBS News*, February 26. Retrieved from http://www.cbsnews.com/stories/2006/02/26/sunday/ main1346174.shtml.

Foltz, K. (1990). Madison Ave. Turns an Ear to Rap Music. *New York Times*, July 6, Section D, p. 5.

Foucault, M. (1977). *Language, Counter-memory, Practice* (D. Bouchard, ed.). Ithaca, NY: Cornell University Press.

Frank, T. (1997). *The Conquest of Cool: Business Culture, Counterculture, and the Rise of Hip Consumerism*. Chicago, IL: University of Chicago Press.

Frith, S. (1981). *Sound Effects*. New York: Pantheon.

Frith, S. (1986). Critical Response. *Critical Studies in Mass Communication* 3(1): 74–7.

Frith, S. (1988). *Music for Pleasure: Essays in the Sociology of Pop*. Cambridge: Polity.

Frith, S. (2002). Look! Hear! The Uneasy Relationship of Music and Television. *Popular Music* 21(3): 277–90.

Frith, S. (2004). Music and the Media. In S. Frith and L. Marshall (eds), *Music and Copyright*. New York: Routledge, pp. 171–88.

Frith, S. and Marshall, L. (2004). Making Sense of Copyright. In S. Frith and L. Marshall (eds), *Music and Copyright*. New York: Routledge, pp. 1–18.

Frith, S. and McRobbie, A. (1990). Rock and Sexuality. In S. Frith and A. Goodwin (eds), *On Record: Rock, Pop, & the Written Word*. London: Routledge, pp. 371–89.

Gans, H.J. (1999). *Popular Culture and High Culture: An Analysis and Evaluation of Taste* (revised and updated edition). New York: Basic Books.

Garcia, P. (2002). Message on thread "Shins hawking McDonald's." Retrieved from http://ilx.wh3rd.net/thread.php?msgid=1935534.

Garrity, B. (2001). Carmakers Gear Up for Music-driven Media Campaigns. *Billboard*, September 15, p. 65.

Gianatasio, D. (2001). Royal Caribbean Spots Set Sail. *Adweek*, January 8.

Glaser, B.G. and Strauss, A.L. (1999). *The Discovery of Grounded Theory: Strategies for Qualitative Research*. New York: Aldine de Gruyter. (Original work published 1967.)

Graser, M. (2005). McDonald's on Lookout to Be Big Mac Daddy. *Advertising Age*, March 28, p. 123.

Greenwald, A. (2000). Nick Drake's Full "Moon." *Washington Post*, October 8, p. G09.

Gross, J. (1987). Pop Culture. *Toronto Star*, April 11, p. S18.

Grossberg, L. (ed.) (1986). On Postmodernism and Articulation: An Interview with Stuart Hall. *Journal of Communication Inquiry* 10(2): 45–60.

Grossberg, L. (1992). *We Gotta Get Out of This Place: Popular Conservatism and Postmodern Culture*. New York: Routledge.

Grossberg, L. (1995). Cultural Studies vs. Political Economy: Is Anyone Else Bored with This Debate? *Critical Studies in Mass Communication* 12(1): 72–81.

Hall, S. (1980). Encoding/Decoding. In S. Hall, D. Hobson, A. Lowe and P. Willis (eds), *Culture, Media, Language*. London: Hutchinson, pp. 128–36.

Hall, S. (2002). Race, Articulation, and Societies Structured in Dominance. In P. Essed and D.T. Goldberg (eds), *Race Critical Theories: Text and Context*. Malden, MA: Blackwell, pp. 38–67.

Hall, S. and Whannel, P. (1964). *The Popular Arts*. London: Hutchinson.

Hammersley, M. and Atkinson, P. (1995). *Ethnography: Principles in Practice*. London: Routledge.

Hanson, I. (1999). Rock for Rock's Sake Is No Longer Enough. *New York Times*, December 5, Section 4, p. 18.

Harris, J. (2000). Media: So, You'd Like to Use One of My Songs on Your Advert …: Well, with Dance Artist Moby, Every Track on His Album Play Has Been Used in a Commercial, with About 600 Currently Using Samples from It. Has the Ad World Gone Mad? *Independent*, June 20, p. 9.

Hart, O. (2006). Bah Hummer: Indie Rockers Reject Big Money from the King of Gas Guzzlers. *Austin American-Statesman*, February 21.

Hebdige, D. (1979). *Subculture: The Meaning of Style*. London: Routledge.

Hesmondhalgh, D. (1998). The British Dance Music Industry: A Case Study of Independent Cultural Production. *British Journal of Sociology* 49(2): 243–51.

Hicks, B. (1997). Orange Drink. From *Rant in E-Minor*. New York: Rykodisc.

Hilton, S. (2001). Behind the Building Boom: A Flotilla of New Ships Means New Choices—and Some Bargains. *San Francisco Chronicle*, April 22, p. T12.

Hoggart, R. (1957). *The Uses of Literacy*. London: Chatto & Windus.

Holden, S. (1989). Madonna Re-Creates Herself—Again. *New York Times*, March 19, Section 2, p. 1.

Howard, T. (2001). Stars Take Center Stage in Oscar Ads. *USA Today*, March 21, p. 3B.

Howard, T. (2003). Coke Turns to Urban Music Stars for Latest Ad Campaign. *USA Today*, January 13, p. 7B.

Howell, P. (2005). Put a Stop to Using Old Music for New Movies. *Toronto Star*, April 8, p. D01.

Huron, D. (1989). Music in Advertising: An Analytic Paradigm. *Musical Quarterly* 73(4): 557–74.

Ives, N. (2002). The Media Business: Advertising; The Odd Embrace of Marketing and Anti-establishment Music. *New York Times*, November 6, p. C3.

Iyer, P. (1988). *Video Night in Kathmandu and Other Reports from the Not-so-Far East*. New York: Alfred A. Knopf.

James, M. (2001). *Moby: Replay, His Life and Times*. Chicago, IL: Olmstead Press.

Jaszi, P. (1994). On the Author Effect: Contemporary Copyright and Collective Creativity. In M. Woodmansee and P. Jaszi (eds), *The Construction of Authorship*. Durham, NC: Duke University Press, pp. 29–56.

Jeckell, B.A. (2001). Spears' Pepsi Ad to Get Online Unveiling. *BPI Entertainment News Wire*, March 20.

Jhally, S. (1987). *The Codes of Advertising: Fetishism and the Political Economy of Meaning in the Consumer Society*. New York: Routledge.

Johnson, A. (1995). Jackson Angers Ex-Beatles: Fellow Artist Who Bought Publishing Rights "Cheapened" Songs by Using Them in Adverts. *Guardian*, November 6, p. 4.

Johnson, D. (2002). Wrangler Missteps with Anti-War Song. *Adweek* (Art & Commerce: Letters), November 11.

Johnson, M. (1987). *The Body in the Mind: The Bodily Basis of Meaning, Imagination and Reason*. Chicago, IL: University of Chicago Press.

Jones, S. (2002). Music That Moves: Popular Music, Distribution and Network Technologies. *Cultural Studies* 16(2): 213–32.

Kanye West and Pepsi Take a Trip around the Globe: Grammy Award-Winning Artist Stars in New Commercial Directed by Spike Lee. (2005). *PR Newswire*, August 25.

Kaplan, E.A. (1987). *Rocking Around the Clock: Music Television, Postmodernism and Consumer Culture*. London: Routledge.

Kielty, T. (2003). CD Report: New on Disc; The Shins *Chutes Too Narrow* Sub Pop Records. *Boston Globe*, October 17, p. D16.

Klein, N. (2000). *No Logo*. New York: Picador USA.

Kohn, A. and Kohn, B. (1996). *Kohn on Music Licensing*, second edition. Englewood Cliffs, NJ: Aspen Law Business.

Kroth, M. (2004). Review of Dirty Vegas *One*. *SF Weekly*, December 1.

Lanham, T. (2004). Lust for Cash: Iggy Pop Makes His Case for Using Punk Music in Television Commercials. *The Wave Magazine*, January 14, p. 53.

Laue, C. (2003). Still Flying High: The Counting Crows Find That Touring Is Helping Them Survive the Ups and Downs of the Music World. *Omaha World Herald*, April 3, p. 4go.

Lazare, L. (2005). Coke Ad Nothing Like Real Thing. *Chicago Sun-Times*, June 30, p. 65.

Lears, J. (1987). Uneasy Courtship: Modern Art and Modern Advertising. *American Quarterly* 39(1): 133–54.

LeMay, M. (2004). The Shins. *Pitchfork Media*, March. Retrieved from http://www.pitchforkmedia.com/interviews/s/shins-04/.

Levitt, T. (1970). The Morality (?) of Advertising. *Harvard Business Review* 48, pp. 84–92.

Lippert, B. (1987). Nike's "Revolution in Motion," Roll Over, John: The Song Fits, and Nike's Wearing It. *Adweek*, April 6.

Lipsitz, G. (1990). *Time Passages: Collective Memory and American Popular Culture*. Minneapolis, MN: University of Minnesota Press.

Lipsitz, G. (1993). Foreword. In S.D. Crafts, D. Cavicchi, and C. Keil (eds), *My Music*. Hanover, NH: Wesleyan University Press, pp. ix–xix.

Loomis, P. (2004). Panel: Music and Marketing—The Role of Brand Image Music, Music Licensing, Contemporary Pop Music and Music Scoring in Advertising and Marketing. Retrieved from http://www.aaf.org/resources/video_nc04.html.

Lukács, G. (1971). *History and Class Consciousness* (R. Livingstone, trans.). London: Merlin Press. (Original work published 1923.)

Lynch, S. (2000). Commercial World Embraces Electronic Music: Fox Network and Ad Producers Know What Teens Want to Hear. *Ottawa Citizen*, May 20, p. I6.

Lyon, R. (1997). The Partnership for a Drag-free America: Creatives and Music Superstars are Collaborating on the "New Classics" as Never Before. *Creativity*, December 1, p. 16.

Macdonald, D. (1983). *Against the American Grain: Essays on the Effects of Mass Culture*. New York: Da Capo.

Magiera, M. (1987). Nike to Keep "Revolution" Despite Suit. *Advertising Age*, August 3, p. 3.

Marks, J. (1998). Shake, Rattle, and Please Buy My Product. *U.S. News & World Report*, May 25, p. 51.

Matthews, V. (1987). The Media: Shoe Loves You, Yeah, Yeah, Yeah—Not Even the Beatles Are Now Safe from the On-song Advertisers. *Guardian*, June 1.

McAllister, M.P. (1996). *The Commercialization of American Culture: New Advertising, Control, and Democracy*. Thousand Oaks, CA: Sage.

McAllister, M.P. (2003). Is Commercial Culture Popular Culture? A Question for Popular Communication Scholars. *Popular Communication* 1(1): 41–9.

McChesney, R.W. (2003). Theses on Media Deregulation. *Media, Culture & Society* 25(1): 125–33.

McChesney, R.W. (2004). *The Problem of the Media: U.S. Communication Politics in the Twenty-First Century*. New York: Monthly Review Press.

McCourt, T. and Burkart, P. (2003). When Creators, Corporations and Consumers Collide: Napster and the Development of On-line Music Distribution. *Media, Culture & Society* 25(3): 333–50.

McDonald, J.R. (1993). Rock and Memory: A Search for Meaning. *Popular Music and Society* 17(3): 1–17.

McGinness, R. (2005). Introduction. In R. McGinness (ed.), *Sponsorship: The Fine Art of Corporate Sponsorship, The Corporate Sponsorship of Fine Art*. Corte Madera, CA: Gingko Press.

McLeod, K. (2001). *Owning Culture: Authorship, Ownership, and Intellectual Property Law*. New York: Peter Lang.

Meyer, L. (1956). *Emotion and Meaning in Music*. Chicago, IL: University of Chicago Press.

Meyers, O. and Zandberg, E. (2002) The Sound-track of Memory: *Ashes and Dust* and the Commemoration of the Holocaust in Israeli Popular Culture. *Media, Culture & Society* 24(3): 389–408.

Michael Jackson Fooled McCartney. (1990). *St. Petersburg Times*, January 27, p. 3A.

Middleton, R. (2000). Introduction: Locating the Popular Music Text. In R. Middleton (ed.), *Reading Pop: Approaches to Textual Analysis in Popular Music*. Oxford: Oxford University Press, pp. 1–19.

Miles, N. (2003). Pop Goes the Commercial: The Evolution of the Relationship Between Popular Music and Television Commercials. *Vanderbilt Journal of Entertainment Law & Practice* 5(2): 121–35.

"Milky Way" is the First Volkswagen Ad to Launch on Web Sneak Preview on the Internet Prior to National Broadcast. (1999). *PR Newswire*, November 11.

Moayeri, L. (2003). Review of Iggy Pop *Skull Ring*. *Miami New Times*, November 6.

Morford, M. (2004). Aerosmith Sells You a Buick: In Which the Rock Icons Waste Their Finest Song, and Rock 'n' Roll Finally Gasps Its Last. *San Francisco Chronicle*, December 10.

Morley, P. (2004). Music on TV: Justin's Secrets and Fries: Paul Morley Imagines a World in Which Fast Food Giants Advertise Their Wares with an Appropriate Soundtrack of Chas'n'Dave, Not Timberlake. *Observer*, August 15, p. 53.

Morris, C. (2000). Ad Gives Drake's "Moon" Rise in Sales. *Billboard*, April 1.

Mundy, J. (1999). *Popular Music on Screen: From Hollywood Musical to Music Video*. Manchester: Manchester University Press.

Odds and Ends. (2004). *Seattle Times*, August 25, p. A2.

Oestreich, J.R. (2002). Schubertizing the Movies. *New York Times*, June 30, p. 1.

Paoletta, M. (2000). Dance Trax: America Gets into the Groove in 2000 As It Embraces Dance. *Billboard*, December 30.

Paoletta, M. (2003). The Newest Soundtrack to the World? *Billboard*, March 22, p. 39.

Pareles, J. (1987). Nike Calls Beatles Suit Groundless. *New York Times*, August 5, Section C, p. 23.

Parpis, E. (1999). Creative: Double Vision. *Adweek*, January 25.

Peterson, L.E. (2002). The Soft Serenade of Sycophancy: It's Time the Captains of Industry Demanded More of Ethics Watchdogs. A Little Chumbawamba Can Go a Long Way. *Ottawa Citizen*, March 13, p. A17.

Peterson, R.A. (ed.) (1976). *The Production of Culture*. Beverly Hills, CA: Sage.

Platt, W. (1996). Two Score Minus 10, There Am I. *St. Petersburg Times*, September 22, p. 1.

Pop Music in Ads Is a Double Sell. (2001). *St. Petersburg Times*, June 19, p. 5D.

Pot, J. (2004). Message on thread "Shins hawking McDonald's." Retrieved from http://ilx.wh3rd.net/thread.php?msgid=1935534.

Potts, M. (1987). Got to Get You Out of Our Life: Former Beatles Sue Over Use of Song in Nike Commercial. *Washington Post*, July 29, p. F1.

Prindle, G.M. (2003). No Competition: How Radio Consolidation Has Diminished Diversity and Sacrificed Localism. *Fordham Intellectual Property, Media & Entertainment Law Journal* 14: 279–325.

Prinsky, L.E. and Rosenbaum, J.L. (1987). "Leer-ics" or Lyrics: Teenage Impressions of Rock 'n' Roll. *Youth and Society* 18(4): 384–97.

Pruett, J. (2003). Review of The Shins *Chutes Too Narrow*. *East Bay Express*, October 22.

Reed, C. (1988). The Media: Pop Too Near Beer—After a Fight, MTV Has Agreed to Show a Music Video Mocking Some of Its Biggest Sponsors. *Guardian*, August 29, p. 19.

Review & Outlook: Sacrilege! (1987). *Wall Street Journal*, August 14, Section 1, p. 14.

Rich, F. (1999). The White Panthers. *New York Times*, February 6, Section A, p. 15.

Ritzer, G. (1993). *The McDonaldization of Society*. Thousand Oaks, CA: Pine Forge Press.

Rose, M. (1993). *Authors and Owners: The Invention of Copyright*. Cambridge, MA: Harvard University Press.

Rose, T. (1994). *Black Noise: Rap Music and Black Culture in Contemporary America*. Hanover, NH: Wesleyan University Press.

Rosen, J. (2000). A Techno Auteur Finds Rock-like Success. *New York Times*, October 8, section 2, p. 36.

Rosenthal, R. (2001). Serving the Movement: The Role(s) of Music. *Popular Music and Society* 25(3/4): 11–24.

Rothenbuhler, E.W. (1987). Commercial Radio and Popular Music: Processes of Selection and Factors of Influence. In J. Lull (ed.), *Popular Music and Communication*. Newbury Park, CA: Sage, pp. 78–95.

Rowan, D. (2002). UK: Chumbawamba's Tune Turns the Tables on US Car Giant. *London Observer*, January 27.

Rush, G. and Molloy, J. (1995). Sneaker Preview: What Jax Told McCartney About Nike Ad. *New York Daily News*, August 15, p. 19.

Ryan, J. (1985). *The Production of Culture in the Music Industry: The ASCAP-BMI Controversy*. Lanham, MD: University Press of America.

Sabella, D. (2004). Panel: Music and Marketing—The Role of Brand Image Music, Music Licensing, Contemporary Pop Music and Music Scoring in Advertising and Marketing. Retrieved from http://www.aaf.org/resources/video_nc04.html.

Saussure, F. de. (1966). *Course in General Linguistics* (W. Baskin, trans.). New York: McGraw-Hill.

Savan, L. (1993). Commercials Go Rock. In S. Frith, A. Goodwin, and L. Grossberg (eds), *Sound and Vision: The Music Video Reader*. London: Routledge, pp. 85–90.

Savan, L. (1994). *The Sponsored Life: Ads, TV, and American Culture*. Philadelphia, PA: Temple University Press.

Scanlon, T. (2002). The Shins Get a Bite from McDonald's. *Seattle Times*, February 21, p. E2.

Segal, D. (2002). "18": Another Commercial Break for Moby. *Washington Post*, May 15, p. C01.

Segal, D. (2003). With "Chutes," The Shins Create a Better "World." *Washington Post*, October 22, p. C05.

Segal, D. (2004). A Steak in the Heart of "Happy Together." *Washington Post*, April 6, p. C01.

Serpick, E. (2006). Doors Ride Again: Box Set, Movie, and Vegas Show in the Works for the Band's Fortieth Anniversary. *Rolling Stone*, May 4, p. 20.

Shanahan, L. (2003). Designated Shopper. *Brandweek*, April 21.

Sheffield, R. (2002). Emotional Rescue: Moby Searches for the Perfect Mix Tape. *Rolling Stone*, May 23, pp. 77–8.

Shi, D.E. (1979). Advertising and the Literary Imagination during the Jazz Age. *Journal of American Culture* 2(2): 167–75.

Siegel, E. (1989). Madonna Sells Her Soul for a Song. *Boston Globe*, March 2, p. 77.

Simpson, D. (2000). Plug and Play: Licensing Pop Songs to TV and Commercials Is Bigger Business Than Ever. *Guardian*, May 5, p. 14.

Sleeve Notes. (1990). *Independent*, June 1, p. 15.

Small, C. (1998). *Musicking*. Middletown, CT: Wesleyan University Press.

Smith, S.B. (1985). There's No Avoiding Music Videos. *New York Times*, March 10, Section 2, p. 29.

So Who Are Those Guys with the Funny Haircuts? (1992). *Adweek*, June 22.

Song About Heroin Used to Advertise Bank. (2001). *The Onion*, April 18. Retrieved from http://www.theonion.com/content/node/38780.

Sterne, J. (1997). Sounds Like the Mall of America: Programmed Music and the Architecture of Commercial Space. *Ethnomusicology* 41(1): 22–50.

Stevenson, S. (2005). What's the Worst Ad Song Ever? *Slate Magazine*, June 6. Retrieved from http://www.slate.com/id/2120229/.

Stockler, B. (2000). Talking 'Bout My Generation. *Creativity*, July 1, p. 22.

Stratton, J. (1983). Capitalism and Romantic Ideology in the Record Business. *Popular Music* 3: 143–56.

Street, J. (2003). "Fight the Power": The Politics of Music and the Music of Politics. *Government and Opposition* 38(1): 113–30.

Swenson, J. (1987). Pop Sells Out: Commercials and Corporate Sponsorship Spark a Music World Debate. *United Press International*, May 4.

Tayler, L. (2003). Rock Stars Move to Corporate Beat: Once Oil and Water, Musicians and Advertisers Have Now Joined Forces. *Ottawa Citizen*, June 23, p. D3.

Taylor, T.D. (2007). The Changing Shape of the Culture Industry; or, How Did Electronica Music Get into Television Commercials? *Television and New Media* 8(3): 235–58.

The List: As the Ad-friendly Moby Releases His New Album, We Remember the Music That Launched a Thousand Products. (2002). *Glasgow Herald*, May 4, p. 6.

Thorncroft, A. (1986). Marketing and Advertising: UK Sponsorship At Last Goes Pop. *Financial Times*, September 18, Section I, p. 20.

Thornton, S. (1996). *Club Cultures: Music, Media and Subcultural Capital*. Hanover, NH: Wesleyan University Press.

Tota, A.L. (2001). "When Orff Meets Guinness": Music in Advertising as a Form of Cultural Hybrid. *Poetics* 29(2): 109–23.

Tyler, L.L. (1992). "Commerce and Poetry Hand in Hand": Music in American Department Stores, 1880–1930. *Journal of the American Musicological Society* 45(1): 75–120.

Usinger, M. (2004). Shins Survive Dark Days. *Straight.com Vancouver*, May 20. Retrieved from http://www.straight.com/content.cfm?id=2780.

Walker, R. (2001). Ad Report Card: Mitsubishi's Commotion. *Slate Magazine*, August 7. Retrieved from http://www.slate.com/id/113077/.

Walser, R. (1993). *Running with the Devil: Power, Gender, and Madness in Heavy Metal Music*. Hanover, NH: Wesleyan University.

Wells, M. (2003). Message in a Bottle of Pop: Last week the BBC Ran into Trouble over the Sponsorship of Its Radio and Top of the Pops Chart Shows by Coca-Cola. *Guardian*, December 8, Media Pages, p. 8.

Wiener, J. (1987). Exploitation and the Revolution. *Advertising Age*, June 29, p. 18.

Williams, R. (1962). *Problems in Materialism and Culture*. London: New Left Books.

Wollenberg, S. (1988). Nike Plans to Drop Ads with Beatles' "Revolution" in March. *Associated Press*, February 23.

Zaleski, A. (2003). Indie Rock Shins Get a Kick out of Surprising Success. *Cleveland Plain Dealer*, November 14, p. 10.

Zivitz, J. (2000). VW Spot Puts Drake in Limelight. *Montreal Gazette*, August 24, p. D14.

Žižek, S. (1989). *The Sublime Object of Ideology*. London: Verso.

Index